MY GRANDMOTHERS AND I

Few children can have had a more contrasting pair of guardians than Diana Holman-Hunt, who was brought up at the beginning of the century by her two grandmothers. On her father's side was Mrs Holman-Hunt, widow of the famous painter, good-looking, mean, terrifyingly strong both physically and mentally and living entirely in the past. On the other side, her maternal grandmother was luxurious, delicious, feminine. Always longing to 'be amused', her life was spent in great comfort surrounded by servants with, at her side, her charming, blind, joking husband.

Luckily Diana was a tough and humourous child and adapted herself well to both households. Mrs Holman-Hunt instilled in her grandchild a great interest in and knowledge of the Pre-Raphaelite Brotherhood by much-repeated stories, visits to the Tate and National Galleries and an exhausting test called 'The Quiz Game'. But Diana was never sorry to return to her other home where the food was always good and plentiful and her Sussex grandparents reassuring in their well-ordered way of life.

My Grandmothers and I

BY

DIANA HOLMAN-HUNT

Illustrated

A HAMISH HAMILTON PAPERBACK
London

To my grandchildren, Theresa and Sebastian, with love

First published in Great Britain in 1960
by Hamish Hamilton Ltd
First published in this edition 1987
by Hamish Hamilton Ltd
27 Wrights Lane, London w8 5TZ

Reprinted 1987

ISBN 0-241-12019-5

Printed and bound in Finland
by Werner Söderström Oy

Foreword

This is a venture in autobiography—true in essence, but not in detail. I have tried to depict my grandparents and others as they appeared to me as a child. All the events described are based on fact but, for convenience of the narrative, they are sometimes transposed.

For the sake of susceptibilities, a few people are left out altogether and some minor characters are amalgamations of several personalities, so do not represent any living individuals.

I should like to express my gratitude to my brother-in-law Guy Strutt for his criticism and help.

Part One

CHAPTER ONE

I KNEW it was early because the birds were chattering in the creepers. 'That wistaria must be cut back, it brings the spiders,' my grandmother would say. No sound came from her room. If she were awake there would be a murmur of voices, while Fowler massaged her legs, or the tinkle of china on the tea-tray.

My list of tasks showed as a dark patch on the curtain against the light. The head of the hat-pin, which stabbed it to the stuff, appeared as a black spot; while I watched it sharpen, I hoped today might be different with no tasks to do at all. It was my birthday.

I jumped out of bed and ran to the window. In the distance a gardener was scratching leaves off the path with his rake: the noise was faint, perhaps imagined. Cherub stood on one toe in the middle of the fountain; his laughing face was turned away, but a trickle of water ran from his dolphin. I got back into bed, hoping to dream. He was my friend, and unlike other people we could fly. If things went wrong he rose from his pedestal and I followed, stepping on air in the nick of time as the grown-ups came rushing down the terrace. 'Stop, stop!' they cried. 'Come here at once! What are you doing? Have you finished your tasks? Just look at your dress!' We flew over the lawn quite low, our feet just over their outstretched hands, while they looked up, beckoning and shouting. Taking a deep breath, we rose a little higher, skimming the flower-beds and old Dan's acre. When we reached Snakes' Wall and the screen of trees on the edge of the cliff, we soared up and up, until the rooks' nests looked enormous. Then we swooped down to the marsh. It was safe there and we sailed low over the dykes and old Timothy's huts, the rushes just brushing our toes, on and on until we reached the sea.

Fowler drew the curtains with a rattle of rings on the pole.

'Many happy returns of the day, Miss Diana, I thought I would find you awake.' She put something down on the bed.

'This is a present from Hannah and me, and Tilly and Mrs. Hopkins.'

I sat up and undid the parcel, fumbling at the knots. Inside was a furry blue animal the size of a pug. 'It's like the ones we saw at Selfridges in London.' To my surprise he squeaked when I gave him a hug. Fowler frowned and looked at the door.

'What's his name?' I whispered.

'It's a teddy bear. I knew they took your fancy, so we wrote up. A lot of palaver it was too, with writing and postal orders.'

'Oh, thank you so much, he's lovely; thank you very, very much.'

'Don't forget to thank the others, it's from them too, and Tilly could ill afford it.' I tried to give her a kiss. 'Now then, you don't want to act soft, you'll have my hair down.' She glared in the glass and patted her bun. No other servant was allowed to scowl; she was the exception to the rule.

'Fowler is a rough diamond,' my grandmother would say, 'but she knows my ways and suits me on the whole. Her manners are appalling, but alas, one can't make a silk purse out of a sow's ear!' She would raise her hands, heavy with diamond rings, and adjust the silver plait which circled her head like a crown, as if to shut out a noise.

She was my mother's mother and called grandmother Freeman. I could never describe her looks, the shape of her face or the colour of her eyes; but her expression seemed to cloud and clear like the sky. She demanded perfection. At the wave of her hand or the touch of a bell, some smiling person would appear and quietly remedy a fault: a dead rose in a vase, a smudge on the window, a weed in a flower-bed, would provoke her to complain. She would protest at a confusion of plans or even a silence: 'What terrible muddles! How dull; my dear, can't you see, I want to be amused.'

We must all, except Fowler, be neat and gay however we were feeling and our hands and tongues must never rest.

'Where is your knitting? I hate to see you idle. If you've lost your tongue you had better read aloud.'

I knew that if I felt worried I must discuss the matter privately with Cherub, or even Fowler, who would listen frowning and perhaps give me a Gregory powder messed up in strawberry jam.

'Birthday or no birthday, it's high time you were up,' said Fowler, returning with my dress. 'You'd better go to the bathroom and wash yourself quick.'

Beside my camel-hair toothbrush in a mug there was a pot of bear's grease, some Pomade Divine and a cool ivory box with a mirror in the lid: it was a delight to unscrew, the action so smooth it scarcely made a sound; whatever the hurry I could never resist picking it up. Inside sat a hard, round, pink velvet ball, with a knob on top and some fluff underneath.

'Hurry up, do!' shouted Fowler, knocking on the door. 'I haven't got all day. You're just fiddling with that box, I can hear you.'

'I'm coming,' I said, clenching my toes in the white fur rug.

She was waiting to fit my harness. While I clung to the back of a chair, she tugged at the white canvas straps and buckled them behind. This was Papa's idea to prevent round shoulders, and everyone but Fowler had long ceased to be aware of the braces under my dress.

As she brushed my hair and coaxed it into ringlets I read yesterday's tasks from the curtain. If I should lean forward to see more clearly, she would rap my head with the back of the brush. I hoped my grandmother would crumple the paper and toss it away. If any items were outstanding, the old list would remain pinned to the new one; this always filled me with gloom. I reached to unpin the list and gathered up my knitting and the bear. Fowler looked me up and down: 'You'll do,' she picked a hair off my collar and then knocked on the door leading to my grandmother's room: 'Miss Diana, madam.'

My grandmother sat in bed, her head against a bank of square frilled pillows. Her silver plaits lay in parallel lines on the turned-down sheet, their tails level with the lace on the hem. There was a smell of wintergreen, and a dead fire lay in the grate.

'Good morning, my love, what an age you've been,' she said,

without looking up. I leant forward to give her a kiss and put my list and knitting on the quilt.

'Such a stupid bread-and-butter letter from Ada Wilkins. Coloured writing-paper is so vulgar—someone should tell her.'

I thought of our grey silurian. 'Ours isn't white,' I ventured. Clearly my birthday was forgotten.

'And most unsuitable the way she discussed our ghost at luncheon in front of the servants. Sometimes I really despaired.'

Things fell under two headings: 'suitable' and 'unsuitable'. Friends, books, hats, marriages and conversations were one or the other. Some unsuitable things were merely 'rather unfortunate' but others were 'very disagreeable', or worst of all '*disastrous* my dear!'

She picked up my knitting and counted the rows from the black cotton mark which she had made the day before. 'Only nineteen! Not very good.' She reached over to the pin-cushion for a needle and thread.

I had only one kind of knitting, white operation stockings for the wounded. They were made like scarves and the edges sewn together. I imagined the soldiers lying in strings of white woollen sausages. She stitched the black cotton just below the needle.

'Try and do better today, my love, I should set yourself a target of twenty-five rows. Although I trust the war will soon be over, the hospitals, alas, will need all we can send, for a long time yet.'

I was surprised. 'I thought there was always a war.'

'How strange; but I suppose it's perfectly natural; even to me it has gone on for years. My beloved will soon be home, God willing.'

She meant my Young Uncle who was fighting. He was born long after my aunt and my mother, whom I never saw, and grandmother loved him better than anyone else. The thought of his return made me uneasy. When he came home, the house was turned upside down and no one paid much attention to me. Long ago I had decided to ignore him.

The lazy young ladies who came to stay were called *jolies laides*. They weren't really jolly. They wore unfeminine hats and never brought any sewing. 'Have you no work?' my grandmother would ask, a false look of concern on her face. 'Of course if you prefer to be idle . . .' She would shrug her shoulders and pick up her knitting. Stammering excuses, they sprang to wind wool, or pretended they had letters to write in their bedrooms.

As soon as they had left she would sigh. 'My dear, how dull, she never utters.'

To utter meant to make conversation. 'Don't let's ask her again. And what *has* she done to her figure?' If Young Uncle were there she would wish me to go off by myself: 'Run along, precious, and amuse yourself. Can't you see I'm busy?'

'You're dreaming as usual.' She raised her lorgnettes now and read through the list. 'Did you cut off *all* the deadheads? Splendid.' She crumpled the list and threw it into the waste-paper basket. She wrote something on the back of Mrs. Wilkins' letter and then stared at me, thoughtfully tapping her teeth with the pencil. 'What have you got under your arm?' She stretched and tweaked at my bear. I felt myself blushing. 'Oh, just a teddy bear —from London.'

'What a hideous thing.' Carelessly she threw him on the bed.

'I like him,' I said, snatching him up. 'Fowler and Hannah and Tilly and Mrs. Hopkins gave him to me; I think he's lovely.'

'Children are too extraordinary! Of course it was kind of the servants—I wonder—why, of course, it's your birthday! My precious, give me a kiss. How forgetful I am. Why didn't you tell me? There are three, no, four parcels and a letter; and a postcard from cousin Priscilla.' Priscilla! My heart gave a jump. 'I have put them aside and we will open them later with George. I do hope the letter . . .' She broke off vaguely. 'Now, where were we?' She picked up the list. 'No tasks today.' She tore the blue paper and threw it in the basket. 'What would you like to recite? Whatever you like, my love, but I should put the bear away.'

I took him to my room and, pushing past Fowler, put him in a drawer, leaving it open to let him breathe. I ran back and climbed on to the dais.

I began in my poetry voice: 'Take a candle child to light your mother through the snow.'

'No, darling, "Take a candle, pause, child, comma, to light your mother through the snow."' She moved about in bed as if in pain. 'No, no, try something else. What about "Little lamb, who made thee?"'

'I hate the little lamb.'

'Whatever you like.' She sighed, closed her eyes and leant back against the pillows.

Fowler tiptoed into the room before I had finished. This was the signal for me to go.

'Run along, precious.' Raising a pale hand to her lips, grandmother blew me a kiss.

Fowler and I had breakfast in the gun-room, which was between the pantry and the gentlemen's cloakroom. The telephone stood like a black daffodil on a seat in the window. We kept the door ajar to hear what they said in the pantry.

Johnstone talked to Arthur in a different voice from the one he used to me. Johnstone was the butler and was horrid to Arthur, because he dropped his aitches and had once worked in the London house as a boot-boy and wasn't strong enough to be a Tommy. Johnstone was supposed to sleep between the furnace and the cellars; but I knew he slept on the library sofa because his own room had no proper window and was as hot as an oven. He drank a lot of port and was fuddled every afternoon. Fowler said: 'You don't want to let on about Mr. Johnstone, we don't want any trouble—least said, soonest mended. If you've finished, say your grace. For what we have received . . .' She rang a little bell. 'Now, you want to go to the piano.'

'Oh, need I? It's my birthday.'

'Well, I don't know, I'm sure, but you want to visit Mrs. Hopkins first, if you've time, and thank her nicely for the bear.'

Mrs. Hopkins was the cook and looked like Mrs. Noah, with black hair painted on her head. She had red cheeks and a moustache. She frightened Annie the kitchen-maid but was always nice to me. When Annie deserved it, she let her watch a sauce she was making; but the rest of the time Annie did horrible things at the scullery sink, or spent hours on her knees scrubbing.

Mrs. Hopkins had a terrible temper and once threw a whole basket of carrots at Dan, the vegetable gardener, because one was muddy. She would slam the doors of the pantry-hatch shouting: 'That there Arthur and his silly expression, "'ark, 'ark, the lark," fair gives me the pip; he picked it up in the dining-room, and his "winkin' merry bugs" whatever they be.'

'Good morning, Mrs. Hopkins, I've come to say thank you for the bear.'

'You're welcome, miss,' she said, wiping the flour off her hands. 'I've kept a bit of cake mixture back.' She handed me the wooden spoon.

Fowler bustled in. She had come for the egg-nog.

'You here? I hope you're not getting in the way? The mistress will soon be down to give you your music lesson.'

This would be the worst moment of the day. While I perched on the stool a pain would burn between my shoulders and the harness would cut into my skin.

My grandmother would draw up a chair on my right and beat time on the side of the piano. There was no varnish left on the case. The brass candlesticks would rattle in their sockets, and the photograph frames would tremble to the sharp tick-tock of the metronome. 'One, two, three, four! One, two, three, four!'

Clasping my teddy bear, I ran along the still-room passage and past the pantry where Arthur was singing 'Swanee'. I let the green baize door to the hall swing wide, and close itself with a hiss and thud. The clock was striking eleven. My grandfather was sitting in the boudoir and his pink head showed over the back of the chair.

'Good morning,' he said. 'I trust I am correct in thinking today is your anniversary? May I offer you my hearty congratulations?'

'Yes, it is.' I gave him a kiss. 'Feel, what Fowler and Hannah and Tilly and Mrs. Hopkins have given me.' I rubbed the teddy bear against his cheek.

He raised a stiff hand to push it away. 'A stuffed toy, like a golliwog?'

'No, no, he's a teddy bear, Fowler said so—from London.'

'Edward Bear,' he said, turning round.

'Oh, is his name Edward?' I could see no reason why it should be.

'Certainly his name is Edward,' he replied, as if he really knew.

I had never met an Edward, but it seemed to suit him very well. 'I love him so much,' I said, pressing him to make him squeak.

'Edward Bear. Cherub's nose will be put out of joint.'

'Cherub's quite different and even he has a dolphin. He won't mind at all.'

'No, I dare say Edward does not compare, as a garden ornament at least, with a good cast of the Verrocchio cupid.'

'It was nice of Tilly to give him as well as the others. Hannah says Tilly has many admirers, but although she's pretty she's got her head *screwed* on.'

'So Tilly isn't silly,' he sang, 'she's chilly to Willy.'

'Billy, Milly, filly!' I cried, bouncing Edward up and down. The door opened and my grandmother sailed in followed by Fowler with a foaming egg-nog, and the pugs who were shut up until now in the boot-room. Arthur walked behind, carrying her bag and a tin of hot water in a grey velvet cover.

'Good morning, dearest,' she said. She put her feet on the tin, Fowler arranged the rug over her knees and the pugs turned round and round making nests in the folds. 'It's Diana's birthday.'

'So I recollect,' he said. 'As it is such a special occasion, I sat in here, hoping we might be spared the ordeal of a music lesson. Is Arthur there? I should like a cigar.'

She sipped her egg-nog. 'Poor child, she has a strong sense of rhythm but no ear I'm afraid. Such a pity. . . . Now dear Walter Pritchard . . .' Walter, Lady Pritchard's son, was nearly fifteen.

'Damn Walter Pritchard. What about the presents?' Arthur lit the cigar. Fowler took a postcard, a letter and three parcels from a drawer and put them on the table.

I seized the postcard from my cousin Priscilla and put it in my pocket.

'Shall we leave the letter until last?' asked my grandmother, snipping the string with her scissors.

'Yes, I should,' he said, puffing out smoke.

'Open the big one first.' She handed it over and I made the paper crackle.

'There seems to be a lot of wrapping,' he said. 'Has it got an Indian stamp?'

'Heavens alive!' she exclaimed, leaning forward in her chair, 'it's a leopard skin, a small leopard's skin—or is it a tiger?' I spread it on the floor and the pugs began to snort.

'What's the good of that?' he asked crossly.

'It's very nice.' I stroked it. 'Feel!' I picked it up and rubbed it on his hand.

'Damned silly present for a child; what's next?'

'Oh look! Aunt has sent me a little silver piano for the dolls' house. It will go with all the other silver things.'

'It's very pretty, my love. How kind! Now, here is our present.'

I opened the white leather box, and a necklace of tiny plaited pearls slipped to the floor.

'Careful, darling! I will fasten it for you. It's certainly very, becoming; a little long . . .'

'"No matter his mother said, for he's a growing boy, I warrant his behind will grow to fit the corduroy!"' This was a favourite song, which he sang often, waving his cigar like a baton.

'Thank you very much.' I stood on my stool and looked in the glass.

'You are sure you like it?' He sounded doubtful.

'Of course she does, it's the very thing. I found it in Vigo Street. She's wearing her new lace dress, made by Miss Dolby, and she looks quite charming—dear George, how I wish you . . .'

'I thought there were four parcels,' he interrupted. She had been going to say it was a pity he was going blind.

'Give it to me, my love.' She slit the letter open with her ivory knife. Her hands were shaking a little when she raised her lorgnettes and read:

'"My dearest Diana,

"I am posting this letter a month before your birthday to make sure it arrives in time."' She looked at the date on the post mark.

'Well, get on with it, Mamie!' My grandfather crossed his feet on his stick.

'"Under separate cover I am sending you the skin of a young leopard I shot in the jungle. It will make a good rug for your room, if you get it properly mounted and lined."' She cleared her throat. '"Some people make the claws into brooches . . ." How extraordinary, do let me see.'

'For God's sake get on with the letter. You're not a savage! Brooches indeed!'

She read on: '"I enclose some snapshots of me and my—"' she hesitated and spelt out a word, 'it looks like "CHIPRARSIES". I wonder if they can be orchids?'

'Of course not,' he grunted.

'"Also of me and my new polo ponies. Their names are Hasty-Hussy, Hot House"—and something I cannot decipher.' She peered into the envelope. 'There are no photographs as far as I can see.'

'Perhaps they were in the parcel.' He poked at the paper with his stick.

'Here's one,' I said, 'of a very big man on a very small horse, wearing a white hat.'

'I presume the very big man is wearing the white hat,' he said.

'It's a topi; I thought you wanted to hear the rest of the letter? "I am pleased to hear my advice has been followed and the groom is teaching you to swim. I hope he will soon teach you to ride. There is nothing like the pig's skin. In a year or two you should learn to play tennis . . ."'

'The pig's skin?' I exclaimed.

'"I hope you spend plenty of time in the fresh air, birds'-nesting and romping with the kids on the farm." I suppose he means the sock-lambs, which you rear on a bottle.'

'Only a couple of old goats in an atmosphere fouled by cigars,' grandfather said, with a chuckle.

'"I don't want you to be a namby pamby."'

'What's that?' I asked.

'It doesn't matter,' he said.

'"I hope you have learnt to do your own hair and dress yourself and aren't molly-coddled any more."'

'I can wash and dress myself but I can't do my hair,' I said, playing with the pearls.

'"Your last letter was very well written. It's good of your grandmother to teach you to read and write so young, and I hope you are getting on with your music. I think you are old enough to pay a proper visit to Grand H-H, of two or three weeks, at least three times a year, instead of sometimes going for the day from the house in Bryanston Square, which I hear may be sold. I wish you many happy returns and I am your affectionate father. Postscript. It is time you knew it is all rot about fairies and Father Christmas."'

They sat in silence until my grandmother sighed and examined her rings. 'Riding, birds'-nesting, tennis,' she murmured.

'The London visits present a more difficult problem and you must face it fairly and squarely; a letter will follow no doubt. In my opinion she should not go alone for at least a couple of years, unless Fowler . . .'

'I couldn't possibly spare Fowler and she wouldn't fit in. She could take her, of course, and be back in time to dress me for dinner—no, the child would have to stay alone and I imagine the discomfort is appalling. One servant if you please! It all sounds most unsuitable to me.'

'I hear the house is run on somewhat frugal lines . . .'

'My dear, she's eccentric and old-fashioned.'

'She certainly lives in the past. You must recollect that Holman-Hunt was born in 1827. He is part of her religion . . .'

It was as if I wasn't there. I would talk it over with Cherub this very afternoon. Father Christmas didn't matter, and as for fairies, Papa was of course mistaken, as old Dan knew and had often told me they lived on the marsh.

'Oh well, we will discuss it later. Run along and get tidy for luncheon, my treasure, the gong will go in a minute.'

I took Edward with me to wash his hands.

Hannah and Tilly were tidying their hair in front of the cracked glass in the housemaid's cupboard, and Polly was cleaning the brass.

'Thank you so much for the bear,' I said, giving them a kiss.

'My little love,' said Hannah, 'he seems a funny thing to me; we just took Miss Fowler's word.'

'His name is Edward,' I said, stirring the polish jar with its wooden spoon.

'Fancy that!' said Tilly. 'He is a swell; just like the Prince of Wales.' There were several pictures of the Prince in uniform pinned to the walls with tiny Union Jacks.

'That's a new one,' said Hannah, pointing, 'isn't he a lovely boy? What a jolly smile! See, he's smoking a cigarette! He wears his cap in a jaunty way, doesn't he now?'

'He looks a bit flighty to me,' said Tilly, 'but every inch a Prince.' We gazed up at the beaming face.

'Ah well, the war will soon be over. Mr. Johnstone says the Hun is on the run.'

'My, aren't you posh today, dressed to kill!' cried Polly.

'You'll turn her head,' warned Tilly.

'Never!' protested Hannah. 'Never, will she dear? There are some as are born with their heads screwed on and some,' she glanced at Polly, '*some* as aren't.'

'Things that screw on, unscrew very easily,' I said, thinking of the ivory box. 'Papa says I'm to go and stay with Grand in London for two or three weeks.'

Grand was my father's mother and Grandpa Holman-Hunt's widow. I knew he was the famous pre-Raphaelite painter and that she was also known as Mrs. H-H.

'Well, fancy you, going to pay a visit all alone,' said Hannah, dusting a wooden chair for me to sit on. 'Careful dear, you don't want to crease that nice new dress.'

'Paying a visit is what Grand calls going to the lavatory, except she calls it the convenience. Unmentionables are socks and drawers.'

'My word, she is refined,' said Polly.

'Grand calls a po an "article". I can't think why.' It was nothing to do with the *Spectator*.

'I don't think po is a very nice word for little girls,' said Hannah primly.

'Well, I call it a chamber and that's that,' said Polly, shaking her tin of Bluebell.

'Now my girl, get on with your work. You've no time to chat,' said Hannah, putting on a prig's face.

'When I go to Kensington Palace, I sit on a commode, when I'm told I'd better, after tea, before the 'bus ride home. I don't think the Princess has got a . . .'

'To think that one of these days you might meet the Prince of Wales!' said Hannah quickly, ecstasy lighting her face. 'You are a lucky little girl! Just think if you was to have tea with Him and His mother . . .'

'I'd rather have tea with you,' I said, 'if Mrs. Hopkins . . .'

'I think I hear Miss Fowler calling,' said Polly, looking up from polishing a can. 'You'd better run.'

Before Johnstone rang the gong, my grandfather was always ready at the bottom of the stairs. 'Come along slow-coach!' He rattled his stick along the banisters. As the gong boomed under Johnstone's beating, the pugs led the way, sniffing for their dinner plates behind the screen.

'Try and walk gracefully, precious, don't be a hobbledehoy,' said grandmother, taking my hand and leading me on. She wore a hat for luncheon. Arthur followed with her bag and the hot-water bottle.

She didn't eat like other people; a fact to which she drew attention every day; holding up a spoon of slops and saying: 'Look, look! This is all I can digest.' After a few sips she would push her cup aside, swallow some pills from a little gold box, and pick up her knitting. I chewed in time with the click of the needles. Sometimes she read aloud from the *Graphic* or *Spectator*. 'Just listen to this, my dear: Break in the Hindenburg Line! Zeppelin's lurid end. Kite Balloon Observers under fire. Hun's savage Revenge...'

Johnstone stood swaying a little with his hands behind his back, staring at the pictures. I knew I mustn't watch Arthur poking food into grandfather's mouth, but out of the corner of my eye, across the silver bowl of roses or carnations, I could see a spoonful of meat or pudding poised under his nose. He talked a great deal and when he finished a sentence, he would open his mouth like a baby bird and Arthur would be ready, like the mother bird with a worm.

Sometimes he would look in my direction and say: 'Let's hear Diana's opinion. Meals are a time for conversation.' It was very important to utter.

'Yes darling, tell us something of interest—something amusing.'

'I expect she's too busy stuffing her tum.'

If he were in a good mood, when asked if he would like another helping, he would answer in a solemn voice: 'No thank you, I am not hungry, but if pressed, I might manage,' and then he would burst into song:

Some mulligatawny soup, a mackerel and a sole,
A Banbury and a Bath bun and a tuppenny sausage roll,
A little drop of sherry and a little drop of cham,
Some roly-poly pudding and some jam, jam, JAM.

Johnstone pretended not to notice, but I knew he was a humbug and took in every word, repeating to Mrs. Hopkins through the pantry-hatch what we said about the food and much besides, flicking a glass-cloth at Arthur, and telling him to look sharp and get about his business.

After luncheon if we were alone, we sat in the boudoir, for half an hour or so. Arthur lit grandfather's cigar and when grandmother had drunk some powder in hot water, her head drooped like a broken flower, and she slept, snoring quietly like the pugs.

'Good heavens!' she exclaimed, rudely disturbing the pugs, 'just look at the time. I must go and dress for tea with Mr. James; it's quite a long drive. How sad I must leave you today, but alas, I had no choice.' She rang the bell. 'Arthur must see to the dogs, their breath is rather bad.'

'We shall be quite all right, my dear. Can someone dispose of my cigar? When you return we shall, no doubt, be treated to a description of your taming of the lion. I must bestir myself. Foster is waiting and there is much business awaiting my attention.'

We all knew we must leave nothing out of place, so that grandfather, feeling with his stick, could thread his way between familiar things. A change of an inch in the position of a chair could cause a frightful fall.

It was raining a little. Fowler was waiting in the hall with my galoshes and a waterproof cape. 'Tuck your hair well into the hood,' she said, snapping the elastic on my forehead and tweaking the rubber frill to frame my face. 'Mind you run about, don't go mooning. You don't want to catch your death.'

Cold gusts of wind blew the leaves into whispering heaps in the corners of the terrace. I read the postcard from Priscilla as I cut across the lawns, past the fig trees and the ruins, to the kitchen garden: it had high brick walls on three sides, and was supposed to be an acre. From dawn until dusk Dan worked on it alone. It was his pride.

'Good afternoon,' I said.

He was bent double, filling baskets with apples from the ground. Like a fat crab he scavenged down the row of trees, which joined hands as far as the low stone wall on top of the cliff. It was called 'Snakes' Wall' because in the summer grass snakes hung from the crevices basking in the sun.

'It's my birthday. I've had a letter from Papa; he says it's not true about the fairies.'

I straddled Snakes' Wall, and smoothed the moss on the coping.

Dan waddled back staring at the ground. He rubbed an apple on his sleeve and squatted by my side. 'Eat it up, it be foine and juicy. They'm no fairies in India, not that I know.'

'But there are on the marsh and the cliff and in the acre, aren't there? You said you'd seen them.'

'Aye, I told 'ee I seed 'em on the marsh, twinkling their little loights.'

'And you did, didn't you?' I persisted, yet not daring to look him in the eye. He might have lied all along.

'Aye,' he said, shaking his head, 'there be good uns and bad uns. To my moind it be so.'

'Oh, I knew it was all right, really,' I assured him, blushing.

'Don't worrit thy papa. It be no good worriting about what be.'

'I knew it would be all right,' I said again, flinging my apple core down the cliff into a group of elders.

He couldn't bear to waste time, so I said: 'Good-bye, and thank you for the apple.'

I walked back through the nuttery. Young Uncle had hung small swings from the hazels, for me and my cousin Priscilla. I sat in hers for a change, but it was dull alone. There was no one in the potting-shed and nothing to do. I stroked the beards of raffia hanging from the walls. As usual on such dismal occasions I knew Cherub would be waiting: I climbed the steps to the fountain.

'There's nothing like the pig's skin,' I declared, my shoes sinking in the soggy grass.

'You can't make a silk purse out of a sow's ear,' said Cherub, wisely.

'There are no such words as "can't" and "don't",' I answered primly. 'You don't want to do that, means you *do*, but you mustn't.'

'They certainly talk in a puzzling way.'

'Not that I care, but Young Uncle will soon be home talking Double Dutch.'

'The jolly ladies will bring their maids to sit in the sewing-room for hours.'

'But they are sure to forget their knitting.'

'And wear *unsuitable* silk stockings in the day-time.'

'They always say "You are a funny girl!" and Young Uncle says, "What a nice, clean dress!" when he means it's dirty. I just shan't listen any more. Fairly and squarely . . . what about the London visit?'

'Pooh!' scoffed Cherub, 'this year, next year, sometime, never!'

''Ark, 'ark, the lark!' said a voice in my ear. It was Arthur with the pugs. He always said this, instead of well, or dear me. 'It don't seem right you sitting' out 'ere in the cold, talkin' to yourself.' He looked round at the fallen leaves. 'It's a dead-alive place in the winter; the same old thing day after day fair gives you the pip. You can't beat London is what I say to Mr. Johnstone, and now I 'ear they're goin' to sell the London 'ouse, just when the blinkin' war's nearly over.'

'It's very nice here in the summer,' I said, stooping to pat the pugs. 'It's quite different when I have Priscilla to play with.'

'Yes, it fair livens the old place up when Mr. and Mrs. 'Ubert are 'ere with the children and Rose. Rose knows what's what and that Master Tom's a caution. It makes a change when my friend's at the Pritchards—'Ark at me wasting me time. Mr. Foster's 'ere with the master, so Miss Fowler says, seein' as you're alone, you can come and 'ave tea in the 'all. Don't let on but Ma 'Opkins 'as baked a cake, special like, with icin'.'

'Oh good,' I said, 'can we play the gramophone?'

'You'll 'ave to ask Ma 'Opkins; if she's got one of 'er 'eads she won't 'ave it, not for the Queen of Sheba.'

'Her heads,' I said, stressing the aitches. 'Mrs. Hopkins' hat,' I paused, 'has hay hinside; you'd better say it after me.'

''Ark at you, all la-di-da! There's two new records, one's a fair scream: it's called "Maggie? Yes Ma! Come right upstairs!"'

'Oh, I do hope Mrs. Hopkins . . .'

The pugs began to snuffle.

'I shall fair cop it,' said Arthur, 'I 'aven't finished shuttin' up.'

'Race you to the garden door!' I said.

When we reached the boudoir, the leopard's skin was hanging over the back of a chair, its tail dangling to the floor.

'It don't seem right, that blinkin' wild animal in the boudoir! Why, it looks fair 'eathen in 'ere.' He unfolded the shutters. 'If I was you I'd take it away.'

I ran upstairs and spread it on my bed. I stood and stared: it crouched and wanted to spring at the wall. . . . It didn't look right. I rolled it up, winding the tail round and round the furry bundle, and put it under my arm.

'Ah, here we are!' said Fowler. 'Run and wash your hands because we're going to have tea in the Hall. You can bring that bear if you like. Now, what are you doing? I don't want that tiger messing up the sewing-room: you want to put it in the cupboard with the Burmese toys.'

'What a good idea,' I said, stuffing it in. 'No one seems to like it much; but the silver piano's very nice.'

'Mrs. Hopkins has baked a cake as a surprise. Don't forget to thank her and mind your P's and Q's,' she whispered as we made our way to the Servants' Hall.

Johnstone was sitting in his shirt-sleeves, wearing silver-coloured elastic bands on his arms and reading the paper. He got up when I came in and led me to the end of the table. 'Isn't this where Mrs. Hopkins sits?' I asked. 'Oh, what a lovely cake!' Johnstone hiccuped.

'You're welcome, miss, I hope it eats well,' said Mrs. Hopkins, pushing to claim her place, 'and where would you like to sit?' She glared at Johnstone.

'Next to Arthur, please.' I hoped Fowler would approve.

'Did you ever?' cried Polly. 'She's starting young!'

'Hold your tongue, Polly,' said Hannah crossly, 'I'm sure it's quite nice, as they're the youngest I mean.'

'Not 'alf,' said Arthur, giving me a wink. We all sat down scraping our chairs on the floor.

'Bread and butter first,' said Fowler, looking strict.

'Aren't the candles pretty?' asked Tilly. 'You must blow them out together. When you cut the cake, you have a wish.'

'I wish to play the gramophone,' I said.

'Oh, you mustn't tell or it won't come true dear,' said Hannah, nervously stirring her tea.

'It will, won't it?' I turned to Mrs. Hopkins, 'or 'ave you got one of your 'eads?'

'You can please yourself, miss, them as has no work to do can play it, but me and my Annie will be busy in the kitchen.' She retired behind the cosy.

''Ark, 'ark, the lark,' muttered Arthur.

'We'll have none of your sauce, my boy,' said Johnstone. We got on with our tea until Polly turned up her cup on the saucer and gave a little scream: 'My! There's a tall dark stranger, and what's that? Is it a present?'

'You'd better be careful,' said Tilly, leaning over to look, 'a surprise packet maybe.' She gave Polly a nudge.

'Yes, you'll get more than you've bargained for, one of these days,' said Hannah darkly. 'The hop-pickers are a rough lot.'

'I'm not one to pass remarks,' ventured Fowler, 'but I grant Mrs. Hopkins has a light hand with a cake. Careful, Miss Diana — you don't want to slop milk on Miss Dolby's dress. Now say your grace like a good girl.'

'Come along, Annie,' said Mrs. Hopkins, getting up and brushing the crumbs off her lap into the fire, 'we've no time to waste like some folks.'

I helped to stack the plates, while Johnstone and Arthur lifted the heavy table back against the wall. The gramophone stood in a corner. Its huge mahogany horn was fluted like a flower. 'You'd better let Arthur do the winding, dear,' said Hannah. 'It's not like the churn, or the knife machine, you can't just go on and on. Shall we start with "Tipperary" or "Roses round the door"?'

'That old thing: it's reely orful! "The Waters of Minnetonka" is a lovely waltz.' Polly tapped time with her fingers. 'Tilly, do come and shake a leg.' They danced together, spinning round and round with the velvet ribbons flying from their caps.

'Why don't you dance, Arthur?' I asked, jigging to the music.

'He doesn't fancy it,' said Hannah, 'singing's more his line; two more records and we'll play his funny song. The next tune isn't a new one—maybe I'm old-fashioned.'

'If you were the only girl in the world,' quacked a lady in the horn.

Johnstone rose from his chair, put on his coat, and crossed the room to Fowler: 'May I have the pleasure?' he asked with a bow and drew her protesting to her feet. She was too fat to dance, but he whirled about, pulling her with him, stretching her short arm and pumping her hand up and down. 'Don't tread on my corns, for Mercy's sake!' she cried, hobbling around like a lame black hen. Her bun uncoiled and hairpins scattered, skidding under the chairs.

There was such a din, no-one noticed Mrs. Hopkins until she shouted: 'The bell's rung twice!' and went out slamming the door.

'Oh lor', now what's up? Blast the blinkin' bell,' said Arthur.

Johnstone straightened his coat and took a comb from his pocket. 'You'd better look sharp, Mr. Foster's off most like, it won't be the mistress yet and don't forget the whiskey.'

'We must get to the sewing-room,' said Fowler, panting and wiping her face.

'Good night, my little dear. Sweet dreams,' called Hannah.

When Fowler and I hurried past the row of bells, the library one was ticking, and wagging its yellow tongue.

Fowler covered Mr. Pim, my canary, with a hood of green baize. His cage hung in the window. The curtains didn't pull, because too many of the hooks were missing. She drew down the blind and noisily made up the fire with shovels of coal. On the chimney-piece my shells and things from Mrs. Rook's shop were arranged in patterns, in front of a flyblown card printed in red: 'Be good sweet maid, and let who will be clever.'

Flat-irons lay on sloping metal shelves on one side of the

grate which Tilly burnished every morning with a chain. A large sooty kettle stood on the hob; it was always hot in the sewing-room. Against one wall was an old brass bed heaped with mending. By it stood a dressmaker's dummy wearing my grandmother's clothes; it was as if she were there, silently watching like God.

I was forbidden to touch the sewing-machine, or anything on the table; the button-box with a picture of King Edward on its lid, the heart-shaped pin-cushion, the shears, the glove-stretchers stilettos and bodkins; all had their special place. The most tempting thing was a strawberry, into which Fowler poked the rusty needles. A large magnet, for picking pins off the floor, was tied to the table with a string.

My dolls' house stood in a corner; it was tall and narrow. Young Uncle had made it long ago when he was home on leave. He hadn't forgotten the staircase; it was still in his room but there'd been no time to fit it in.

The piecebag hung from a hook, its lumpy body bulging out from the wall. My scissors on a long red ribbon were shaped like a stork. I cut bits of stuff or ribbon with its beak and gummed them in the dolls' house.

'Mind that glue now, you don't want to make a mess,' Fowler would say, looking up and frowning.

The ground floor was richly furnished with silver, a black velvet carpet and white lace curtains. The rest was rather bare, as the things people gave me didn't look right.

Old Dan made me some chairs out of conkers. Fowler was shocked when I threw them on the fire: 'You're spoilt, that's what you are, folks take a lot of pains and I gave him my best steel pins. I don't know what to make of it, sometimes you act real bad.'

When the whole house was tidy, I sat back and put in the people. They uttered all the time and I moved them about. When I was falling asleep, they began to do things alone. Of their own accord, they behaved unsuitably, shouting and hitting each other, and jumping out of the windows.

The fire blazed hot and the machine buzzed like a bee. If Fowler were pressing grandmother's clothes, there was a smell of scorched paper and a windy noise when she swung the crimping tongs round and round to cool them. I could hear the iron thud and swish to and fro and sometimes a sizzle, when she spat to test it for heat.

Arthur knocked on the sewing-room door.

'The master's alone in the library; 'e'd like to see Miss Diana.'

'Ah, here you are,' said grandfather, 'how late your grandmother is.'

'Perhaps the lion has eaten her,' I said.

'It wasn't a real lion.' He fumbled for his glass of whiskey. 'You would weep if you thought a real lion had eaten one of the pugs. Is *The Times* on the stool?'

It was, still just as Arthur had ironed it.

'Open it in the middle.'

'It's so big, I'd better lay it on the floor.' I sat on my stool and bent over the vast sheets, shifting them to rights.

'You will see some things are printed larger than others; try and read those out. Mark the unfamiliar words with your pencil and tomorrow you can copy them down in your vocabulary, when I have explained their meanings to you.'

'It's not like a story,' I said, beginning to read: 'L-U-D-E-N-D-O-R-F-F dismissed guard against Spanish I-N-F-L-U-E-N-Z-A on the way to Mons learn the Hesitation W-A-L-T-Z no promise of offal Swiss feelings outraged register at Liptons for jam Bovril gives strength to win a D-I-S-A-P-P-E-A-R-I-N-G husband how to feed a pig quick sale for dear matches B-R-U-G-E-S under the yoke H-O-R-A-T-I-O-Bottomley will speak in ruined village Mr. Wilson's reply drink after the war Lord d'Abernon's S-U-G-G-E-S-T-I-O-N . . .'

'It's a trifle confusing unless you pause between the headlines.' He seemed to be amused. I slid off the stool and scrambled about on the paper, searching for what he wanted.

'That was capital. Ring for Arthur, I should like a cigar.'

'Oh, need I?' I coaxed the crumpled *Times* into its folds. 'He gets fed up when you go on ringing the bell.'

'Damn Arthur and his reactions to the bell!'

'Oh, let me try.' I picked the knife off the table and opened it, breaking my nail.

'Put that knife down—you will succeed only in cutting your fingers. I told you to ring.'

'I can bite it off,' I said, sinking my teeth in the end of the cigar. 'Arthur always does when you're in a hurry . . .'

'Good God,' he exploded, 'do you mean to say that rascal . . .'

'Now, here it is,' I pushed it into his mouth, 'and here's a match—go on—puff. You see? It's easy.' I hoped Arthur was playing his 'Maggie, yes Ma'.

'H-mm,' he said, drawing on the flame, and blowing out smoke in grey funnels, 'hmm, I fear you will be something of a flirt. Ah well, Mamie's very late. Although it appears that in your and Arthur's opinion I am a blind old fool, I am well aware it is past your bedtime. However, I must confess, I am at a loss as to how to amuse you . . .'—he looked for me in the wrong direction.

'Shall we play Blind Man's Buff, like I do with Priscilla? I promise not to run and you can feel your way about and catch me if you can!'

'What folly! Certainly not. You had better write a letter to your father and thank him for the present.'

I sat at the writing-table, sucked the pen and began to scratch at the grey silurian.

There was a sudden commotion in the hall; the pugs uncurled, like fried whitings under a fork, and ran to the door yapping. My grandmother was suddenly with us again, wearing her furs, and filling the room with a smell of violets.

'My treasures!' she exclaimed, patting the hand which held our cigar, 'I'm shockingly late'; she crossed the room drawing off her gloves. 'I couldn't resist calling on Lettice Spragg. The dear girl was overjoyed and gave me such a welcome! She showed me her work; great piles of most elaborate comforts. When I think of my own pathetic efforts, I must eat humble pie.' She leant over my shoulder and read: '"Dear Papa, thank you for the leper's skin, it was just what I wanted." Oh, my precious, how comical you are.'

'I think she should go to bed; she waited up for you, you know.'

'But of course.' She bent over my chair, letting her sables brush against my cheek. 'Dear George, I have so much to tell you, but alas, now it is time to go and dress.'

I fetched Edward from the sewing-room. 'It's far too late to have a bath,' called Fowler, 'you just want to do your teeth and wash your face and hands.'

There were no tasks to tick off and I didn't bother to say my prayers, which were only a list of names, with 'God bless' at the beginning and 'please help me to be a good girl amen' at the end.

Edward and I got into bed and I put Priscilla's postcard under my pillow. I heard voices through the door and slow rhythmical strokes when Fowler brushed grandmother's hair. I took the wicked Kaiser out of *Punch* and made him do a goose-step. Suddenly, to my surprise, he threw his helmet in the air and began to whistle 'Tipperary'.

CHAPTER TWO

It was not until Fowler and I were crossing London in a taxi-cab that I began to feel uneasy. I knew she disapproved of Grand and of the house in Melbury Road, where she had taken me many times before but only for the day. When we drew up in front of the tall, grimy, brick and stucco house, I pointed out my name on the blue plaque let into the wall: 'And see the O.M.? It means the Order of Merit.' She was not impressed: 'O.M. Pooh! What's the good of that? A title now, a title would be nice.'

'Grand says . . .'

'Grand fiddlesticks!' she snapped. 'A barrack of a place, no butler, no proper staff. I don't know I'm sure.' As she rang the bell, she shook her head with disapproval and the cabby nodded. He put my hamper on the step and left us there waiting for Helen.

'I expect she's downstairs,' I said after a while, perturbed by the delay. 'When she climbs from the basement, her face gets very pink, as pink as her dress.' For her sake I wished she would hurry.

'Seeing as it's afternoon, it's to be hoped she's changed from her print and washed and put on her blacks.' Fowler tapped her foot, as if we'd already been there an hour.

At last, there was a rattle of chains and a scraping of bolts. Helen peered round the door wearing her pink print dress.

'Ah, good afternoon,' said Fowler, scowling.

'Like a cup of tea, miss?' asked Helen, shyly. I sensed she was afraid of Fowler.

'I'll not trouble you,' said Fowler, her nose pointing in the air, 'but I'd be obliged if you'd tell the under-housemaid to steam

Miss Diana's velveteens and mind she keeps her kettle off the lace.' She knew, of course, there wasn't anyone to tell. She turned to me: 'Well, I haven't got all day. I must bustle back to the station. I'm sure you'll be all right.' Her expression showed she thought it most unlikely.

'Oh, don't go,' I cried in a panic, throwing my arms round her neck. 'Please don't go, don't leave me.'

'What a way to go on!' she said severely, adjusting her hat. Her face was very white and her eyes were shining when she pressed my hand and pecked me on the cheek. Helen and I watched her walk down the steps to the cab but she didn't look round.

'Well, miss, you haven't shrunk,' said Helen. This was the only joke she ever made. She bolted and barred the door. My throat was sore with worry. I stared at our dim reflection in the glass of the portrait of Grandpa Holman by Sir William Richmond and saw I was nearly as tall as Helen.

'The mistress is in the sitting-room. You know your way, miss, don't you?' Helen vanished down the basement stairs.

In the inner hall one jet of gas burned low and blue on an iron bracket, casting a glinting light on the brass plates, copper trays, daggers, scimitars and swords that dotted the walls, between oil paintings. Grandpa Holman's portrait of himself as a boy, Christs, virgins and saints, great-uncle Waugh who was drowned; all gazed down at the Burmese gongs, supported by gilded dragons —these were a present from Papa and didn't look right. A pair of tall church candlesticks, festooned with rosaries, stood each side of a massive table which was draped with altar cloths and shawls. On it stood a red chalk drawing and Chinese bowls filled with silver money. There were no flowers or signs of life: no coat flung down in a hurry, no secateurs, gloves or parasols.

The sitting-room door opened slowly. Suddenly Grand was there with her arms outstretched like a cross: 'My pet! I thought I heard voices. Come and give me a hug.' She was straight and bony; her brooches, chatelaine and buckles pressed sharply into my ribs.

Nothing was changed in the sitting-room; perhaps the leafy Morris paper was a little darker. The Della Robbia, covered with dust, still hung over the fireplace, the vases held the same sprays of honesty and peacock feathers, and the spindly bamboo tables, as before, tottered under the heavy weight of papers.

A purple taffeta curtain was pulled across the Van Dyck crucifixion. Grand had said long ago that Crucifixions and St. Sebastians were less valuable than Holy Families. Sensitive people couldn't bear to see the blood, or the cruel arrows sticking into dripping wounds. I couldn't bear it either. I spun round on my heel; another curtain of faded orange silk was drawn across the Bellini; a small piece of St. Joseph showed in a corner.

In the day-time, the more precious pictures too were covered, to prevent their fading by the sun; this precaution gave the effect of many windows of odd shapes and sizes, placed at different levels on the walls, through which peeping Toms could pry. I hated this sensation and wished all the pretty wallpaper was showing but I knew of course, as Grand had told me, that only poor uneducated people didn't like pictures on their walls.

'Shall we draw the curtains?' I asked, taking off my woollen gloves.

Without speaking she whisked a muslin veil off the Byzantine black Madonna, revealing the dark face under its jewelled crown.

'The gold background is nice,' I said, flinching from the wicked squinting eyes.

'The furious seascape below is by Mr. Ruskin.' She leant forward to examine it more closely. 'His waterfalls and rocky coasts are better. Take off your coat, my pet.'

An inverted coolie hat, filled with catalogues and crumpled paper bags, lay on the Moorish throne which was made of ebony, inlaid with ivory stars and little bits of glass. Grandpa Holman had painted this in his picture of *Isabella and the Pot of Basil*.

'Everything's the same,' I said, stroking a huge oak chest.

'The Hobman chest, remember?' She raised the lid which was carved inside. 'Made in the Spanish Netherlands as a travelling altar. It once held the sacramental vessels but now, as you see, it's crammed with clothes which the models wore; in fact, when it stood in the studio, Holman called it his "prop box". See, here is Miss Siddal's dress for Sylvia.'

'Guggum's dress,' I said, fingering the folds. Danish ancestor

Hobman had used the chest as a trunk when he brought his furs to England. He must have had a lot—fur coats, fur hats, fur boots, fur gloves, fur trousers, fur combinations, fur . . .

'I told you, I hope I did, I always forget, Holman's name was really Hobman? It was his Christian name; he was never called William. One day, looking up some papers in connection with a lawsuit, he found the clerk had written "Holman" by mistake. From that day he used no other name, and when I heard that Queen Victoria said: "We consider Hunt too ordinary a name for such an *extraordinary* man: we would like you to use a hyphen," I naturally used the double-barrel. Beloved Holman . . . Come my pet, it's only four o'clock, for a whole hour we will do as you like.'

'I should like to do my museum.'

'Capital! There is no fire in the drawing-room but if you keep your coat and I put on my paisley, all will be well. We'll take these candles—there is no need to light the gas, but first I'm sure you should go and pay a visit.'

'I'll take a candle with me,' I said, thinking of poor Edward stifling in my stuffy box. I crossed the inner hall to the front door and set my candlestick on one of the Waugh chairs which had wheat-sheaves carved on their backs. I undid the leather strap and raised the creaking wicker lid. Edward's nose was poking up between the tissue paper. I pulled him out and I stood for a moment undecided. Perhaps she disapproved of bears. I took off my coat and wrapped him in its folds. With the bundle under my arm I made my way to the drawing-room.

'Take care, my pet, not to drip grease on the Persian rugs; they are silk pictures on the floor.'

'Yes, I know,' I said, shielding my flame from the draught.

'You're sure you're warm enough without your coat?'

'Yes, quite warm, thank you.' I shivered and laid Edward on a table.

My museum was a glass brass-bound cabinet lined with dingy velvet. It stood at the far end of the room on the left of the French windows: I had helped to curtain them with beads.

With a tinkle of keys from her chatelaine, Grand opened the cabinet doors; a frowsty smell arose from inside. Each item was labelled. While I took the things out and put them on a table, Grand read their descriptions from the list which we had made one rainy afternoon.

'The bottle of Jordan water in which you were christened. I saved it to use again. Oh, how I hoped you'd be a boy! I expect you've often longed for brothers?'

'I've never thought about it really.' Did she mean that no-one wanted me?

'The humming bird—see the exquisite colours of its plumage? A mud trap made by a spider. Look at that hinge, the spider made it. A silver necklace of Fatima's hands, each one is saying its prayer and here's a prayer wheel—see how it turns? The thunderbolt Holman picked up on the downs at Fairlight with Edward Lear and Jack Millais when Thackeray came for the day. A mandoline—how pretty it is—tortoise-shell, gold and mother-of-pearl; I bought that years ago in Naples. An Irish sea urchin—I filled it with plaster of Paris; an ink horn, a brass shell from the Crimea, a bundle of Lord Kitchener's letters—he was such a good friend. A South African medal, a fossilized fish found by Mr. Ruskin in France, a Chinese puzzle, a phial for kohl—orientals paint their eyelids. An enamelled hobble-ring—an Eastern prince wore this to show he never worked. Ivory chessmen, spillikins, how delicate they are. A set of Maundy money, even a silver penny. A scarab from Mr. Leonard Woolley, glass bangles from Egypt: they're very brittle but slip them on your wrist. Silver anklets, with tiny bells—your Aunt Gladys wore these as a child in *The Flight from Egypt*. A piece of papyrus, it's indestructible, just you try and tear it! A moving picture—see how ingenious—a thick pack of cards . . . flick and the girl is dancing! Give it to me, I'll do it for you . . .'

'The velvet's very dusty, I think I should brush it before we put everything back.'

'Yes, of course, there's a little brush hanging on the fire-screen. . . . Good gracious, what a cloud.' She sneezed. 'On Friday we have this room to turn out and, what do you think? Such treats! On Saturday, dear Anstey Guthrie is giving a children's party.'

'A party?' My voice rose with alarm. 'Will it be like the

Thackeray Ritchie party at Wimbledon, when the children acted *The Rose and the Ring?*' Fairy Blackstick had been nice but Gruffenuff was horrid and I didn't know anyone at all.

'Such a clever book! Why you prefer that rubbishy *Alice*, I simply cannot conceive. I never cared for Lewis Carroll, dabbling in that photographic rubbish was such a waste of time. No, it won't be quite the same but I think there'll be a conjurer, or perhaps a Punch and Judy and lots of jolly games.'

'I don't want to go,' I said, by now thoroughly disturbed.

'You are a goose, of course you do, and now it's time for tea. You'd better run and fill the kettle in the cloakroom. It makes the tray lighter for Helen. One must always consider the servants and remember the poor creatures are human. I hope you shook hands when you arrived? No? A gracious gesture makes such a difference. Holman was so gracious, a saint, always putting the happiness of humble people far before his own.'

Holding the candles she walked with me across the hall to the cloakroom for the kettle. 'When Helen brings the tray shall I tell her to carry up my luggage?' I asked, pointing to the hamper.

'Tell Helen to carry that heavy box, up all those stairs? My dear child, I've never heard of such a thing! One doesn't tell servants to do things. One asks them politely. Your box can stay where it is. Why should an elderly person wait on an active child? You can take out your nightgown, your loofah and your tooth-brush, and if you're not going to wear that coat you'd better hang it here.'

What would Fowler say?

'Oh, I think I'd better put it in the sitting-room. I mean it might get damp if I left it in the hall . . .'

'Damp in the hall!' Her eyes flashed with indignation. I might have suggested there were cobras crawling up the walls.

'This house is as dry as a bone, perhaps a little damp in the basement. I hope you're not a fusspot. Your grandmother may be a delicate woman.' She sounded doubtful. 'I hear she has ulcers caused, no doubt, by rich food. Central heating's unhealthy and it's folly to take so many pills. There are but three remedies to which I turn; senna-pods, brandy and vaseline. Ah, here's Helen with the tray. While the kettle boils you can toast the buns. Don't drop them in the fire as there aren't any more.'

'Miss Diana's milk, mum,' said Helen, lifting a steaming jug with lumps of skin hanging from its lip.

'Oh, I don't want any hot milk,' I said, dropping the bun off the toasting-fork into the fender.

'Of course you do,' said Grand, 'boiled milk is free from germs and nourishing as well.'

'I hate boiled milk,' I said, blowing the ash off my bun. Grown-ups always thought they knew exactly what one wanted.

'Unboiled milk is exceedingly dangerous; in fact it once made you very ill with infantile tuberculosis. That will do nicely, Helen. We can manage. Now my pet, careful how you spread the margarine. I expect you have butter in the country, but margarine is just as good; indeed I believe it's better. You may take a little gooseberry jam.'

'At home they have gooseberry jam in the Servants' Hall; we never have it in the drawing-room. Priscilla says it's full of fur. I know what she means,' I said, trying to swallow a hairy skin.

'Dear me, I hope you're not a fad? Food is only important as fuel; whether we like it or not is quite immaterial. It's just fuel; like coal for the fire.'

'Well, I love food,' I said, munching away: having had no luncheon I was hungry.

'Oh, come now, you can't love food; you love God and I hope you love Grand! We love food for the mind, such as pictures and poetry.'

'I love food to eat,' I insisted, licking the crumbs off my fingers, 'I love roast lamb and Addison's strawberry ices.'

'Don't be ruled by Brother Ass, he's only your body and a nuisance. Be like St. Francis; ignore him!'

She had often talked about Brother Ass before. High-minded people stifled their greed, their sneezes and hiccups and suppressed other noises to imitate St. Francis who was what Polly called 'refined'.

'Now my dear, you can make yourself useful; there are many circulars, envelopes and paper bags ready on the Moorish throne.'

'Which do you need most, spills or lavatory paper?'

'Let me see—the latter I think, as none has been made for so long. Here is your knife.' It was engraved with the name Helen Faucit. 'You will find the stiletto, the template and string in the Indian box over there.' She settled at the writing-table, and with a pin-like nib, scratched away at her letters.

I ripped the blade through the stiff paper folded round the template. 'Some of these bags from Palmer's Stores are very thick and covered with writing.'

'Print is all right on one side you know. Try not to talk.'

When I had cut a hundred sheets, I pierced their corners and threaded them with a string; I tied this in a loop to hang on a nail by the 'convenience'. I made a mental note of the softer pieces and put them together in the middle, between the back of a calendar from Barkers and an advertisement for night-lights. This task had always seemed to me constructive and I preferred it to the one at home of threading thousands of old stamps, with a needle, on to yards of cotton. When six snakes were done Fowler packed them in a box and posted them to London. I liked to think that when they felt a little better, the wounded soldiers wore them after tea.

'What time d'you have dinner?' I asked, when I thought I'd cut enough sheets of paper for a month.

'Dinner?' She peered over her pince-nez. 'I don't have any dinner. My good Helen will soon be up with the trip-wires, booby-traps and bells and, although it's only Monday and I usually bath on Friday, I thought it would refresh you if we took a bath tonight.'

I was shocked. 'Don't you bath every night? I do, at least nearly always.'

'Hot baths are so devitalizing.' She rose from her chair and before I could stop her, picked up my coat. With a squeak of surprise Edward fell on the floor.

'Good gracious! What's that?' she gasped.

'That's Edward,' I said, bracing myself for an attack.

'He's not beautiful, is he?' She looked suspicious: 'So that's why you kept your coat. I'm afraid, my pet, you behaved in a deceitful, scheming way: ugly things corrupt and lead to evil deeds.'

'I don't think Edward's ugly,' I said, clenching my fists.

She hesitated before she spoke. 'My pet, how sad it is that you are an only child.' It didn't seem sad to me. I rescued Edward and let her draw me to the fire. 'I think you should have a dog. I once had a noble dog, a bulldog, his name was Caesar. I was fined, the only time I ever went to court, because he strayed without a muzzle. "But my dear Judge," I protested—I had dined with him, a delightful man, the night before—"ten shillings! Surely you know Caesar never wears a muzzle?" "In that case," he replied, "I fear it must be a sovereign!" How dear Holman chaffed me later for my ingenuousness!'

'There are two pugs at home,' I said, 'but they aren't really mine and I'm rather frightened of bulldogs; at least of the ones I see in Punch.'

'Ah! I expect you mean the cartoons by Bernard Partridge? Remind me to take you to call. He lives down the road and said he'd like to make a sketch of you one day, as Peace or France, I can't remember which. What was I saying? Ah yes, a fear of dogs is nothing of which to be ashamed. Edward Lear, an enormous man, found even small ones most alarming. You know who I mean by Edward Lear?'

'Oh yes—the Owl and the Pussy-cat man. He called Grandpa Holman "Daddy", or "Papa", and he called him ...'

'"Infant!"' she prompted.

'And Edward Lear gave Queen Victoria drawing lessons but it didn't do much good ...' I glanced up at her framed illustrated letters on the wall.

'My pet, I do believe you have Holman's memory! He never even forgot a conversation. I have Lear's letters put away; they're really quite amusing. He wrote to at least thirty people before breakfast every day. Hark, I think I hear Helen with the bells.'

I ran to the hall. Helen stood there, puffing as usual. Lengths of wire, with sharp prongs at each end, were wound round her neck, and bells on metal rings were hanging from her arms. In one hand she held a hammer and in the other a basket full of tins.

'The trip-wires first,' Grand said, briskly, 'bring a candle, dear.'

'Take a candle child to light your mother through the snow!' I giggled because Helen looked so funny. Grand stretched the wires across the room and hammered the sharp pegs in the floor between the Persian rugs. She made piles of tins here and there about the room.

'What is she doing, Helen?' I asked.

'Them's for trapping the thieves what come in the night,' she whispered. 'We don't want to be murdered in our beds now, do we?'

'I should think not!' I exclaimed, much startled. The old Monk at home was bad enough. 'There aren't any thieves in Bryanston Square—at least we don't set any traps,' I boasted loudly.

'The things there are all very well in their way,' Grand condescended, 'but they don't compare with the treasures here; what with menservants, telephones and electric light, such precautions would be perhaps superfluous: electric light, thanks to Sir Joseph Swan, who was your godfather's father you know. Gabriel Rossetti was once offered a post in a telegraph office. He declined of course. In my opinion the discipline would have done him good. Now for the bells.' She hooked them over the doors.

'You'd better fetch what you need from your box and say goodnight to Helen. Take care not to walk on the paint.'

There was a notice tacked to a tread: 'Edith H-H painted this staircase in 1905'. I picked my way with Edward and my nightgown under my arm, swinging my new check sponge-bag.

In Grand's bedroom the windows were open so that when we opened the door, the curtains billowed like sails. She lit the gas with a pop and said: 'You will sleep on the Chesterfield dear. Do as I do, we can both be modest.' Turning her back, she drew a huge white tent over her head.

I sat down and unlaced my boots. Grand was performing amazing contortions, writhing under her tent and kicking strange garments aside: a pair of stays shot across the room.

I managed to undo my dress and, shaking with cold, fingered the straps of my harness. It was buckled at the back. I saw some scissors on the table, and after a moment's reflection, with two quiet snips, cut through the canvas. I crumpled the contraption in a ball and hid it with Edward under my blanket. I felt wide awake and wicked. It was the slyest thing I'd ever done. I discarded my petticoats, lawn and flannel, my silk vest and my drawers until but for my socks I stood naked.

Grand turned round: 'My dear child! Where is your kimono? The one your father sent you last Christmas from the East?'

I had forgotten to fetch it from my hamper.

She picked up the paisley shawl and draped it round my body. She was still wearing her tent. 'Wait while I turn off the light but bring the candle.'

We climbed another flight of stairs. After much rattling of matches she again lit the gas and turned it very low. An elaborate illuminated notice was nailed over the bath: 'Edith H-H painted this bath with white enamel and varnished the mahogany surround in 1906. After use visitors are requested to clean gently with brush provided and polish with soft cloth hanging on the right. Kindly confirm that taps are not dripping.'

'Stand well back!' she ordered, approaching the geyser, 'just in case it explodes.' A sinister hissing was followed by a violent bang and a roar. 'Keep well away till the water runs. You never know.' She held up a warning finger.

I cowered in the doorway. A thin stream of boiling, rusty water cascaded into the bath, filling the room with steam. My hair clung round my neck in a damp, sweaty mass and my nose felt full.

She shouted out of the fog: 'Stay where you are! Shut your eyes! I'm going to get in when I've turned on the cold.'

I sank to the floor coughing. I couldn't see a thing but I could hear a dragon snorting and then a long agonized sigh, followed by sudden pandemonium: pipes thumping and banging and invisible water gurgling in torrents.

'Look alive!' she cried. 'Your turn next. The water isn't dirty; it's only lather from the Castile soap.'

In a daze I sponged my face and washed myself a little in the narrow bath.

'That's enough!' She pulled out the plug and, blinded by steam, flicked a huckaback towel in my eye. 'I'll scrub, you can polish. Here's the soft rag.'

I wiped with frenzied dabs but water appeared from nowhere; dripping from the ceiling and running down the walls. The faster I mopped the enamel, the wetter it became.

'That'll do! I think you must be tired?'

'I am rather,' I confessed. Pushing my hair off my forehead, I followed her down to the bedroom. She held the candle, which wobbled and threw our grotesque shadows on the walls.

I collapsed on the sofa and drew the scratchy blanket up to my chin. The harness was curled up in a nest by Edward.

'But what about your prayers?'

'God bless,' I said, lying where I was, 'God bless . . .' I mumbled the list of names, 'and help me to be a good girl. Amen.'

'My pet, you should be reverently on your knees, but perhaps this once . . .'

Although I was tired, I stayed awake, missing my smooth linen sheets, quilt and pillows. No wonder Fowler was reluctant to leave me in such a dangerous place, where hot baths devitalized and geysers exploded; and robbers came in the night to murder one in bed. Grandmother would think it quite unsuitable, possibly disastrous. At this moment, I was sure, at least forty thieves were lurking downstairs. No, not lurking, tumbling about over the wires, stubbing their toes and barking their shins on the sharp corners of Italian tables. Inflamed with rage they would seize weapons off the walls, which Grand had imprudently left at their disposal, and creep up the stairs and come in without knocking. Fowler knew she would never see me again; that was why she was crying. Surely we would have some warning. The bells would ring! Would the bells ring? Would we have time to hide in the cupboard?

I sat up. 'Grand?'

'Yes dear, what is it? Aren't you asleep?'

'When the bells ring, what shall we do?'

'I will tell you,' she said, in a confident tone. 'You will spring out of bed and twirl this large wooden rattle, round and round, out of the window, and I will blow several short sharp blasts on that whistle tied to the end of my bed.'

'Then what'll happen?' I asked, anxiously clutching at Edward.

'The good police will come to our rescue. The dear, brave men—what admirable patience they show with the smallest problem—telling foreigners their way about and what omnibus to take . . .'

'I don't think they'll get here in time to catch the thieves.' I was breathing deeply. The trip-wires were wrong and would only make the thieves angry. I could see their eyes smouldering with revenge as they reached for the daggers on the walls.

'It is to be hoped they'll sprain their ankles,' she said with a shrug. 'I assure you we can always rely on the police. I contribute to their funds.'

'Are you sure?' I persisted.

'Quite sure,' she said, reaching to snuff out the candle. She hadn't said her prayers.

When I awoke, Edward and my blanket had fallen on the floor. Scattered flies had settled on the ostrich eggs that dangled in a bunch from a plaster rose on the ceiling. The clock struck six.

Grand's head had rolled off her pillow; her mouth was open and formed a dark hole. Her scalp showed pink through her thin white hair. She looked tired and scraggy. It was high time she had a treat. What was the use of all that money in the hall—real silver coins, not just coppers to throw to the gate-boys—unless it would buy delicious food?

Like the walls, the door was covered with pictures: they swayed on their cords and clattered when it opened. Helen came in with a bucket and broom.

'Good morning, Helen, you are early!' I said. She hushed me and then threw handfuls of wet tea-leaves on the floor. Poor thing, she was obviously loony.

'I shouldn't do that,' I said kindly, 'you see, it's only making a mess.' She paid no attention and swept the tea-leaves into heaps.

'The thieves didn't come, thank goodness. If I were you,' I went on, looking round, 'I should try and clean up the fender. It's much worse than the floor.'

'Shush!' she hissed, shaking her broom out of the window. 'Them's the mistress's invitation cards, and I'm not one to meddle. She never throws one away.'

'What's for breakfast? I'm terribly hungry, but I'm not very fond of bacon.'

'Bacon?' She spat out the word as if it were strange. 'It's an egg you'll get if you're lucky, a Chinese egg I daresay, with Foreign stamped on its shell.' She went out, rattling her pail.

'Ah, good morning my pet,' said Grand, rubbing her eyes, and gulping at something that made her face fatter. 'I hope you slept soundly?'

'The sofa's like a canoe, a canoe made of iron.'

'We'd better say our prayers,' she said.

'Prayers in the morning? I never say prayers in the morning, nobody does.'

She knelt on a stool, facing the wall on the right of her bed. 'Dear me, what a heathen.' She gazed at the shelf, on which stood a vase of plaited palm crosses and a framed drawing of hands, lifted in prayer.

'This is Dürer's famous drawing, only a reproduction of course. D'you know,' she asked, turning round, 'Mr. Ruskin said that, in his opinion, Holman was the best draughtsman since Dürer? And,' she pointed to a glass case over the shelf, 'this is Holman's Order of Merit and, in that frame, are his palette and brushes.' She closed her eyes and her lips seemed to gibber. She had told me all this before.

'I was thinking,' she said, getting up, 'what a pleasant surprise it would be for your grandmother, if while you were here, you learnt the Lord's prayer in French or even Italian.'

Fowler wouldn't like it. She would call it tommyrot.

'You've outgrown that childish prayer you said to me last night. Really you should put your father first, not last after the pugs and Mrs. Hopkins, whoever she may be. I expect Arthur is the Pritchard boy? I noticed he came early on the list and I must confess, I was rather hurt not to hear my name.'

'Oh dear, I didn't think . . .'

'Notre père qui est en ciel,' she murmured, 'it distresses me, your religious education is not, well not exactly . . . Ah, I hear Helen with our breakfast.'

The egg wore a red flannel cap: I attacked its shell with gusto, hammering 'Foreign' into splintered letters. When I dug my spoon in the top, I drew back in disgust: 'It smells!'

'All eggs smell,' said Grand.

'But it smells bad,' I explained, 'like . . .'

She picked it up and sniffed: 'It's not new-laid but it's fresh and perfectly wholesome. It might have been more prudent of Helen to fry it. I should use plenty of salt and pepper.' She set the egg back in its cup and walked round the room, sipping her tea.

'Now what delightful thing shall we choose to do today?' She surveyed the invitation cards stuck in the looking-glass frame, letting some more flop in the fender.

'The Arthur Somervilles are at home tomorrow—you must take your music, I haven't heard your new piece—also the dear Israel Gollanczs. We must try and do both. No end of people have asked us to tea, Lilian Bayliss, she's so gifted! George Henschell . . . even Mr. Russell Flint. Here's a note from Annie Swynnerton. She says: "be sure to bring Diana", and we must remember to call on your Aunt Mary Millais. She is Jack Millais' daughter you know, and sat in your family pew, as a child, for his popular pictures: *My First and Second Sermon*.'

'*I* sit in that corner now,' I said.

Aunt Mary lived in Argyle Road and could be relied upon to produce buns and cherry jam. Once she had meringues, left over from the day before when her nephew Raoul had been to tea. She covered her furniture with sheets and we sat amongst a lot of shapes that might be people listening. Her nose was red, and she complained: 'Although your grandfather called my father Johnnie, you should call him uncle Jack, or *Great* uncle Jack would be better. Remember he was *Sir* John Everett Millais.'

Grand always broke in: 'Without meaning to sound offensive, Mary, how typical it was that your father rejoiced in an ostentatious title; whereas my ever-modest Holman preferred the more subtle and distinguished honour of the Order of Merit—a privilege to which few . . .'

'We've an invitation for Thursday,' said Grand, interrupting my thoughts, 'from Lord Leverhulme to see his pictures.'

To me he looked like an apple. . . . What could I do with my egg? Would Helen give me away if I poured my hot milk into the tea-pot?

'Why, I do believe we're free this afternoon. You choose, my pet, we'll do exactly as you like.'

'I should like to go to Selfridges,' I said, without hesitation.

'Selfridges? Who, where and what are Selfridges?'

'It's a wonderful place,' I said, feeling excited. 'Fowler took me there one day to have an ice and you've no idea how interesting it is, and, and . . .' I faltered, seeing her face stiff with disapproval, 'what lovely things they have.' I patted Edward.

'A shop! I scarcely think—no, no. I would suggest the Zoological Gardens, if we must indulge plebeian tastes. Your father is a Fellow, indeed he has presented some exhibits so we should be admitted free of charge.'

'I'd rather go to the Serpentine and feed the ducks, if Helen has some crumbs.'

'I'll tell you what,' she exclaimed, as if she'd had a sudden inspiration, 'we will go to the National Gallery or the Tate; and then, if we feel inclined, we'll pay a call. Now there's no time to dawdle, when you're dressed and we've made the bed you can run downstairs to Helen. I'm sure she would appreciate a little help. Later I thought you could put on a pinafore and sweep up the leaves in the garden. Would that appeal to you at all?'

'Yes, that would be nice,' I said, leaning out of the window and throwing my egg at the elm, which had a notice chained to its trunk: 'William Makepeace Thackeray and his children played round this tree.'

'Was it in this garden that Grandpa Holman boiled the horse?' I stripped off my nightgown while she wasn't looking.

'You gruesome child,' she said, making a face in the glass, 'I believe it's your favourite story.'

'Tell me again,' I pleaded, putting on my clothes.

'Well, when Holman was working on the *Flight into Egypt*—which was afterwards called *The Triumph of the Innocents*—I sat at first for the virgin and your father, an adorable babe in my arms, was Jesus—that canvas gave enormous trouble wrinkling and shrinking and . . .'

'Go on about the horse,' I urged, lacing up my boots.

'When we returned from the East he felt that the anatomy of the ass . . .'

'The anatomy of the ass!' I echoed, rejoicing to hear the silly words again.

'. . . presented an insuperable problem,' we chanted together.

'He made endless studies in pencil.'

'Do go on.' I was seized with giggles.

'So he went to a knacker.'

'But the knacker said he hadn't got a donkey,' I recited, swinging my legs to keep time, 'so instead, Grandpa ordered a large dead horse.'

'It seems to be your story,' she said dryly, 'but at last it, the horse I mean, arrived in a cart—somewhat odoriferous . . .'

'Very smelly!' I shrieked, 'like the egg.' I smothered my nose in the blanket.

'The carcase was cut into huge red joints, which we carried through the drawing-room, down the steps, and laid on the grass in the garden . . . '

'You forgot to say you dropped some bits on the rugs,' I interrupted.

'After much confabulation, we went out and bought some bricks, and a large old copper, which we found abandoned in a builder's yard. Holman borrowed a barrow and we wheeled everything home, causing some consternation in the streets—dear Holman was quite unselfconscious. We carried jug after jug of water out of the house . . .'

'You couldn't get the fire to burn. The water wouldn't boil!'

'Indeed it wouldn't. Holman had imagined the flesh would soon fall from the bone and he would assemble the skeleton with ease in his studio.'

'But you couldn't cook it all at once. The head was so big. It didn't have a tail, the knacker had sold it already. It rained; the fire went out; the sticks were damp. You cooked and cooked, day after day and then?'

'And then the police arrived.' This was the incredible fact for which I'd waited.

'I must admit,' she said, 'the stench was indescribable. The whole neighbourhood complained.'

I rocked with laughter. I could see Grand prodding the dead horse with a poker, to test if it were done; her eyes smarting with the smoke.

'Look, here is the engraving.' She reached up and took a picture from the wall.

'There *you* are, but it isn't very like you as the Virgin on the donkey; and there's Papa as Jesus. He told me you smacked him over and over again because he wriggled. He was cold without any clothes. I'm sure his hair was never curly. It looks awful on a boy. You can't really see the donkey with all those cherubs dancing about. Boiling the horse was just a waste of time.'

'My pet, they're infant spirits, not cherubs. This one examining a tear in her dress is your Aunt Gladys, my daughter. Perhaps you've never met? See the silver anklets you have in your museum? The scene is the Philistine plain.'

'I'm sure there weren't really soap bubbles, not that size, in the stream.'

'What you call the stream is the River of Life. The bubbles are symbols of faith, Jewish beliefs. If you look at the largest, you'll see the Tree of Jesse. Mr. Ruskin said that the Della Robbia, even the Donatello children, were only rivals of Holman's. When I think the models are my very own babes . . .'

There was a knock on our bedroom door and Helen came in with a letter. It wasn't on a salver.

'If you please, mum, one of the footmen from Holland House has just left this.'

'Ah, let me see,' said Grand, putting on her spectacles. 'Oh, how charming of her! Dear Lady Ilchester, how thoughtful and considerate! "It occurs to me,"' she read aloud, '"that your granddaughter, who is accustomed to the country, might like to play in the grounds. I enclose a key to the gate at the back of the glasshouse walk. I have told the head-gardener that she is to come and go as she pleases as I am sure you have many rival claims on your attention," etcetera.' She handed over the large iron key. 'I must get dressed at once. Are you ready? Brush your teeth. There's common salt and grated pumice in the bowl.'

While she was squirming under her tent I left the room with my harness. She called: 'Come home for luncheon when the clock strikes twelve.'

I was pleased to find Helen had already lit the fire. I threw my harness in the flames and watched it blaze. I knew I should be steeped in sin for ever more.

It was easy to scoop handfuls of silver coins from the Chinese bowls and pour them in my pockets. I slammed the front door and ran down the steps, turning right to Kensington High Street, instead of left to the back gate of Holland House.

I walked quickly until I found a policeman. He was tall and standing in the middle of the road.

'How d'you do,' I said, peering up at his face which was shadowed by a helmet. 'Is your name Percy?'

'My name happens to be William,' he replied, 'and what can I do for you?'

'I thought all policemen were Percys,' I confided, 'like the one at home.'

'You're the little girl who visits the old lady up the road? We think the world of her.' He beckoned to a nanny with a pram, who was waiting on the kerb.

'I wish to take a cab to Selfridges,' I said, adopting Fowler's manner. 'I thought I would buy an ice for Grand, and perhaps have one or two myself.'

'It's a long way to go alone,' he said, pulling his moustache, 'and I doubt if you can buy an ice to take away.'

'I've plenty of money,' I retorted, 'I can buy a dish to put it in.' I held out some silver in my palm.

'That's queer money, that is,' he said, inspecting it and picking out a coin. 'You can't buy nothing with that. It looks antique to me.'

'Do you mean it isn't any good?' I asked, dismayed.

'Well, it's no good for buying things,' he said, looking sympathetic.

'What stupid money!' I cried and threw it on the ground.

'Now then miss, there's no need to upset yourself, you know.' He stooped to pick it up. 'I expect your Granny's worried. I'd better come along.'

'I'm quite all right. I'm really on my way to Holland Park. I've been before. There are sheep and cows just like we have at home. Good-bye.' I offered him my hand; he shook it solemnly and made a little bow. I felt he would come at once, if Grand blew her whistle and I whirled my rattle round and round out of our bedroom window.

The next morning it was raining. 'What a deluge!' Grand complained. 'Alas, you can't go and play in Holland Park, you'd better help Helen in the kitchen. Give her a whistle and she'll be ready with some matches at the bottom of the stairs as it's rather dark in the basement.'

I pulled the cork from the speaking-tube and gave a blow: 'I'm coming down,' I yelled. 'Can you light a match?'

There was a strong smell of fish throughout the house. 'That fish is bad,' I said, groping my way into the kitchen.

'It's a wee bit stale,' she admitted. 'Fourpenny worth of skate, I got it off a barrow; but, you'll see, a curry sauce will make it very tasty.' She gave the range a poke.

'So the frescoes are finished at last.' I examined the walls. 'Grand's done the peacocks very well. "Hitch your wagon to a star",' I read from the painted blue ribbon writhing round the moon. 'I wonder what it means?'

'Don't ask me,' said Helen, stirring something wholesome in a basin, 'the mistress must have her little fancies.'

'We don't have frescoes on the kitchen walls at home. Mrs. Hopkins wouldn't like it.'

'Now, out of my way if you please.' She pushed me aside with a pot of smelly fish.

I opened the larder door. 'Oh!' I shrieked. 'What's that?'

'Now what is it?'

'A horribly crawly thing like a huge brown prawn or a . . .'

'It's only a cockroach—the brute!' She pounced forward with a rolling-pin and burst it on the shelf.

'Oh!' I shuddered. 'How awful . . .'

She shrugged. 'You should see the floor at night. It's a living mass.'

'A mass of what?'

'Black beetles,' she said grimly, putting the rolling-pin back in the drawer, without wiping off the bits.

'But where are they now?' I edged towards the window. A cat was mewing in the area.

'I don't know where they are now,' she said.

I knew. They were hiding, watching us and waiting. The cat was crying louder. I opened the back door and went out into the rain.

The coal-cellar door was broken. Just inside stood an enamel bucket full of water and . . . I bent down and peered in. No! I couldn't believe my eyes. 'Helen!' I shouted. 'Do come, there are lots of tiny little pigs in the milk-pail. I think they must be dead.'

'They're kittens, not pigs; I drowned them all this morning. That's why the cat is making such a fuss.'

'Do you mean to say,' I fought to control my voice, 'you stole the cat's kittens and drowned them?' I was blinking in horror.

'What else could I do?' She clattered at the sink.

Dumbfounded, I fled from the kitchen and stumbled blindly up the stairs.

'Grand,' I cried, flinging open the sitting-room door.

'Whatever's the matter?' She looked up from her writing. 'Your eyes are popping out of your head!'

'It's Helen,' I gasped, 'she's wicked, the wickedest person I know!' I shut the door quietly and crept over to the desk. 'You must send her away.'

'But my dear child, have you taken leave of your senses? Good Helen is a treasure!'

'She's been drowning kittens,' I whispered, clutching at her arm.

'Well?' She shook away my hand and pushed her spectacles up her forehead.

Poor thing! She was old and rather dense. I must be patient. 'She stole them from the cat. The cat is their mother and crying.' I couldn't make it any clearer.

'But my pet, what else could Helen do? We can't have the house overrun with cats! What would they eat? They would only go astray.'

'They could have my fish. I think it's dreadful.'

'What nonsense! It's perfectly proper . . .'

'Proper!' I exploded. 'D'you know, grandmother sent away Lizzie, the maid, when she burnt a mouse on the fire? She threw the trap on the blazing coals.' I choked. 'The trap was a little cage with the mouse alive inside. When grandmother came down at eleven to have her egg-nog she saw the wires glowing in the grate. She picked them out with the tongs.' I was breathless, as I recalled this fearful occasion. 'I was sitting at the piano. She rang the bell. I shall never forget. She was terribly angry. Hannah said: "I will tell Lizzie, madam, to pack her box at once." Lizzie was sent home and Polly came instead. Her mother works in the dairy.'

'But I call it monstrous! D'you mean the wretched girl was dismissed for such a trifle? I've never heard of such, well, such callous behaviour. I suppose she should have set the creature free to eat valuable plants in the herbaceous borders, or perhaps she should have released it in the room, pursued it round and round, and beaten it to death with the poker?'

'Oh no,' I cried, staring wildly at the peaceful Della Robbia. 'I don't quite know what she should've done, but . . .'

'She should have drowned it in a bucket!' Grand declared, with a triumphant smile. 'All unwanted young creatures are dealt with in this way. It doesn't take long I assure you. It's quite humane.'

'Are you sure?'

'Quite sure. My pet, what a storm in a tea-cup or should I say a bucket? Come and give me a hug.'

I drew near and saw to my confusion the charred buckle of my harness lying on the desk. Her eyes followed mine.

'Ah, yes, I'd forgotten. Helen brought me this. It looks like the buckle of a belt. Is it yours?'

'Where did she find it?'

'In her sieve when she riddled the cinders.'

'Riddled the cinders? I'm sure Polly never riddles ours.' I looked guilty.

'I daresay,' she said dryly, 'but thrift is encouraged in a well-conducted house. We are wandering from the point, I feel you know something about it. Indeed my child, you are blushing.' She wagged an accusing finger and chucked my chin.

I didn't answer straight away. If I admitted what I'd done, she would write and tell Papa and I was sure that he would answer sternly: 'A worse and stiffer harness must be bought and worn at night as well.'

'I know nothing about it,' I lied. 'I don't know what it is.'

'I think you do. Come, look me in the eye and remember "From Truth Unswerving" is our motto.'

I looked her in the eye and dumbly shook my head. Nothing would induce me to confess.

'Very well, we'll say no more about it.' To my relief she picked up the buckle, turned it over in her hand and then threw it into the waste-paper basket. I sighed. If only Fowler knew, I was growing more evil every day.

Waiting for breakfast on Friday morning, Grand studied the invitations round the looking-glass over the fireplace. 'So today has come at last, with Anstey Guthrie's party. He's such a generous dear. You've read his stories? *Fallen Idol*, *Vice Versa*, *The Brass Bottle*, I can't remember all the titles. His delightful nephew Eric always helps him entertain.' She turned round; her eyes were shining. 'I've kept my surprise until now, a surprise for you, my pet.'

My hopes rose. Could it be a kipper?

She went to a drawer and pulled out something that looked like a choir boy's surplice. Helen came in with the tray. The egg had been fried.

'Diana's classical dress,' cried Grand, 'it's fit for a Goddess!' She shook out the stuff and displayed it over the sofa. The egg on the tray was congealing. 'The hours, the golden hours I've spent on the embroidery! I know I shouldn't boast, dear Holman was so admirably modest, but look at the crescent moon, Diana's symbol, made of silver beads! They were so fine I couldn't thread them on a needle. I used my own hair and a magnifying glass, stitching under the lamp, night after night, longing for your visit. As I worked I recalled the charming brown wedding dress Holman designed for pretty Ellen Terry when she married Mr. Watts and I remembered the exquisite embroidery he worked on the sleeves of—was it Orlando's blouse? No, he wore the armour which was lent by Mr. Frith. The maid said, 'There's a tin weskit and trousers in the hall . . ."'

'You used your own hair?' I interrupted and stared at her in wonder.

'And look at the sprigs of daphne which I worked into a border round the hem. Two yards at least. I copied the design from a book in the British Museum—Montague House as Holman always called it. The other day I caught the custodian reading the *Weekly Herald*. I reported him of course; he was clearly a scoundrel . . .'

It dawned on me slowly that I was to wear this horrible garment at the party. 'But I have a nice dress. It isn't unpacked. Red velvet, and Fowler says the collar is Brussels lace—it's in points like this.' I traced a zig-zag on the table. 'I've got a white fur coat with cord frogging—the lining is satin—and black kid shoes with silver buckles and white silk socks. Everything's there in my hamper. Helen, I mean someone, should have steamed the velvet; Fowler gets so cross if anything is creased.'

'But of course you must wear this dress and be a little Goddess. Hop out of bed and let me hold it against you.'

It had no shape and hung in limp folds from my shoulders to the ground.

It looked like a curtain. 'Please Grand,' I pleaded, 'don't make me wear it!'

'My dear child!' She dived back to the drawer and pulled out coils of silver ribbon. 'To make it becoming we bind the classical folds to your body, and your curls . . .' She swept up my hair in her hands and drew me to the glass. I looked like a poor skinned rabbit. 'Your curls must be dressed like this'—she picked up a silver brush, and stuck some hairpins in her mouth, 'bound here and there, and tied high at the back in a tuft of ringlets.'

'No, no, I don't want to be a Goddess!' The dress had fallen on the floor. I ruffled my hair and I stamped in temper on the beads.

'Youth is cruel,' she whispered sadly, picking up the dress and sinking on the sofa. We sat panting and staring at each other. Her eyes were wet with disappointment, and I felt defeated. Tears rolled slowly down her face. 'It's all right, Grand,' I seized her skinny wrist, 'don't you worry, I'll wear it.' I would wear it as a sacrifice for burning my harness and lying. After all it wasn't asking much; I might have had to drown a kitten.

When four o'clock came, it was foggy. A fuzz of yellow wool seemed to press against the windows. 'We can't go to the party,' I announced, with gloomy satisfaction.

'You are a kill-joy, of course we will,' contradicted Grand. 'Holland Park Road isn't very far. We will fetch Holman's lantern from the studio—the brass one he had made for *The Light of the World*. It cost over seven pounds.'

In spite of being bloused and bound with silver ribbons, my classical dress was very long and would, I feared, hang below my rabbit coat.

'That Grecian style is most becoming,' she said, with an appraising stare.

'The moons are nice,' I admitted, 'but my neck feels cold with my hair tied up on top, as if I was going for a bathe.' I twisted and turned before the glass.

'Those black kid shoes don't look right, nor those white silk socks. I think it would be prudent to wear your boots in this inclement weather.'

'Boots at a party? I can't wear boots at a party!'

'My dear goose, of course you can't wear them at the party. There are no sandals to fit you in the prop-box so it's obvious your feet must be bare. How I wish we had a bow and arrow.'

'Bare? I can't have bare legs at a party! Fowler wouldn't like it.'

'Limbs, not legs. Tables have legs, such an ugly word.'

'Well, I call them legs,' I retorted, sulking and kicking my reflection until it swung to and fro, 'and I don't want a bow and arrow.'

'Come along, cross-patch, I can see a little black dog on your shoulder.'

'No you can't!' Grand was so silly.

It was a long walk to Mr. Anstey Guthrie's. The candle fell from its socket and rolled about the bottom of the lantern. We arrived very late; motor-cars were lined against the kerb. A starched maid, rather like Tilly, answered the bell; a noise of merriment could be heard behind a door. I took off my boots and Grand knelt beside me, coaxing off my socks. 'You have a classical foot.' She stroked my toes and invited approval from the maid. The maid didn't care. I was a martyr but they didn't care a fig.

'When we go in,' Grand whispered, 'hold your head high and say "prune". You must learn to make an entrance and it makes your mouth look smaller.'

They were all dressed in proper clothes. No one paid attention until I shouted 'Prune' and a small man rushed up and shook us by the hand.

'Dear child, I didn't mean you to say it aloud! Ah, this is Diana Daphne, my little Goddess—Mr. Anstey Guthrie.'

'Charming, how charming and original!' As he drew us aside he purred, and blinked through his pince-nez. 'Lady Rachael, pray come and meet this fair one from Olympus!'

Lady Rachael, a friend of Grand's, who appeared to have dipped her face in flour, rose from a little gilt chair: 'You're just in time,' she said, waving a white jewelled hand to a queue of children winding round the room. 'Chop, chop, chop, chop. Which would you rather, oranges or lemons?' I clasped a child round the waist and followed. All of a sudden, the human arch formed by two grown-ups holding hands above our heads, collapsed and caught me in a trap.

'How d'you do. I'm Eric,' said the man. 'No one wants to be a lemon but I need a girl like you.'

'No, no, do be an orange,' cooed the lady, tickling my cheek with her hair.

'I wish to be a lemon.'

When there was no one left to catch we had a tug of war.

'Hurrah!' cried Mr. Anstey Guthrie, clapping his little hands. 'The answer is a lemon.'

'Bravo!' cried Eric, giving me a pat. 'A Herculean effort.'

'What about nuts in May?' asked someone.

'I shan't know what to do,' I said, hitching up my dress, 'I've never played before.'

'Here we come gathering nuts in May!'

'We want Oswald for nuts in May!'

'Who will you send to fetch him away?' They swept towards us singing in our faces.

'Oswald's so large,' said Eric after consultation, 'we'd better send the Goddess. She's a Spartan,' he added, giving me a nudge.

I tried to hitch my dress above my knees. I was taller than any of the boys. Their pumps slid across the floor. I stood firm, my feet apart, my toes gripping the carpet. One after another I pulled them over; they slipped and slithered to my side. Our line, unwieldy by now, surged forward again and again, everyone laughing and singing: 'We'll send the Goddess to fetch him away!' No one seemed to mind that they never had a turn. My hair tumbled round my face. The silver ribbons came undone and my dress flapped round my ankles.

'You look like a Bacchante,' said someone. I wondered what it was.

'By jove, you've earned your tea,' said Eric. Grand was balancing a cup and talking to some ladies in the corner.

Gay clusters of balloons hung above the tables, which were laden with brightly coloured food. I seized a chair, and gazed at Eric. Brother Ass was hungry and wanted to begin. Mothers and nurses stood behind their children tying bibs and tucking paper napkins into collars. 'Bread and butter first,' they cautioned. 'Remember Mr. Manners.'

'What would you like?' asked Eric. 'Bread and butter's very dull; iced buns with cherries, pink sugar mice?'

'Yes please,' said Brother Ass.

'A jam tart? A gingernut, a scone?' He reached for plates of éclairs and jumbles filled with cream. 'Or would you rather a meringue?'

'Yes please. Yes please.' My mouth was full of chocolate biscuits. I helped myself from a little silver dish to some brown potatoes made of marzipan.

'By jove, you've got an appetite,' he said, shifting round the plates. 'Keep some room for the jelly and fruit salad. Have some more cream?'

'Yes please,' I grinned. I had almost forgotten that meals were a time for conversation. 'I'm never very hungry at home but in London, well, it's different. For luncheon we had dumplings and gravy and then only porridge for pudding. I couldn't eat the dumplings so Grand says I must try again tomorrow. At home

Mrs. Hopkins makes very nice gravy from bones in a big copper pot with a little tap at the bottom but Helen . . .'

'Helen's gravy is different?' he asked with an understanding smile.

'Oh, everything's different in London. I hate porridge. Grand sprinkles it with salt. That's because she was a Waugh. They call it Walf to rhyme with calf.' I wiped away some crumbs. 'Is the milk boiled?'

'I doubt it. Have another cup to wash down that banana.'

'Yes please.' It was like the milk at home.

The other children were already saying grace. I gulped down some orange jelly.

'What a lot you eat!' said a small boy on my right. I hadn't noticed him before. 'You eat as much as—' he began to giggle, 'as much as—an elephant.'

'Elephants don't eat much,' said a girl the other side, 'one bun at a time, but pigs . . .'

'I like pigs when they're little,' I said, scraping the pattern off my plate.

'What about pulling the crackers,' interrupted Eric. 'I hope you've had enough. I should stoke up if I were you. Sure you wouldn't like a macaroon?'

'I couldn't eat any more, thank you very much.' I leant back in my chair sighing, while they crossed hands and banged the crackers. What a mess they made. Grand appeared with a paper crown and set it on my head.

'Now children!' Mr Anstey Guthrie had to shout above the din. 'Ten minutes from now there will be a wonderful surprise.' He flashed a warning at the nurses, 'Ten minutes, in case sticky fingers need a wash.'

We scrambled from our chairs and pressed towards the door.

'Do you want to go to the convenience?' murmured Grand, pinching my arm to make me pay attention.

'No, not at all,' I said, pulling away and rushing on ahead.

The room was almost dark. 'It's only a magic lantern,' piped a little boy.

'It *is* a magic lantern in a way,' said Mr. Anstey Guthrie, dodging a beam of light which cut across the room, 'a rather special magic lantern.' He spoke slowly to impress us. 'I present you with a moving picture,' he turned to the grown-ups who came crowding round the walls, 'a cinematograph of animated drawings: Felix the Cat.'

There was a whirring noise behind and suddenly a small black creature flicked on to the sheet that was pinned to the opposite wall. He walked with his head bowed and his hands behind his back, up and down, up and down. He left his footprints in the snow. He had a tail, but he wasn't like a cat.

Grand came to stand behind my chair. 'Quite remarkable! The same principle as the picture pack in your museum; but this is made of drawings. Think of the work it will provide for unsuccessful artists. Between ourselves,' she confided in a lower tone, 'this is a trifle crude, indeed it's somewhat vulgar, but in the right artistic hands, if only dear Holman . . .'

For some reason I had an awful pain. 'I think we'd better go,' I said, reluctant to tear myself away. 'I'm afraid I may be sick.'

'What a nincompoop you are, you must have over-eaten. Can't you control your Brother Ass?'

'No, I can't,' I answered firmly, rising from my chair.

'Sit down, sit down!' cried someone, 'your head is on the screen.'

'It's that greedy old Goddess,' grumbled the girl who said I was a pig.

'A calamity!' whispered Grand to Mr. Anstey Guthrie, 'an attack of nervous indigestion. We will creep out quietly. Pray don't disturb yourself at all.'

'Thank you very much for having me,' I said, making my bob and looking round for Eric.

The fog was worse. I groped my way along the railings while Grand tapped the curb with her umbrella.

'You poor child!' Grand held my head with her bony hand while I retched into the article. 'After an hour of sickness I'm sure you've nothing left to vomit.'

Sixty sick minutes. . . . 'Such a pain,' I moaned, 'such a dreadful pain.'

'My pet, how hot your forehead is; I fear you have a fever.

Where, oh where is my thermometer?' She fiddled in a cupboard, 'Here we are. Tuck it under your tongue.'

I lay still and listened to the clock.

'Now, let's see.' She held the thermometer under the gas. 'No, it can't be right! We'd better try again.' She jerked it up and down.

'This is no common bilious attack,' she said at last, staring at me gravely. 'One hundred and four! We must keep our heads.'

Her anxiety flew across the room and fluttered at my ribs, like a horrid moth. 'I want Fowler, I want to go home . . .'

'Curse Brother Ass!' She looked like a witch with white hairs scrawled on her black kimono. 'I must get dressed at once and fetch a physician.'

'But you can't go out in the fog.'

'Indeed I can brave the fog, with God's help.' She sank to her knees on the prayer stool making the sign of the cross. After a while she rose and said: 'I shan't be very long. May your guardian angel keep watch. Perhaps I had better wake Helen.'

'Oh no, don't get her,' I shuddered. While the angel hid and spied, Helen might drown me in a bucket. Grand patted my head and went out. There was silence until she slammed the front door.

I lay in a daze; the blanket was itchy, so I tossed it away. Why had I got such a pain? If Fowler were here she would ask: 'Have you been a good girl?'

'No, not since Monday.'

'Monday? Never in all my born days, never have I heard of such a thing! You want a grey powder in gooseberry jam. What, no grey powders? Gooseberry jam for drawing-room tea? Senna-pods, brandy and vaseline? As if them dratted things was any good. What a God-forsaken place with no butler and no proper staff! Just you run along this instant. Look sharp, I haven't got all day. Not since Monday—the very idea!' Still grumbling she would help me on with my coat. 'Mind how you go with that candle. Thieves on the stairs? Don't talk daft!'

Grand hadn't cheated over the paper. The softest pieces were still where I had put them in the middle: 'PLEASE POLISH THRONE', said a notice pinned to the wall.

I crept back to our room and lay down on the sofa with Edward.

Fowler wasn't there; it was only a dream. My pain had gone so the doctor was coming for nothing. I would pretend I felt ill and I hoped he would say: 'London is so unhealthy, I think she had better go home.' Everything would be all right.

'Now my pet,' said Grand, when the doctor had gone. 'I want you to be very brave. Doctor Wills wishes to telephone a surgeon. He will be back and I've given him my key to the front door.'

'A surgeon?' What did it mean? I was fuddled.

'When he returns he will take us in his motor-car to the home —the best in London—no expense shall be spared—thanks to forethought, I have ample wherewithal for this.'

'Whose home? Why? I don't understand.'

She put her hand on my shoulder. 'I believe in telling the truth. I'm sure you would prefer it. As I said, you must be very sensible and brave.' She pressed her long nails into my skin. 'You-have-got-to-have-an-operation.'

'An operation?' Still I didn't understand. Operation stockings were the long white woollies that soldiers wore when they were wounded. 'What is an operation?' I stared at the jewelled clasp winking on her cape.

'While you are asleep, the surgeon will cut you open and remove something inside which is inflamed, may be diseased, and has given you pain. He says you have acute appendicitis . . .'

'Cut—cut me open,' I stammered, 'just because I had a pain?' It was monstrous. 'You don't cut people open because they have a pain. You give them a grey powder, you—why Fowler would know . . .' I was outraged and began to shout. 'I haven't got a pain. I had. I haven't now. I said I had but I was lying; I wanted to go home.' I was incoherent, and sprang off the sofa in alarm.

'Don't touch me! You're bad—mad!' I backed against the wall clasping my hands across my stomach. She came towards me smiling, showing her teeth and stretching out her hand as if I were a dog. I darted past her to grab the rattle and rushed to the window yelling: 'William! I'm going to get William!' I leant out clutching the rattle. Fog belched in my face and the curtains flapped to and fro.

She was behind me in a flash, gripping my elbows. I kicked and squirmed, trying to twirl the rattle round and round. She was tugging so fiercely at my arms that I lost my grip. The rattle was too heavy for one hand and fell with a thud in the garden. I burst into tears.

'My poor child, control yourself. Remember who you are. Dear God, what should I do? Your William, whoever he may be, cannot help us now.'

'Yes he can!' I dodged her to the bedpost, knocking the palm crosses off the shelf. 'I shall whistle and scream for William. I'm sure he'll come.'

'No, no!' she cried, 'the neighbours will hear.' Her hair hung down and her bonnet was askew. Fog clouded the room, fuzzing round the gas. My nightgown was torn as we struggled for the whistle. I was beside myself with fear. 'You're wicked!' I shrieked. 'This house is bad. Fowler knew it was.' Bad eggs, buckets, beetles . . . 'I hope the thieves come and murder you in bed. I hope they cut *you* open.'

'No hysterics please!' She smacked my face. Her rings stung and bit my cheek.

'I hate you!' I roared and fell on the sofa sobbing.

A tremendous draught announced the opening of the door. The ostrich eggs danced a jig, and the dusty invitations shifted in the fender.

The doctor towered above us. We watched him in silence. He shut the window and reached up to flare the gas. 'It's dark in here,' he said. 'Everything's arranged. I must impress on you that we have no time to lose.'

Grand whispered: 'It's been a shock, you'll understand, but I know my grandchild will be very brave and true to our family tradition. I will rouse my maid.' She retied the strings of her bonnet, twisted up some straggling hair and left the room.

'Brave? Do I see tears?' He gently held my wrist and sat beside me on the sofa. 'My poor scared child.' He stroked my forehead. 'Do you always sleep here? You can't stretch out. This couch is far too short.'

'Oh no, I have a bed at home, a brass bed all to myself, with sheets and things. I have a room of my own, it's very nice with roses on the walls. I would like to go home to Fowler.'

'And so you shall,' he said, 'when we've cured your pain.'

'But I haven't got it any more.'

'Not now perhaps, but I assure you it hasn't gone for good. When we take it away, you won't feel a thing, you'll be fast asleep. Will Teddy come too?' He picked up Edward and laid him on his knee.

'His name is Edward, like the Prince of Wales.'

'Well, well, he looks rather pale.' He bounced him up and down. 'He doesn't squeak?'

'No,' I sniffed, 'he used to but now he only clicks.'

'Poor chap, he is in a bad way! He needs an operation. Squeak-itis I fear. A very urgent case.'

'Would it do any good?' He was only joking.

'I should just think so. In no time he'll be as right as rain. We'll remove the trouble while he's fast asleep, put things right and sew him up again. It'll do him a power of good to get away; he needs a change from this gloomy house. A nice light room with a little white bed, grapes and chicken, pretty nurses—I think old Edward's a bit of a one, keen on the girls, don't you?'

'He's rather flighty,' I admitted.

'I bet he is. He's got a roving eye. Where's your dressing-gown? I think I hear your Granny.'

'My kimono's still in my hamper but here's my rabbit coat.'

'The very thing.' He wrapped me up. 'Heave ho.' He pretended we were heavy and staggered, sagging at the knees, as he carried us downstairs.

'Look out!' I cautioned. 'You're treading on the paint.'

'You're really wonderful, doctor,' murmured Grand, who followed with a candle.

Six weeks later Grand and I were sitting on the hard Waugh chairs in the front hall, waiting for Fowler. We were both dressed for going out.

'I think it scarcely credible,' said Grand, 'that a servant should take a cab all the way from Victoria. You can't be right—it's not as if she'll have luggage.' Yet again she searched for her spectacles and my grandmother's letter in her muff. '"Fowler will come in a cab about three and fetch my precious," underlined, "precious grandchild." Extravagant in every way,' she muttered and then continued reading: '"I cannot describe to you, who after all have seen so little of her, the hideous," underlined, "anxiety I and my husband have suffered. The delayed shock . . ." etcetera. Ah well, you may be right and we are, like the Scouts, quite prepared to leave at once.' She placed her hand on my knee. 'So as to benefit to the fullest extent from the drive to the station—I shall of course take an omnibus home—I think we should play the quizzing game, don't you; which building is what, and who lived where?'

'Oh no, I don't think Fowler would like it—although I suppose we could give her the easy ones like the Albert Hall and Wellington Arch. Grandmother says the Albert Hall looks like a plum pudding.'

'Indeed!' She seemed offended. 'Now we mustn't waste time. Like the busy bee we must try to improve the shining hour.'

'I love wasting time. In the nursing home I wasted my time all day.' I got up and ran about. 'The Quizzing, Bizzing, Tizzing game! Those plates up there are Spanish lustre. This brass seahorse came off a gondola in Venice: it's only a stupid old doorstop now and keeps falling over, and that,' I gave it a kick, 'is my hamper and this,' I thumped my chest, 'is Brother Ass and me!'

'I notice you put him first, and the doctor said you shouldn't run about.'

'The nurses thought Brother Ass was a perfect scream. A perfect scream, they said.'

'A vulgar expression that makes no sense!'

'They used to ask: "Will he be a good boy and take his medicine?" At first sister got muddled and thought he was Edward—Edward had his stitches out the same day as me.'

'It was extremely kind of Dr. Wills to humour you, he's such a charming man.'

'The big tacks were done with black cotton, but if you look closely in his fur, there's a little seam of blue stitches. He squeaks better than ever. I showed our scars to Priscilla. It was nice to see Priscilla. She got the giggles too, about Brother Ass.' I was excited and threw caution to the winds. 'I love her best in the world.'

'Surely not,' protested Grand. 'Come, come, not more than your father.'

'Far, far more,' I said, stretching out my arms, 'as much as this.'

'She always seemed to me,' she paused, 'a silly little thing – like a doll.'

'I love silly people. She said she'd come and stay in the summer. I do wish it was now.'

'Hush! I think I hear the cab.'

I ran to open the door. Fowler was waddling up the steps.

'Careful now,' she said, warding off my kiss. She carried a fur rug over her arm.

'Good afternoon,' said Grand, glaring at the taxi. 'I can hear the meter ticking, we must hurry. Here, cabman, kindly fetch the box.'

'Good day, madam,' said Fowler. She looked me up and down, her lips set in a line. I knew what she was thinking: my hair was greasy, my nose red and sore, my coat creased and my boots dull from lack of polish.

'It's a great pity,' said Grand, by way of excusing my woebegone appearance, 'that just the other day Miss Diana caught another cold.'

'Not me, but Brother Ass!' I giggled, pressing Fowler's hand.

'The fortnight's convalescence has been a very pleasant time, instructive yet not strenuous. We paid some charming calls.'

'If you ask me, it's fresh air and feeding up she needs. I don't like the looks of her at all,' said Fowler frowning. She didn't say 'madam' this time. 'Not but what I'm not pleased to see her.' She squeezed my fingers with affection.

'Not but what I'm not!' I echoed, jumping up and down.

'We've had wholesome invalid food,' Grand boasted, as if in some way she wished to justify herself. 'My good Helen steamed a cod and boiled a fowl – so filling, garnished well with rice. Now, this is no time for idle chatter. I had considered coming to the station, but on second thoughts,' she forced a smile but she was crying, 'I think you might prefer to be alone. My pet, give old Grand a hug. I shall count the days, the hours, until you come again.'

'Good-bye and thank you for having me,' I said, stiffly because I felt embarrassed. I took Fowler's arm and walked down slowly to the cab.

'If you ask me, these steps could do with a good scrubbing. What a scarecrow!' She tucked the rug round my knees.

CHAPTER THREE

THE train was crowded but we found a corner. At first it was I who did all the talking, relating my adventures. Fowler was aghast, clicking her tongue and interrupting with: 'You never?' or 'You don't say?'

When I'd finished she exploded: 'You must of known you didn't ought to of burnt the harness? Not that I held with the dratted thing . . . Did you put the money back—what you took from the bowl?' She sighed. 'Sometimes you act real bad. Of course you had a pain, you hadn't been a good girl for five whole days! I've never heard of such a thing. I don't believe it was a Pendix. It was just that doctor's tommyrot.'

'Oh yes, it was a Pendix, it's in my museum and looks like a worm in a bottle. I put it next to the Jordan water but Grand doesn't like it much.'

'Well, I don't know what to make of it all; my head is busting. You want to keep quiet a bit now, for mercy's sake.'

She sat in silence, frowning out of the window, thinking matters over. 'You want to be careful what you say,' she said at last, sucking her teeth, 'we don't want any trouble. If you told the mistress the half—why mercy me, I don't know what she wouldn't do, the letters she'd write to your Papa! There's no love lost and the fat'd be in the fire. You don't want to go blurting out a lot of things what she doesn't want to hear. Why, most like she'd have one of her attacks.'

She met my bewildered stare with fierce black eyes. 'Nothing deceitful mind; that Helen, and the couch, the Pendix, that's what gets my goat—to think they had the nerve!'

I felt depressed. We had reached the marsh, and I could hear the sad wailing of the gulls. They seemed to know the truth must be wrapped in a soft web of lies. It was a grub which, for all they cared, could die in its cocoon.

'Cheer up dear,' said Fowler, patting my hand. 'All I meant was, least said soonest mended.' She stretched her little legs. 'There isn't much news except we've got a crystal set; I've no use for the dratted thing, but Arthur, he's keen. The mistress forgot and jumped up with the earphones on; she pulled the whole thing over. Mercy, the way its squeaks! If you ask me the master's right when he calls it dibolical and the young master's home. . . . It was him what brought the contraption.'

'Oh him! Any *jolies laides*?' I leant forward and pricked up my ears.

'Only Mrs. Whosit, what doesn't bring a maid, if you call her jolly and I doubt if she's a lady. I've never held with widows, they're deep. The way she takes the mistress in with all her silly talk. This time, if you please, she's brought some secateurs and rubber boots and as I said to Hannah, if you ask me, that bit of sewing, why, she never did a stitch!'

'She says she writes letters in her bedroom, but doesn't really,' I admitted. 'When Polly held the blotter up to the glass . . .'

'She never? With you in the room? I'd like to give that girl a piece of my mind. Just you wait. . . . What did it say?'

'I think she's only making lists of things to talk about because she finds it hard to think of things to say. One line was very clear.'

'What was that? Not that it matters!'

She might as well know. 'It said: "Pig dung. Phlox are greedy feeders."' I would never forget this sentence.

'Well!' She was astonished. 'What d'you make of *that*? The dirty thing! I always said she was no better than she should be. Look sharp, we've arrived. Mind how you go.'

The front door was opened by Arthur. The pugs wriggled and slobbered round my feet.

'Winkin' merrybugs, she doesn't 'alf look porely.' Arthur laid the fur rug on the chair, under the carriage box of pennies which we kept to fling from the motor or pony trap to the gate boys on the marsh.

'Mind the radiator there; the heat'll crack the pelts,' warned Fowler.

There was a smell of roses, beeswax and cigars; the fireplace was banked with pots of cinerarias.

'How's Johnstone?' I asked, taking off my coat.

'Sleepin' it orf. 'E'll be ticketyboo for dinner.'

'Hush you, what a thing to say! Will you never learn?' Fowler glared at Arthur. 'I expect he's busy in the pantry . . .' She produced a comb and tried to drag it through my hair. I winced and staggered backwards, so instead she rubbed the smuts off my forehead with her handkerchief and spit.

'You'll have to do,' she said at last, pushing me towards the boudoir door.

When I came round the Coromandel screen, grandmother flung down her knitting. An odd-looking box crashed off the table with a screech. 'My precious, precious love!' She took me in her arms. I buried my face in the violets pinned to her dress. 'Give George a kiss and then tell us how you are.'

'So you're back? About time too! I've missed our reading.' He grunted.

'Yes, I'm back.' It sounded foolish.

'What a sight!' she cried. 'A fright! Your hair—it's just a lifeless frizz, it hasn't any shine!' She picked up her lorgnettes. 'Unbrushed, unwashed, unkempt . . . '

How, where could one's hair be washed in London—in Helen's bucket? Fowler always singed it with a taper.

'Poor lamb, your nose is very red—dreadfully unbecoming—you'd better dab it.' She produced a scut of cotton wool from her bag and drenched it with cologne.

'I can hear she has a cold,' grandfather said, 'I should put some more logs on the fire.'

'No darling, ring. What are the servants for? Sit down, my love, and tell us all about it. What I've been through—with Johnstone's help—he is invaluable you know—I *telephoned* the surgeon!' She sniffed her smelling salts and sighed. 'The nursing home—my poor, poor lamb, how I suffered for you.'

I watched Arthur stack the fire.

'The nursing home was very nice, and everything was nice at Melbury Road . . .'

'Very *nice*? For heaven's sake tell us something of interest. Can't you see we want to be amused? I'm sure you met some fascinating people.'

'I don't think so. I can't remember.' I wriggled on my stool. 'I had a bad egg for breakfast.'

'How disgusting! Like your poor mother the day you were born. She would have you in that wretched house, much against my will . . .'

'Hush Mamie, let her continue.'

I searched for something suitable to say, not wanting any trouble. 'Helen taught me how to make a tart . . .' I ventured.

'A tart, shut up in a damp basement with a skivvy?' She shook with irritation. 'What's the use of that?'

'I cleaned the brass upstairs and cut a lot of . . .'

'Brass? Let me see your hands. Appalling! George, d'you hear? I shall certainly write to her father; it all sounds most unsuitable. No wonder she was ill!'

'I may be blind but I'm not deaf,' he said. 'For God's sake let her get on.'

'We had tea at an A.B.C. one day,' I volunteered.

'Stingy old thing! She could at least have taken you to Gunters.'

'Please,' said grandfather, quietly staring at the fire.

'She's not stingy.' I could see her shabby little purse and her tear-stained face when I said good-bye. 'It's not her fault that she hasn't any money.'

'Don't be such a goose!'

'What rubbish! She's got pots of money,' grandmother declared.

Not pots, Chinese bowls in the hall. 'I know, but it's not worth anything, not for buying things.' I tried to explain and at last succeeded in making an impression.

'Good heavens George! Does it mean she's bankrupt? Rouse yourself. Pay attention!'

He cleared his throat. 'My dear, must you listen to the idle chatter of a child? I recollect, Hunt confided that Charles Dickens advised him over business, and Dickens was astute. It is amusing to recall that it was Augustus Egg who founded Hunt's fortune, with a cheque for a paltry fifty pounds. I would hazard, indeed I think we can assume, that her assets are still as safe as houses and if not, well, she can pluck a picture off the wall . . .'

I wished she would, there were far too many. They went on talking until grandmother yawned. 'Bad eggs and dirty brass. So boring. I must go and talk to my beloved and then, when I've changed for dinner, I'll come and say goodnight to you.' Would she be pleased if I recited 'Not repair'? 'I shall tell Fowler you're to stay in bed tomorrow. People are coming to luncheon. Your head can't be washed with that heavy cold and your hair isn't fit to be seen.'

Grandfather and I sat in silence for a while. 'She loves Young Uncle much more than me,' I said, fighting back my tears.

'It's because she finds him more amusing. You must learn to extract the essence of a thing and serve it up in palatable form. You can't always be a goldilocks sitting on a stool. Recollect moreover that he is never here for very long.'

I would pretend he was never here at all.

Fowler and Hannah stopped talking when I opened the sewing-room door. 'My little dear,' said Hannah, clasping me to her and rocking me to and fro on the old iron bed. 'Am I glad to see you back! There's been no pleasing the master, so Mr. Johnstone says, and Arthur spends all his time tinkering with the wireless. They've been sending out dish after dish. You should of heard Mrs. Hopkins carry on. I said just you wait till Miss Diana's back, I said, then everything'll be all right.'

'There's the dressing gong,' said Fowler. 'Hannah'll give you your bath. I'm that behind.' She scuttled along the passage.

'And Miss Fowler! Why I wouldn't of believed it, she did take on. Old Dan and Whaler called twice a day to ask for news, they did, and of course Miss Dolby.'

'I've something to tell you,' I said, when she was drying me later. She hadn't asked any questions and wouldn't make any trouble. 'I went to tea again with Princess Louise at Kensington Palace and who do you think was there?'

'Not HIM?'

'No, not Him, but his brother Henry.'

She was delighted. 'Well, I never! Just you wait till I tell the others.'

'We had crumpets for tea with honey. The Princess wanted to talk to Grand so she said: "Dear boy, can you amuse Diana next door?"'

'Whatever did he say?'

'He didn't say much but he asked me what I'd like to do, so I said: "I would like to feed the birds on the Round Pond, there are some moorhens there, I know," and he said: "I don't think we can."'

'As if he could be seen standing in the cold, with a bag of crumbs, by a messy old pond in a public park! Why, you shouldn't of suggested such a thing,' she looked shocked, 'not to royalty, why, he's a Prince, he couldn't stand there feeding those dirty old birds.'

'I think they used to,' I said, by way of an excuse, 'it's a nice pond and was once in the palace garden. There are tunnels of trees and holly bushes cut to look like puddings. I wish Priscilla had been there but anyway we just sat and looked at a photograph album. There were lots of photographs of Him. I said: "At home in the housemaid's cupboard we've got lots of photographs of your brother pinned to the walls."'

'Whatever did he say?'

'He just said: "Oh!"'

'Is that all?' Her face fell. It was all but it wasn't what she wanted.

'Then he said,' I lied glibly, '"how *very* interesting, I must tell my brother that. I'm sure He would be pleased . . . One day He'll call."' Of course He would. 'Arthur will open the door and He will say: "Pray lead me to your fascinating housemaid's cupboard." You must fall to your knees like this,' I grovelled on the rug and pulled her down beside me. 'He will say: "What a delightful place!" and then,' I grabbed my new loofah and hit her on the shoulder, 'he will say: "Arise my Lady Hannah."'

'Whatever are you two at?' shouted Fowler, rattling the handle of the bathroom door. 'You want to look sharp, the gong will go any minute and the mistress wants to say goodnight to Miss Diana.'

One summer morning, as the clock struck eleven, grandmother walked across the hall, her heels clicking on the parquet. Fowler opened the boudoir door and they both came in, followed by Arthur and the pugs. I spun round on the music stool. Grandmother stirred her egg-nog and the others disappeared. 'What a beautiful day! It is sad Priscilla isn't here for you to play with.' She threw open the window. 'But Lettice Spragg has promised to invite you to tennis one Sunday. I confided my worries to her and read aloud your father's latest letter.'

'Tennis!' I was astounded.

'Her cousin, Major Someone, his wife died—so dull, she never uttered—he and the daughter both play. I said you could go early to help her prepare.'

'But I can't play tennis; I shan't know what to do.' I felt sick with alarm.

'It's quite easy, my dear, you just run about with a bat and hit the ball over the net. Anyone can do it. Just watch Lettice and do what she does.' She gazed into the garden. 'I long to get out to the roses. Madame Butterfly and Betty Uprichard. . . . Alas, my love, you must go to the village. Fowler will take you to try on your cream shantung . . . Ah, good morning, Hannah.' She sounded surprised.

Hannah stood, as she always did, with her hands clasped together staring at the floor: 'Oh madam, I don't know how to tell you . . .'

'If it's something disagreeable I'd rather not hear.' There was froth on her lip and her face was clouded.

'Oh madam, it's Polly. She's lost her head, she's in trouble.'

'Polly Wolly Doodle!' I sang.

'In trouble? Why wasn't I told?' Grandmother turned to me and said sharply: 'Don't sit there staring. Can't you see I'm busy? Take the pugs for a run.'

Once outside the pugs went mad and raced round the lawn in circles; possessed and pursued by devils we tore round and round. At last I was too tired to follow and flung myself down by the fountain. The pugs rolled on their backs crushing the daisies and waving their paws in the air.

'A grasshopper sitting on a railway track, singing Polly Wolly Doodle all the day. Polly's lost her head. She stuck it out of the window . . . It turned round and round. It came unscrewed and fell off. . . .'

'I knew it would—like the ivory box.' Cherub was delighted.

'It dropped on the terrace and rolled plop—on to the lawn. It bowled over the grass with its hair unwinding like a ball of wool.'

'No, like a silly old pink velvet puff.'

'It rolled through the acre—Dan gave it a kick!'

'It bounced over Snakes' Wall and hurtled down the cliff.'

'Polly jumped out of the window to look for her head. Her legs ran across the lawn, jumped the wall and tore their black stockings on the brambles. They couldn't find it anywhere. It wasn't down a hole.'

'It was floating in a dyke on the marsh, under the rushes—poor pretty Polly was nibbled by eels. Fare thee well, fare thee well . . .'

'It's time to go to Miss Dolby's,' shouted Fowler from the terrace, 'to try on your cream shantung.'

We walked slowly up the drive. 'Now you don't want to let on to Miss Dolby that you didn't have a cold last Sunday—not that I liked the looks of you at all.'

I wasn't deceived. I knew she hated going out on Sunday afternoons, preferring to sit by the sewing-room fire in all weathers with her shoes off and her knobbly toes up on the fender or soaking in a foot-bath.

It made no difference to me whether I went to Sunday school or not, except that Miss Letty Spragg gave us all large coloured stamps, which made pictures to stick in the dolls' house. When we went we were always late and had to scurry up the aisle in squeaking boots, past many curious eyes, to sit in front where there weren't any hassocks.

Miss Dolby sat behind with the village children, whom she kept in order with her umbrella, poking fidgety-Phils with its sharp ferrule and hissing: 'Shush, or I'll tell your Dad!'

Miss Letty played the organ while a village boy, called Tommy

Rook, pumped the handle up and down. It made a long embarrassing noise at the end of each hymn, causing Miss Dolby to get busy and jab the gigglers in the ribs.

Mr. Duncan, the vicar, came halfway through to read about God.

'God's temper is worse than Mrs. Hopkins,' I said, after reflection, when we crossed the churchyard. 'He's always angry and jealous, punishing people with plagues and making them kill their doves . . .'

'For mercy's sake!' cried Fowler, propping herself up on a grave, 'you don't want to talk like that! Don't forget He can hear every word.'

God looked like Mr. Duncan and wasn't even married, although he had a son, and Jesus turned a poor man away from a wedding party because he was wearing shabby clothes.

'I expect that Miss Letty gets it all wrong,' said Fowler. 'Don't you go talking religion, it doesn't do at all.'

Miss Dolby lived over the sweetshop. A little bell rang when we opened the door.

'Good afternoon, Mrs. Perkins. We've come for upstairs, but seeing as we're passing, two pennyworth of peppermints please.'

'Oh dear, I haven't any money,' I said. The big jars glistened with tempting coloured sweets.

'What would you like?' asked Fowler.

'Four nice soft caramels for a penny?' suggested Mrs. Perkins, who was very fat.

'I'd rather have a liquorice belt.'

'Tut, tut,' said Fowler, 'that nasty common stuff—blacking your teeth and messing you up!'

'It's funny the children like it, if you ask me,' said Mrs. Perkins, slipping four caramels into a bag from her little brass shovel.

I liked to visit Miss Dolby although she bristled with pins and smelt musty. Her church umbrella stood in a vase. There were two white china lambs, covered with curls, on her dresser. I wished they were mine.

'It's too tight under the arms,' I said, when I tried on the cream shantung. 'I must be able to wave them about.' The lambs were nicer than ever: their curls very prickly.

'If you stand still, miss, I'll scoop out the armhole a little. We know our own minds, don't we?'

'It mustn't show her knees,' said Fowler.

'I can drop it from the waist,' said Miss Dolby, patting my legs. 'You've grown since the velvet, quite the little lady, you'll soon be coming to Matins.'

'You should see Miss Priscilla,' said Fowler. 'She *is* dainty.'

'Her mother's very chick and much admired by all accounts,' said Miss Dolby through her teeth. 'Of course I never gossip or repeat things but . . .'

'You're pricking me!' I cried.

'Well it's gone very well for the first time on. Don't you think, Miss Fowler? Over your head now, careful. Oh I've pinned the petticoat—what pretty drawers!'

'Yes,' said Fowler. 'Real lace it is, but the bows will come undone.'

'I do hear our Miss Letty is courting. Vicar's nose'll be put out of joint. I'd always hoped they'd make a match of it, seeing as she's an orphan and got a bit of money.'

'Mr. Duncan's too old to get married. If you ask me it wouldn't do at all. Although she must be over thirty I'd say, that would be scraping the *bottom* of the bin . . .'

'There's bins and bins,' said Miss Dolby, winding her tape-measure. 'I'm not one to pass things on, what's no concern of mine, but at the Institute the other day, Mrs. Rook was saying Miss Letty's giving up the Sunday school for good and when I said to Miss Letty, casual-like, after the meeting: "See you next Sunday afternoon," did she colour up?'

'I don't know what to make of it all, I'm sure,' said Fowler sniffing.

How they talked.

'Would you like to give me those lambs?' I asked.

Miss Dolby's mouth dropped open, a pin stuck to her lip.

'They were my mother's. Well I never! What would Mr. Manners say?'

'They're so pretty,' I explained, putting on my skirt.

'You don't want to mind her,' said Fowler. 'She comes over silly sometimes. Now Miss Diana, say "Good afternoon."'

She bustled me out and we clattered down the stairs. She frowned at Mrs. Perkins and then slammed the door.

'I could shake you, that I could, I feel so vexed! Asking Miss Dolby for her lambs—the very idea! I don't know I'm sure. What comes over you—sometimes you act real bad! Whatever will she say? Now pick up your feet and walk nicely.'

'I thought she might be tired of them.' I had thought nothing of the kind.

'Don't talk so silly! You know you must never ask for things or pass remarks, it's very rude.' We walked in silence, until we saw my grandmother gliding towards us up the road followed by the pugs. She was holding a white parasol lined with bottle-green silk.

'My love, what a hot day! You can carry my bag and come with me to call on Percy.' She dismissed Fowler with a nod. 'Polly's run away,' she added, when we were alone. 'So tiresome, she's going to have a baby. Aprons *are* so deceptive—poor silly girl! But I must say it will be quite a change to knit some little vests instead of those boring operation stockings.'

'But why shouldn't Polly have a baby, if she wants one. I mean?'

'I don't expect she wants it at all.'

'Oh well, I suppose she'll drown it in a bucket. It doesn't take long.'

'Heavens above! My dear child . . .'

'Well, Grand says kittens are drowned in a bucket because nobody wants them and it's quite . . .'

'Babies are never drowned in buckets. Never! D'you understand? What a shocking idea!' She pressed a hand to her breast.

We arrived at the police station. 'Weeds, weeds,' she grumbled, poking at them with her parasol. 'You wait outside. I must be quick if he is to find Polly in time and bring her safely home.' Picking up her skirts she mounted the steps and pushed open the door.

I decided to call on Mrs. Rook, who kept the ironmonger's shop. If I remembered to take a penny, I bought tiny brass screws for my collection. I examined everything with care. I picked up a knife. To open the blades, there was no need to break one's nails, one simply turned a ring at each end. The knife was slim and smooth: it was marked one shilling. 'I must have it,' I said aloud.

Mrs. Rook stepped through the bead curtain from the kitchen. Her nose was always dripping and she blew it on a bit of paper.

'Oh dear, I haven't any money.' I ran to the door and looked up the street. Grandmother was still at the police station. There was no time to run home and take twelve of the gate boys' pennies from the carriage-box in the hall.

Lady Pritchard was waving from her gate. She and Walter came down from London to their country house every summer.

'Good morning,' I said, bobbing. 'Please have you got a shilling?'

'A shilling?' She looked rather startled.

'Yes, a shilling.'

'But of course, for sweets I suppose.' She led the way into the house and rang a bell. 'Tell Clara to give you my purse,' she instructed Arthur's friend.

He returned with it on a salver and she picked out a shilling and handed it to me saying, 'It's already washed.'

'Thank you very much. Does Fowler wash our money, I wonder?' We walked back together to the road.

'Ah here you are at last!' Grandmother was waiting. 'Forgive me Mabel, but we must hurry home to luncheon.'

'Don't forget your P's and Q's this afternoon,' said Fowler, when we walked to Miss Letty's. 'You don't want to go asking her for china ornaments, nor passing remarks. She's given up the Sunday school you know and least said soonest mended!'

'I shan't want anything of hers,' I protested grandly, because I had a shilling in my pocket.

An elderly maid opened the door and it shut behind me like a trap. I was making a face in the glass when Miss Letty marched in.

'Hello!' she said, jerking my hand up and down.

'How do you do?' I bobbed.

'How quaint,' she murmured.

'Have you got a headache?' Why was she wearing a bandage?

'A headache? No. My bandeau,' she explained touching it and blushing.

'Oh I see!' I was tempted to giggle.

'Where are your plimsolls?' she asked.

'Plimsolls?'

'Shoes like mine. Yours will make marks on the grass.' She looked upset when I followed her into the hall. 'What a brain-wave—you can put on my galoshes. Your feet are quite big.'

'They are heavy!' I said, making large awkward strides in her galoshes.

'They will do very well,' said Miss Letty, and looked at her watch. 'We've got an hour or so before the others come and there's the lawn to mark out and all kinds of jobs. We'd better set to work.' I followed her into the potting-shed, dragging my strange heavy feet. She stirred up a pudding of white stuff and water.

'It's like cooking,' I said, taking the stick and splashing my cream shantung.

'Don't leave lumps on the bottom of the pail! Scrape the bottom of the bin.'

'I think it's quite smooth now,' I said, 'rather like sauce.' She poured it in a machine and wheeled it on to the lawn. 'It should have been mown, but it can't be helped now.'

'I've paced it all out and put in the pegs; it must be right because I used a ruler. Fix one with your eye and walk forward slowly in a straight line and don't wobble on the bumps. Here is the first peg and there, and then there,' she pointed, and ran about, flapping like a gull about the lawn.

'That line's very wavy,' she complained, looking back at the trail. 'You must try and do better; and keep moving or it'll make another puddle.'

'It's rather hard. I've never done it before.'

'Never mind, it'll have to do. I must go in and get out the china as Janet's off on Sunday afternoons.'

I trudged round the lawn in my galoshes, pushing the little white wheel. It was a difficult task; there were so many pegs. I threw my straw hat on the ground. I was sure Miss Letty would be pleased with what I had done.

'Do come and see, it looks just like a Union Jack!'

'Oh!' she cried, running towards me. 'What have you done? There shouldn't be any *diagonal* lines!'

'Oh dear, does it matter?'

'Well, it's not right,' she looked angry, 'but I suppose it'll just have to do. Didn't you see how I tilted the machine when I wheeled it out from the shed?'

'I didn't notice, I'm afraid; you just said: "Make straight lines from peg to peg."' She was impossible to please.

'Oh well, I suppose it will just have to do,' she said again. 'Now we'll take out the pegs, and while I get the tea you can whiten the balls. Here's a bit of chalk, rub them with it until they look clean.'

'They *are* dirty, quite black, and this one is split.'

'It makes up the six, it'll just have to do.'

'I haven't a bat of my own,' I said, hoping that wouldn't do at all and I might not have to play the dratted game.

'It's not a bat, it's a racquet,' she snapped. 'I have an old one, two or three of the strings are gone but it will do quite well for a beginner.'

'It's not a bat, it's a racquet, it's not a bat, it's a racquet,' I repeated, as I worked, chalking the balls.

I had just finished when a gentleman in white came out of the house with Miss Letty—her cousin the Major. She was blushing and looked rather silly. A large girl followed and was introduced as 'Our Elsie'. She stared at my galoshes.

'Diana's never played before,' said Miss Letty, as if this needed excusing.

'Got to start sometime,' said the Major, spinning his racquet like a juggler. 'Elsie's only a beginner, aren't you my girl?' He whacked her on the behind.

'I've played six times,' said Elsie primly. I hated her already.

'It's nice for the kids to meet,' said the Major. 'I'm only a rabbit myself—you're the champion, old bean; you'd better play with the kid.'

'Oh no!' she protested. 'You're far better than me.'

'Don't talk rot—we'd better toss.'

They threw their racquets in the air and stooped to examine

them for something. 'Rough!' they shouted and threw them up again. They were mad. I tittered, nervously twisting my bat.

'I say!' boomed the Major. 'Court's a bit rum—the markin' I mean.'

'That's my fault I'm afraid!' I said, when Miss Letty began to explain. 'I did it all wrong.'

'I see,' he smiled. Miss Letty looked embarrassed. He measured the sagging net. 'No good cryin' over spilt milk, eh, or should I say whitewash?'

Elsie looked so superior that I decided to ignore her the whole afternoon.

'What do I do now, Miss Letty?'

'It's Henry's service, you stand on that line,' she pointed with her toes, 'and hold out your racquet like this.'

'Same as the egg and spoon race!' I giggled.

'Stand firmly with your feet apart, bend well forward,' she stuck out behind, 'whatever you do, keep your eye on the ball, and hit it as hard as you can.'

I stood still, holding my racquet before me. A ball sailed over the net and landed in a cloud of chalk. 'Line!' they cried, 'you must *run*!'

He biffed it again at Miss Letty; she thrashed it back at Elsie, who tripped over a peg and grazed her knee badly.

'Oh dear!' cried Miss Letty. 'That peg must have been overlooked; I'm terribly sorry.'

She frowned. I wasn't sorry. It served Elsie right.

The sun shone in my eyes and the balls soared up in the air like kites, or into the net. It was blazing hot. My socks fell down and my ankles felt tired. I tried to run but I stumbled about, as my feet were like lead in the galoshes. The cream shantung was covered with stains. What would Fowler say?

'Bad luck! Well tried! *Run!* Shot! Service! You must buck up, kid. Thirty—no forty love'—it's not a bat, it's a racquet, it's not a cat, it's a jacket, or a rat or a packet. I felt quite dizzy. A ball flew up in the air so high . . . I hoped it would never come down.

'Wait for it!' panted Miss Letty, prancing about. My head well back, I watched it fall . . . the sun was dazzling. I shielded my face but the blow knocked me down. I lay, still as a stone. The ball had landed in my eye.

'I say! What jolly bad luck!' said the Major, vaulting the net and breaking it down. 'You'll have a shockin' bruise.'

I sat up blinking. 'Oh I say,' he helped me limp to a seat, 'wounded soldiers never *cry*!'

'I'm not a soldier,' I said, crying louder than ever.

'Oh Henry, what shall I do?' asked Miss Letty. 'D'you think I should telephone?'

'I shouldn't,' I said. 'Johnstone's asleep and Fowler will fetch me at six.'

'It's past five now,' said Miss Letty, 'let's go in and have tea.'

'I think she should bathe that eye,' said the Major, taking my arm.

'Can we play three after tea?' asked Elsie. She despised me, but I didn't care. No one replied. I shuddered with sobs but the Major pretended not to notice, because he was nicer than the others.

'Shall we leave her to rest?' asked Miss Letty, when we'd finished the cake. '*We* could knock up. Perhaps Elsie would stay with her?'

'Oh, need I, Dad?' whined Elsie.

'Please don't. I'm quite all right.'

'It seems so heartless to leave you alone, you poor little thing.'

'Keep your pecker up,' said the Major, 'brave soldiers never say die. Ha, ha, it's not to question why, it's just to do or die. Once more into the breach.' He bounced a ball up and down.

'Very well,' said Miss Letty, 'I will draw down the blind. How I wish Janet was here! When your nurse arrives, do shout out of the window.'

I was thankful they left me alone. I got up and looked in the glass; my eye was a bilious colour and my face blotchy with tears. I bent down to take off the galoshes. My eye throbbed. Would it burst? I raised my head slowly and sat very still. My feet felt curiously light.

Waiting for Fowler was a waste of time. I would creep out and call on Mrs. Rook.

I went round to the back because the shop was shut on a

Sunday. As soon as I knocked Mrs. Rook opened the door. She looked me up and down and wiped her nose on her sleeve. I handed her the shilling. She took it without a word and disappeared through the bead curtain to fetch the knife off the counter.

When I got back to Miss Letty's, Arthur was there. His buttons shone in the sun. He had clips on his trousers. 'Are you ready?' he asked. 'Miss Fowler was busy—Winkin' merry-bugs! What 'ave you done to your eye?'

'A tennis ball hit it,' I said, tears of self-pity making it smart. 'Let's go.' We walked a little way, his bicycle ticking between us.

'Good evening, Miss Diana.' It was Miss Dolby out for a stroll. She looked very smart and was carrying her Sunday-school umbrella. I thought of her lambs.

'Mercy me!' she peered at my face. 'What have you done to your eye?'

'A tennis ball hit it.'

'Well, well!' she said. 'That's what comes of playing games on Sunday. Whatever will they say? I am surprised at Miss Letty. Her head's been turned by that cousin of hers.'

'I'm afraid we must hurry.'

'You're walking very odd,' said Arthur.

'My eye hurts and my feet are sore.'

''Ark the lark, you are in the wars. Shall I lift you onto the bike?'

'Please do!' He wheeled me along, softly whistling the tune of: 'Daddy wouldn't buy me a bow-wow.' We met Polly on the drive.

When we reached the front door Arthur left me alone. I hobbled across the hall. Grandfather was sitting in the library.

'So you're back at last. Did you enjoy it?'

'No, I didn't.' I sat down and cried.

'For God's sake what's the matter?'

I could only answer with sniffs.

'Confound it!' He felt for his stick and rose from his chair. I stayed where I was, for once not attempting to help him. He found his way to the door and shouted: 'Mamie! Arthur!' There was a sound of doors opening and footsteps across polished floor.

'Yes sir, coming sir,' said Johnstone thickly.

'Fetch the mistress and be quick about it.' He came back to his chair and sat down. 'Oh, dear, what can the matter be?' he sang.

Grandmother swept into the room. 'George . . .' she began. 'Good heavens! My poor lamb, what have you done?'

'Well, what the hell has she done?' he shouted. 'Here I am, left in the dark, and you tell me nothing!' He banged his stick on the fender.

'She's got a black eye: it's horribly swollen—she's quite disfigured!' She examined me through her lorgnettes. 'Her knees are grazed, her dress is filthy—covered with stains—grass I suppose; and it looks like paint. George, can you pull the bell: twice for Fowler.'

'Damn her dress, what's happened to her eye?' He pulled the bell savagely; the cord sprang back against the wall and wriggled like a snake.

'Now my love, calm yourself; if you cry like that you will only get a red nose. Tell us what happened.'

'She was going to tell me when you came in.'

'Really George, there's no need to be offensive. Think what a shock, you shouting like that—I imagined all manner of horrors.' She held some smelling salts to her nose.

'A tennis ball hit me in the eye,' I said, aware I must avert a quarrel. 'When I bend down it's awful, but my ankles are worse.' I didn't mention the galoshes.

'Your ankles?' she echoed in alarm. 'Ah, here's Fowler at last. Come quickly!'

'Mercy!' cried Fowler, bustling about. 'What has she done? That Miss Letty should be downright ashamed.'

'I should fetch a cold compress,' said grandfather sharply. 'You women do nothing but chatter. You must look after her properly.' He cleared his throat. 'I trust you still insist on her milk being boiled?'

Grandmother murmured vaguely: 'Boiled milk is so revolting.' Boiled milk in London was enough.

'Do look at my new pocket-knife,' I said; 'although it was Sunday I bought it from Mrs. Rook's shop. I asked Lady Pritchard for the shilling.'

'You *what?*' they exclaimed in one voice. 'D'you mean you actually asked Mabel for *money?*' The atmosphere was thick with disapproval. 'Whatever possessed you to do such a thing?'

My grandmother rose from her chair, flushed with agitation. 'Surely you know you must never ask for *money?*'

'But I told you I wanted to buy a knife from Mrs. Rook's shop.'

Grandfather stared; he too seemed interested in nothing but the shilling. 'You must never ask for money. Neither a borrower nor a lender be. Pocket-money.' He whacked his shoe with his stick. 'Mamie, perhaps she should have a regular allowance.'

'What ever for? Dear me, how very unfortunate, I must write a note to Mabel at once, Arthur can take it round before dinner.'

'She wasn't cross,' I said, smarting at their injustice, 'she has plenty of money and it's washed every morning.'

'Ha ha! I must pull Pritchard's leg about his filthy lucre!'

'It really is rather droll now I come to think of it.'

Grandmother smiled to herself as she left the room to write to Lady Pritchard. They had both forgotten my eye.

'We met Polly on the drive,' I said, after a gloomy silence. 'I hadn't seen her for ages. She lost her head and ran away, but Percy found her. She's got terribly fat. At first I thought it was a pillow, but when I gave it a jab she said it was a baby. Did you know? I think there must be several but she says there's only one and she's going to lay it like a hen.'

'Indeed? Quite remarkable!'

Grandfather raised his eyebrows politely.

'I know how an egg comes out but how does it get in? She doesn't seem to know.'

He said nothing, as if he hadn't heard.

'How did it get in?' I repeated, thumping a cushion in time with the words.

'I used to know,' he said at last, 'but for the moment I must confess the answer has escaped me.' He paused. 'For the life of me I cannot recollect.'

'Oh do try,' I wheedled.

'It's no good,' he said, shaking his head, 'I can't recollect, but

I shouldn't ask Polly again, she might get it wrong. Mamie is younger than I am. One day perhaps she will tell you.'

'One day! What's the good of that? Why not now?'

'What a fidget you are!' As I ran from the room he called: 'Remind her, Mr. Duncan is coming at seven.'

She was sitting at her writing-table twisting the note to Lady Pritchard in a *chapeau de Napoléon* round the shilling. Arthur stood by, holding a salver. 'Quick as you can, remind Johnstone we are expecting Mr. Duncan and tell Fowler to hurry with the compress. Miss Diana's eye looks very bad.'

'I know how babies come out, I want to know how they get in. Grandfather says he's forgotten but he thinks you may remember.'

She gazed at me.

'Is that what he said?'

She picked a little mirror off the desk: 'Look at that!' she pointed at her jaw, just above the lace. 'Old age is a disaster. Who would believe I once was a beauty?'

'Yes, but what about the baby?'

Of course she was old but what did it matter?

'My love,' she sighed, gently drawing me to her, 'I have forgotten too. It is so long ago.'

'But what about the *baby*?' I insisted. 'Do try and remember!' For some reason there were tears in her eyes but she forced a smile, and whispered in my ear: 'I've lost the book of directions, yes, that's it—I've forgotten . . . The bell! It must be Mr. Duncan. Come and say goodnight in a quarter of an hour. He will be sad about Lettice. Ah well, such is life.'

She sailed into the hall. 'Oh, good evening Mr. Duncan, how very nice to see you. I hope I am forgiven my little peccadillo? How right you were about the tennis!'

Although my eye was throbbing I hunted amongst the plant catalogues and papers for *The Book of Directions*. It would of course be leather bound with its title stamped in gold. It was nowhere: I left the boudoir in impatience, opened the library door and crept to the largest bookcase. Mr. Duncan was talking about the church and deathly beetles watching in the roof. They might flop on our hats and wriggle down our collars, or swarm like the locusts in the bible, who ate every living thing. I climbed the library ladder and methodically ran my finger along the spines of the books, shelf after shelf.

'So knowing your real interest in the—er—*fabric* of the church . . .' Mr. Duncan rolled his r's as usual.

'Yes, indeed,' said my grandmother, 'such an exquisite building must be preserved at all costs.'

'At some cost, Mamie, or we might say, at a certain cost.' Grandfather sipped his whiskey. 'You may rely on a contribution from us but get more than one opinion; all these people are rogues and think I'm made of money. Ask the Pritchards for some of their filthy lucre.' Suddenly he roared with laughter.

'Ah, hah! said Mr. Duncan, looking round. 'I've heard you were a book-worm, child, and now I see it for myself.'

I climbed down the steps to say how-do-you-do. 'I'm looking for a book which is lost,' I said, bobbing.

'But that's a serious matter, young lady. Not a rare first edition, I trust, or a valuable binding?' When he saw my eye he gave a start.

'What's that?' asked grandfather. 'It's the first I've heard of a book being missing. Here I sit in the dark and you tell me nothing!' He was angry.

'My dear George, calm yourself, it's news to me too . . .'

Could she have forgotten?

'But you said you'd lost the *Book of Directions*.'

'*Book of Directions* for what?' asked Mr. Duncan, raising his eyebrows.

'Oh, I've dropped a stitch,' grandmother cried, before I could answer. 'Why it was nothing at all, a mere trifle, temporarily mislaid—a trashy little thing—say goodnight to Mr. Duncan. Where *is* Fowler? For heaven's sake ring!'

'But you said . . .' I began.

'Now give me a kiss, and run along to Fowler without another word.'

Mr. Duncan was perplexed because she was blushing, but I knew she was lying about the book. It wasn't lost at all.

'Ah, here's Fowler at last! How disgusting!' Grandmother flinched and shaded her eyes.

'Now Miss Diana, you want to put this on to draw out the bruise,' said Fowler, nodding politely to Mr. Duncan.

I squinted at the bloody bit of meat, which she bore in a dish. She held it up: it was dripping. The pugs snorted with excitement and Mr. Duncan looked away.

'It's like the horse,' I said, 'the one they cut up in London.'

'Not here, I can't bear it! Good night, precious. I should spend the day in bed. You really look a sight!'

'Yes, you'd better run along.' Grandfather gulped at his glass of whiskey.

Hannah was waiting by the green baize door. 'My poor little love,' she cooed.

'There's no call to be soppy,' said Fowler, when the three of us stood in the lift.

''Ark, 'ark, the lark!' sang Arthur, tugging at the rope and bending his knees with the effort of sending us upstairs.

'I'd just like to give that Miss Letty a piece of my mind, games on a Sunday indeed—the very idea!'

'It wasn't her fault,' I protested, 'it was jolly bad luck. God punished us for annoying Mr. Duncan.'

'It's a shame she's got no one nice to play with,' said Hannah.

'Yes, it's a pity she hasn't got a friend.'

'But I have!' I protested.

This wasn't quite true but lately I had marked one down—not Tommy Rook—and decided to make his acquaintance.

Old Timothy lived on the marsh alone with his dog, and his donkey, in a cluster of black wooden huts which we passed on our way to the beach. Priscilla and I had often seen him out shrimping.

He wore gold rings in his ears and his hair was long and matted; strangest of all, one of his hands was a hook. I asked my grandfather if Timothy had once been a pirate, retired now of course.

'That old rascal! He's a fisherman and no doubt will one day be brought before us on the Bench, for smuggling. . . . Perhaps not, in a place like this . . .'

'What do people smuggle?' I asked.

'Brandy mostly, and silks I suppose,' he answered vaguely.

I wanted to find out more, but when I went to old Dan all he would say was: 'Be askin' no questions thee'll be hearin' no lies,' and even Arthur was useless.

I decided to pay Timothy a visit. I set out one Sunday afternoon wearing my red silk stockings. I climbed Snakes' Wall and dropped on to the cliff. It was steep, pitted by hundreds of rabbits, overgrown with brambles, hazels and elders. I slithered down the slope, grabbing the tufts to break my fall.

It took some time to pick my way across the marsh. The dykes were a maze and the few rotten planks hard to find in the rushes. I tried not to cut my legs on the reeds or lose my buckled shoes, but my feet were soaked.

A dog barked when I reached the huts. I peered through the cracks in the boards, hoping to see some bottles of brandy, but all I made out were some barrels.

A fire was burning in the open. A strong smell of tar and bad fish mingled with the smoke. Broken glass and rusty old pots lay about with a litter of mussel shells and bones.

Old Timothy was mending his nets. His cart stood between stacks of driftwood. There was no sign of the donkey.

'How d'you do?' I said politely, wiping my hands on my dress.

'And what be thee a-doing of here?' He leant forward with the net caught on his hook. His ear-rings shone through his hair.

'I've come to pay you a visit . . . and have a look round,' I answered lamely, as an excuse.

'There baint nothin' here for the loiks o' thee,' he said rudely.

'What a pretty glass float.' I stooped to pick it up. 'Have you any more?'

'Aye, they'm plenty more. Have it if it take thy fancy.'

'Thank you *very* much.' I had been going to ask him for it anyway.

I breathed on it and rubbed it on my skirt; it was cloudy, having lain in the mud.

'I've seen you on the beach,' I said.

'Aye, I seed thee too with Jim Whaler and thy nurse. I talks to

Diana Holman-Hunt aged five

Diana aged seventeen

Mr and Mrs Holman-Hunt leaving Windsor Castle after a Royal Garden Party (*Daily Mirror Photograph*)

Grandfather Freeman

Grandmother Freeman

Portrait by Holman-Hunt of his first wife Fanny, née Waugh, who died giving birth to a son, Cyri Benone, a month after it was completed

Companion portrait by Holman-Hunt of his second wife Edith, Fanny's sister. She was mother of Hilary (Papa) and Gladys (Big Aunt)

Diana aged seven with Cherub (showing her black eye after the tennis party)

Diana in Young Uncle's car

Diana's father, Hilary, and Grandpa Holman

auld Dan about the rabbits, and I talks to cook in the kitchen when I brings a ketch of eels.'

'Grandfather likes eel pie but I don't; and rook pie is horrid.'

'Would they know thee be on the marsh?'

He moved over to one of the huts, closed the door and clipped a padlock on a chain.

'They sort of know,' I said, kicking at a tin.

'Don't go near them huts,' he shouted, 'they'm covered with pitch, thee be already mucky.'

'Oh, that doesn't matter,' I said. 'D'you mind if I take off my stockings and dry them by your fire?'

'Thy legs have a raw look in them stockings,' he said.

'Look at my feet!' I held them out in the warmth; they were stained bright red. He picked up the stockings with his one good hand and hung them on a wire. They dripped pale blood from the toes, like the meat I had put on my eye.

'They'm silk,' he said with a wink, holding his hook to the side of his nose, 'foinest silk—but they do be torn.'

'That doesn't matter,' I said, 'only Fowler likes them and now they're too small.'

I walked over to a little hutch; inside was a strange animal, pale and long with lively pink eyes. I was just going to poke my finger through the netting, when Timothy sprang forward and knocked me aside with his stiff wooden arm. I staggered and fell. Was he bad? My green glass ball rolled slowly away. The dog pricked his ears.

'Why did you do that?' I asked, pretending I wasn't really frightened.

'That's Jack Ferret, that is. Never seed 'im before?'

'No, is it a stoat?'

'Treacherous beastie; he boite to the bone. Stand back now.' He opened the door and put in his hook. Jack Ferret ran up his arm, arching his spine, gracefully twirling round and round like a live fur cuff.

In the distance I heard the church clock strike. 'I must go.' I held out my hand. 'Thank you for having me. Next time I'll bring a leather glove and then I can handle Jack Ferret. May I come again?'

He grunted. He and his dog came to the foot of the cliffs to show me a short cut across the dykes.

'Old Dan says there are fairies on the marsh,' I ventured.

'A fairy thyself,' said Timothy grinning.

He waved his hook as I scrambled up the cliff.

I felt it would be unwise to say where I'd been, so I hid the glass float in a warren. When I got home everyone was busy.

'Polly's baby has arrived already,' said Fowler, looking flurried. 'You don't want to make a noise. . . . Mercy me! What have you done to your stockings?'

'Oh, may I go and see?' I pleaded. 'Is she sitting on it?'

'Sitting on it! Don't talk silly.' She was clearly excited and led me up the little stairs to Polly's room.

Her mother, Molly Brown, from the village, was crouching by the fire, boiling a kettle. Polly was in bed, her pale hair sticking to her forehead.

'Where's the baby?' I whispered, looking round.

It was muffled in shawls lying in a drawer.

'It came quickly,' said Molly, 'nothing was ready. When it's a month old, it'll come and live with me.'

'Is that all?'

I was astonished. It was as small as a doll. The egg must have been all shell.

Whenever I could I went back to visit old Timothy. He wasn't always there and the huts were locked but I cleaned the hurricane lamps, lit the fire and tidied things up, just as if we were married. I got to know him very well and became fond of his new donkey. Her name was Anne, which Timothy said was what they called donkeys in France. He knew a lot of French because he had a French fisherman to stay with him in bad weather.

We took Jack Ferret out rabbiting with a tangle of snares, which Timothy taught me to set. He said it didn't hurt the rabbits. If they weren't quite dead, he hit them on the back of the neck. I slit their legs with my knife and threaded one foot through another to make them easy to carry between us on a stick. Sometimes Jack stayed down the hole. In my mind I could see him curled up asleep, with blood on his whiskers. He was bad, but it wasn't his fault; God made him like that. Hidden in fringes of rushes we watched geese and duck flying over, and heron by the dykes teaching their young to fish.

Timothy taught me how to mend nets, splice ropes and clean the fish—he kept the point of his hook as sharp as a pin. He could rip open the herrings and scrape them out in a flash. We caked them, and sometimes even hedgehogs, with clay and baked them in the fire. I helped him lift his traps from the dykes; soggy lumps of wool wriggling with eels, their teeth caught in the fibres. He peeled them from the neck in one go, like a stocking from a leg.

Now I had a friend as I had intended, and I could talk to him, instead of Cherub, while he sat cross-legged smoking his white clay pipe.

Old Dan got to know where I went but he never said much; when I passed through the acre he went on digging.

'You stink of fish,' said Fowler, when she changed my dress, which I pretended had got muddy in the garden. She suspected something. 'You're a sly puss and no mistake,' was all she ever said.

CHAPTER FOUR

'THERE'S no *Children's Newpaper*,' said Fowler, frowning at the bookstall, 'the mistress said you was to have either that or *My Magazine* or *Little Folks*.'

'Please, I'd much rather have a *Tiger Tim*.'

'Now remember what I say,' she cautioned, as we walked towards the train, 'if you do have a bath, you want to keep away from that geyser and dry between your toes and if you have any trouble, just take a spoonful of this.' She tapped the new bottle of syrup of figs which was tucked in a corner of my basket. 'And if I was you,' she went on, 'I'd keep this cake to myself and tell that Helen these eggs is for boiling; and see you unpack: respectable folk don't live out of boxes.'

She turned to the guard who stood by with a green flag under his arm. 'As I said before, when the young lady reaches London, someone must send a wire or telephone a message to the mistress. She'll be taking on that badly and we don't want her to have one of her attacks. Her Gran will be there, it's all written down.'

She handed him a piece of paper and some money.

The guard led me to a little red cupboard in the van. There was no window and the seat was hard and prickly.

'Oh dear, must I sit here?'

'You'll do as you're told, Miss Diana,' said Fowler firmly.

The guard climbed in and slammed the door. I leant out and looked into her eyes. She was worried. 'I'll be all right,' I said.

As the train drew out, I waved and waved until her dumpy black figure disappeared. I was off to another world with Brother Ass.

The guard took the basket from my lap and put it on top of my hamper, beside yet another piece of my luggage.

'There's nothing like a Gladstone bag,' he said, giving it a pat, 'a nice bit o' leather.'

'Mr. and Mrs. Gladstone were very huffy to Grandpa at breakfast,' I said, opening my *Tiger Tim*.

'Were they now, why so?' asked the guard. He wrote something down in a notebook and then looked curiously at me.

'Grandpa Holman liked boxing but they didn't approve of it at all.'

'Is that so? I like a good fight.'

I was reluctant to admit that sometimes I fought with my cousin Priscilla and that I was always afraid she might break my nose; Thackeray had had his nose broken at school. But this was a private worry and of no interest to the guard so I settled down to read.

When the train reached London I spotted Grand at once. She was waiting on the platform with a smart gentleman who was wearing a top hat.

'That must be my Papa!' I said, jumping up and down.

'Is that lady your Gran?' asked the guard. 'It's His Nibs the station-master with her. Surprised there's not a red carpet?' He winked, and nudged me in the ribs.

'My pet, it was my idea! What an advance to travel in charge of the guard! Now you're older I'm sure you'll agree a chaperone's fare is needless expense. This is my only grandchild, Diana Daphne. Good gracious, what a quantity of luggage!'

I bobbed to the station-master. 'Fowler says please can you wire or telephone at once, to say I have arrived?' It was impossible of course.

'*Telephone!*' Grand made a face. 'What an ordeal! Perhaps this good man can come to our rescue? I've never used telephonic apparatus and I'm far too old to learn.'

'It will be a pleasure madam; if the young lady gives me the number . . .'

'Here it is; please just tell Arthur, "Miss Diana has arrived".'

Surrounded by porters His Nibs led us to a cab. I whispered to Grand: 'Here's sixpence, Fowler said we must give it to the . . .'

'Hush my dear.' She shook hands with the station-master. 'I shan't forget your infinite kindness to an old lady in an appalling dilemma. I promise to send you a greetings card or a calendar at Christmas.'

'It has been a privilege, madam,' he murmured, bowing very low. I couldn't help grinning at the porters.

We were still playing the quizzing game when we reached Melbury Road. Grand let us in with her key and we groped our way to the sitting-room door. 'Good Helen will have lit the fire and do look, she's even filled the kettle. At last we're alone. Give me a hug.' She unclasped her cloak and flung it on the Moorish throne. 'Another blessed fortnight together!'

'There's a very nice cake in my basket, shall I go and fetch it?' I asked, wriggling to free myself from her embrace.

'A home-made cake? How capital! It will do so well for Sundays.'

I was already feeling my way back to the luggage. 'Here are some eggs, and this bag's full of lavender and this is some pot-pourri—a sort of porridge of roses—grandmother sent it as a present and there's a letter from her too.'

'Pot-pourri, how delightful. And what have you got in that bottle?'

'Oh that,' I blushed, 'that's only syrup of figs.'

'It sounds delicious! I recall that handsome fig tree which grew against the ruins in your garden. We will keep it for the guests on Sunday.'

'Oh no, the syrup of figs is for *me*.'

'My pet, do I detect a hint of selfish greed?' Her tone was reproving. 'A pleasure shared is a pleasure increased. Lady Gollancz has promised to bring her children. I've noticed that Jews are susceptible to sugary confections.'

Jews? They were as strange as Hottentots to me. 'Do they look like Rabbis?'

'Good gracious no; you're thinking of *Christ in the Temple*; Lady Gollancz has a very fair skin and bright red hair—such a talented woman. I hope she'll entertain us at the piano. Holman had a great admiration for the Jews, such a charming cultivated race . . .'

'Here's the letter,' I interrupted. It would be best to get it over.

She opened the letter and as usual read most of it aloud: '"I hope it will not clash with your plans but we are coming up to London next week, as George insists I consult this wonderful new doctor. I have arranged for Fowler, my maid, to take Diana and Priscilla to the circus on Tuesday, unless I hear that this doesn't suit; the motor will call about two. . . . Although I know that your domestic arrangements are not" something crossed out, "elastic, might I venture to suggest that the child sleeps in a proper *bed* instead of curled up on a sofa? A hump is so unfortunate in girls. Also Fowler, who is rather a dragon, is anxious the child should hang up her clothes and unpack her things into a chest of drawers. Although of course she will have her own maid later on, I'm sure you'll agree that early training in fastidious habits . . . Also perhaps you could engage a hairdresser to visit the house? I enclose the address of a reliable man who has come for years to Bryanston Square, rather than expose her to germs in a public place. Regular singeing of the ends . . ." Dear me.' She read no more but tore the letter into shreds and threw them on the fire. 'The road to hell is paved with good intentions. It would be most unbecoming for me to criticize your other grandmother in any way and I'm sure she means to be kind but I have always thought her a very *worldly* woman. It so happens the Forbes-Robertsons have invited us to tea and dear Gertrude has especially arranged for Jean to be there. Oh well, just as the dragon Fowler must be appeased, so we must not neglect our good Helen. While I write some letters, take a candle and your basket to the kitchen and don't forget to . . .' she paused, 'to what?'

'Shake hands!' I shouted.

'Bravo! When you return, I shall be at your disposal and for a whole hour we will do as you like.'

I crept down the basement stairs. 'Good evening, Helen, here are some new-laid eggs,' I opened the box, 'they're brown and each one has a date written on it in pencil.'

'Country eggs,' said Helen. 'Haven't you grown!'

'And these lavender bags should go in the visitor's drawers or at the bottom of the beds and this stuff is pot-pourri. If I were you

I should throw away that dirty silver money in the hall and put the pot-pourri in the Chinese bowls. Mrs. Hopkins made this cake but Grand wants to keep it until Sunday. Is the cat all right?' It looked very swollen.

'Expecting as usual,' said Helen.

'Expecting what?'

'Never you mind.' She put my cake in a tin.

'I must go and unpack. Good-bye.'

The hamper and Mr. Gladstone's bag were too heavy to lift, so I undid them both and unpacked Edward and some oddments into the hamper lid which served as a tray. I carried it upstairs with the candlestick wedged in a shoe. There were several other doors on the landing besides the one to Grand's room but I had never been into any of the other bedrooms. This time, I saw a key was in one of the locks, so I turned it and walked in.

It was like a room in Mary Millais' house—horrid dust-sheets over shapes. I put the hamper lid down on the bed and holding up my candle, lit the gas. The room was blue and white. The chintz and the wallpaper patterns were the same. After a good look round, I dragged off some sheets, raising a cloud of dust. There was a chest of drawers under the window with a label gummed to the top: WORTHLESS SENTIMENTAL SOUVENIRS. I opened the top drawer. It was crammed to the brim and covered with a piece of sewing, on which Grand had pinned another notice: IT IS DANGEROUS TO OPEN THIS DRAWER! I shut it quickly and pulled out the next. It was extremely heavy and revealed yet another notice: BEWARE! OPEN THIS DRAWER AT YOUR PERIL.

I drew back breathing deeply with frustration. What would Fowler say? Beware, indeed! It was all tommyrot. Of course I must unpack. I would put whatever was inside the drawers under a dust-sheet on the bed. I tugged at the second drawer. There was a crack. The bottom collapsed and a wide clattering stream of gold gushed onto the floor. Coins poured from the chest; they bounced off my feet and rolled noisily about the room. I stood stock still, up to my ankles in money.

'Good gracious, child, what a meddlesome matty you are!' Grand must have *run* up the stairs.

'I'm only unpacking,' I said, as calmly as I could. I was frightened.

'The oak lining of these drawers is very thin. I didn't lock it on purpose, in case some jackanapes . . . Calamity! How catastrophic! The whole bottom of the drawer has given way. What it will cost to repair!'

'I'm terribly sorry, but Fowler said . . .'

'Oh bother Fowler,' she snapped, 'fetch a pillow-case at once.'

I did as I was told without speaking. Grand wasn't often cross.

'Stretch open the mouth.' She took a shovel from the grate and scooped the gold off the floor. Soon the pillow-case was nearly half full.

'Is it any use for shopping?' I asked.

'No, not for shopping.'

I sighed. It was as I had suspected. Poor thing, her money was never any good.

'Why don't you sell some pictures?' I asked, getting up and looking round the walls.

'Hark at the Philistine!' she cried, sinking on the bed. 'As if I would ever sell a picture! To what purpose? I have everything I want. I've bought no clothes for thirty years, I've enough books, enough . . .'

But not enough to eat, and I was hungry.

'We could buy roast lamb, you've no idea how nice it is with onion sauce, or peas and new potatoes and . . .' I could scarcely bear to think.

'Roast lamb! Why, only today I bought an ample piece of salted silverside *and* an excellent turnip for Helen to boil for tomorrow's luncheon. What could be more wholesome with dumplings? My pet, you really must try to curb your gluttony: it's one of the seven deadly sins. Let us talk of something else. Food and money are scarcely elevating topics. As I always tell you, *ignore* Brother Ass.'

'Oh well, I like food and shopping and I ought to unpack; I promised Fowler.' I looked gloomily towards the other bedroom doors. Perhaps all the furniture was full of worthless sentimental souvenirs.

'My dear child, for now, why not let it be? I had thought

tonight we might go through our treasures. Like the boy scouts, I am prepared. I always carry bits of string—one of General Baden Powell's rules.' She tied up the mouth of the pillow-case and together we heaved it to the landing. What a joke, if the thieves came and didn't know the money wasn't any good.

'We'd better put it under my bed and tomorrow we can slide it downstairs on a tray; perhaps it might be more prudent if I took it elsewhere. We didn't turn out the gas.'

I ran to do so and fetched Edward, while Grand unlocked the bureau in her room.

'Sit in front of the looking-glass,' she said.

'It's not at all like our dressing-tables,' I objected. 'It's so high you can't see yourself at all.'

'That chest of drawers is the one in *Morning Prayer* and I had this box made to fit the top. It has made it rather high. It holds every dear letter that Holman ever wrote to me. Some of them begin, "My sweet contentment", some "My beloved gracious wife", some "My true Love".' Her eyes were full of tears. 'Since his death I have always stood to do my hair as there's no interest any more, no pleasure to be gained from my reflection. Push that cheval glass over here and you can perch on a corner of the sofa. Undo the collar of your dress. Can you slip it off your shoulders?'

I put on *The Bride of Bethlehem's* crown; it was studded with jewels and dangling with chains and silver coins.

'It goes rather well with the coral clasps. No, on second thoughts, these ropes of jade and amber are better and these lapis lazuli beads.' She stood behind me watching the effect. 'You're really too fair for the oriental things. Try this necklace and the pearl tiara—these are Bianca's pearls—you should really have her mandoline as well. Just look at this beautiful Florentine work and this huge star-sapphire.' She held it under the candle. I took it and put it on my thumb. My fingers were already loaded with rings.

'All yours, my child, one day, or almost all; I've tied on the labels.'

'I like this carved ivory belt.' I clipped it round my waist. 'It's much too big but very nice.'

'Yes, it's Indian, most unusual. This moonstone and crystal crescent is a symbol of Diana and that circle of amethysts and emeralds simulating Daphne was from Lady Constance Leslie: she had such a lovely face. I have always much admired this rosary of semi-precious stones. Your poor step-uncle Cyril sent the box of opals, fire opals from Ceylon and all this mother-of-pearl. I must think of a use for it some day. This cameo brooch was my sister's. Holman gave it to her on their marriage and when she died it came to me.'

'Grandmother's jewellery is different and so is my aunt's.' It shone more and was cleaner.

'I expect they like diamonds; I've never cared for them myself.' She opened the well of the bureau and took out a lot of leather cases. 'This bird is very pretty but it's the setting which appeals, although the silver gets tarnished; these brooches are early Georgian. I often wore this diamond and turquoise necklace at receptions: dear Holman simply showered me with gifts. Look at this Normandy work, a gold filigree sprinkled with diamonds like a cobweb with dewdrops in the sun!'

The room was like Aladdin's cave with all the jewels about and the bag of gold under the bed, but I began to yawn. The treasures weren't as nice as my museum.

'We'd better put the things back. We'll save up the miniatures for another day. I think I hear Helen with the bells. As it's Saturday tomorrow, we will take a bath then, after our exertions. There are the big rooms to turn out before the party.'

Two boy scouts always came to help with the Sunday parties.

'Are 'Erb and Fred coming as usual?' I asked.

'You mean Herbert and Frederick? No alas, they've failed me, but the scoutmaster has promised he'll send another two. He says the company regard it as an honour. In all the years I've employed boy scouts for my parties only one turned out to be a scallywag. We must say our prayers and then I will write my journal. Look at these rows and rows of volumes. I've left strict instructions that all are to be burnt when I die.'

'Oh, but what a waste of time!' I crossed over to the bookcase.

'Not at all, Diana, nightly my dear Holman and I share our

ideas on art and religion. He had such lofty inspirations. I don't burden him with just any tarradiddle.'

'My diary is different. I write what I have to *eat* and what happens every day.'

'I don't think you need put on the kettle. Just give your hands a rinse and splash your face: soap is so bad for the complexion. *You* shall sleep in my bed and I will sleep on the sofa.'

'You won't find it very comfortable,' I warned.

'I'm no sybarite.' She smiled.

While I undressed she turned tactfully away. I put on my nightdress and kimono. With creaking knees she knelt on the prie-dieu. I had forgotten the Lord's Prayer in French that Grand had taught me: Not Repair Key Ate; and could only repeat my list of names. I began with cunning: 'God bless Papa first and then Grand . . .'

'I am much honoured to find myself promoted to second place from oblivion, or below the pugs! I see Fowler and Hannah are tied and a new friend, called Timothy, is honoured and high up on the list. Would he be the Pritchard boy?' I shook my head. 'Ah, so he's another neighbour's son. Have they an estate or are they tenants?'

'Timothy hasn't got any parents,' I said, climbing into bed.

'Oh, poor little boy! An orphan? I suppose he must live with relations?' How inquisitive she was!

'No, he lives alone with Anne and his dog.' I was on the defensive.

'An elder sister, you mean, or an aunt?'

'Anne is French for donkey. A Frenchman comes to stay now and then.'

'Dear me, a *Frenchman*! And you admit that this Anne person is a donkey? Poor boy, it doesn't sound a desirable background for a child.'

She compressed her lips. It was useless trying to explain. The less said about Timothy the better. I snuggled down with Edward: I had saved up a secret thought: on Tuesday I would see Priscilla.

'But this isn't one of my eggs!' I shouted angrily at Helen. 'It says FOREIGN—you really are the limit! No supper last night and now a smelly egg—I won't eat it, so there!' I threw its red felt cap on the floor.

'Good gracious, what an outburst!' Grand sat bolt upright on the sofa, without her teeth. 'That's no way to speak to Helen!'

I was prickling with annoyance. While Helen had banged her broom against the bed, and swept the tea-leaves off the floor, I had been looking forward to breakfast. 'She can take it away. You must *please* tell her to get me one of mine.' I thumped the pillow.

'Must! I apologize, Helen. Clearly Miss Diana has forgotten who she is!'

Helen was unruffled and turned to Grand: 'There's still nine foreign eggs, mum, and they'll go off if they're not eaten, and Miss Diana's eggs will last a month, and if I've done wrong I'm sure I'm very sorry but using country eggs, when there's foreign eggs to finish is, to my mind, as bad as throwing out good money.' She was thinking of that stupid money in the hall.

'You did quite rightly. I'm much shocked and distressed by Miss Diana.' After a meaning glance at me, Helen left the room.

'My dear child, words fail me! Holman so detested arrogance and,' she paused, looking at me closely, 'as I've told you, Gabriel Rossetti's friends were gluttons; they ate poor Holman out of house and home. He would, I'm sure, feel deeply grieved. I think you should forgo breakfast altogether and pay especial attention to your prayers. I will deny myself your conversation, but remember it is I who make the sacrifice: I, who have looked forward with such pleasure to your visit. For two hours we will remain completely silent.'

'I don't want to talk and I don't want the boiled milk either; grandmother says it's disgusting.' I got dressed without troubling to be modest. How unreasonable she was. I was sick of Holman this and Holman that.

With much gesticulation she instructed me to wear a pinafore and tie a duster round my head. We went downstairs and Helen puffed up from the basement with brooms, mops, dustpans and brushes. She had put a heap of dirty rags and some tins of polish in the lift.

When the clock struck ten, Grand put her arms round me and said: 'My pet, now we will let bygones be bygones.' She was nicer than I was. 'We must set to work. The dining-room is easy; shall we start here? I shook the rugs last week. This huge sideboard was a gift to Holman from Augustus Egg, but in the first place it came from Kensington Palace.'

'Did it belong to Princess Louise?'

Closing my eyes, I could see it laden with hams and pies. I could imagine the silver dishes of devilled bones, kidneys, eggs and bacon . . . there were friend soles, salmon fish cakes, kedgeree. . . . 'I wonder if Mr. Garibaldi asked for macaroni?'

'No, of course not, Holman met Garibaldi at breakfast with the *old* duke; Princess Louise was married to the son.'

'I hope one day someone will ask me to breakfast,' I said, sniffing.

'I've filled the shelves with books of reference, like *Who's Who*, and the *Peerage* and Fox's *Book of Martyrs* and the *Encyclopaedia Britannica*; you will find the answer here if you have any problem.' She flicked the dust about.

My interest was aroused: 'Is there a *Book of Directions*?'

'What's that? Don't look now, I'm sure there is, but we must concentrate first on our work. Work. You see this chair? It's English, quite early. Holman carved this motif on the back, with his own dear hands. He wouldn't tolerate vulgar Regency fashions—hideous, heavy, mahogany. He designed these chairs in the fifties; inspired by an Egyptian stool at Montagu House. Look at the bone inlay!' She polished it with care. 'It was certainly due to Holman's inspiration that William Morris took to domestic design; he never painted seriously after he married that silly woman. She had looks of a kind, but she should never have married an artist. Never! That portrait by Romney is of Jack Russell, the hunting parson. Can you climb up and stand carefully on the sideboard? I'll hand you a chammy leather to rub over the Tintorettos. If only you could reach Titian's portrait of his daughter, but alas, we haven't got the steps. Titian hair, as you see, is gold, not red.'

'Yes, I know.' She'd said it all before, and I wanted to find the *Book of Directions*.

'Let us move our paraphernalia to the drawing-room. Run and ask Helen if she has any milk. It's so good for ivory. This cabinet is yours, I gave it to you at your christening. See the label: "Diana Daphne 1913." These loose doors must be attached one day. And ask Helen for the linseed oil; as you're here to help, we'll treat the Etruscan vases and this Damascus lamp could do with a wash.'

'Tilly always says parties make lots of work,' I said at last, squatting on a dust-sheet between the rags and saucers.

'Parties! The parties which I've been privileged to attend! I kept every invitation; and unbeknownst to Holman, who would, I know, have disapproved, I kept a scrapbook of cuttings, referring to my own modest entertainments. This Portuguese cabinet—it was made for an Indian Rajah—is chock-a-block with such-like souvenirs.' She stepped over our cleaning things and found a bulging book. 'Listen: "The charming rambling fascinating house, full of rare works of art, Eastern bric-a-brac . . . Hungarian band. . . . Delicious music . . . the gracious beautiful hostess. . . . Distinguished guests, well-known artists, writers, critics, singers, lords and ladies, men of fashion. The picturesque daughter of William Morris and the beautiful Stillman girl were talking to Hall Caine and Theodore Watts." Hall Caine I remember had a tawny red beard and such a gentle manner. The carriages came and went by the score.' She turned over a page. 'Here's another cutting: "The rooms filled with Eastern rugs, tapestries, oriental lamps, bronzes, ornaments, knick-knacks . . . the walls graced by Tintoretto, Titian, Bellini, Velasquez, Della Robbia," and see this charming programme, of a Lauriston party July 5th 1888, shaped like a small green leaf, describing the diversions: "Mrs. Shaw will whistle from the terrace at 4.45, 5.15 and 5.45."'

'Why? Who for?' I looked up from oiling an Etruscan urn.

'She whistled quite beautifully. Don't interrupt, "and Professor Elihu Thomson will demonstrate electric welding on the tennis lawn and Robertson's Writing Telegraphic Apparatus. . . . An exhibition in the conservatory, specimens of ortho-chromatic photography and photo-engravings. . . . Orchestra at intervals in the garden." A delightful day—I recollect that stupid Gabriel Rossetti said that to him music was just a *noise*—I know I was looking my best. Vanity is the root of evil, but look at my portrait over there, painted by Holman when I was only twenty-two.'

'You'd better explain,' said a voice, 'how you made Edward Hughes darken the eyebrows and redden the lips, when fathe was too blind to know what you were doing, and how you made him take in the waist. It's not a portrait any more, it's a contemptible Fancy Head.'

I looked round in amazement to see a very large lady in the doorway. Why did I feel this had happened again and again? Grand was struck dumb. The scrapbook slid off her lap amongst the tins of polish.

'And I hope,' went on the lady, who sounded very angry, 'that the fine companion portrait of aunt Fanny, your sister, which you keep in the attic and pretend isn't finished, will be brought to light when you are dead. Cyril would have hung it in the place it deserves if you hadn't banished him to that God-forsaken tea plantation in Ceylon.'

She strode into the room and Grand glanced nervously at me.

'Perhaps you have also admitted how behind father's back you got Edward Hughes to improve *The Lady of Shalott* and what you made him do to the *Tracer* after Millais had advised . . .'

'This is your Aunt Gladys,' said Grand, collecting her wits and adjusting her duster turban. 'This is your niece Diana. You saw her as a baby.'

'How d'you do. Yes, I'm your aunt.'

I sprang up and bobbed. She was the biggest aunt I'd ever seen. I knew that Grandpa Holman had first married Grand's sister Fanny, who had died young, and that Fanny was the mother of my step-uncle Cyril.

Clicking her tongue with disapproval, Fowler had said: 'To think your Grandpa married two sisters—the very idea—so the first wife Fanny is your great-aunt *and* your step-Grand as well. I don't know what to make of it all, I'm sure.'

'I didn't hear you ring, Gladys,' said Grand. 'I suppose Helen let you in. We're very busy.'

She hovered round and made great play of dusting the piano,

blowing on the cast of my hand, which weighed down the sheets of music.

Big Aunt's hat was like a saucepan. I sat down on a dust-sheet and went on polishing the urn. Neither of them spoke but I could hear them breathing.

'On Tuesday I'm going to the circus with Priscilla,' I said at last, feeling someone should utter.

'Oh, are you!' With a wild look, Big Aunt turned to me and then fumbled in a shabby leather bag. 'You'll find *me* standing outside with the leaflets. Look! No, those are for anti-vivisection, but read them all the same. Here are the circus ones. How do you suppose the animals are trained? What d'you think they endure between the acts, cramped in their cruel cages?'

She flung a lot of papers on the floor on top of Grand's invitations. I picked up one photograph after another.

'Oh, no!' A large thin dog with its tongue lolling out and a hole in its stomach was strapped to a board; there were spread-eagled monkeys with terrified eyes, cats with no skin or covered with sores, donkeys . . .

'Don't!' cried Grand, trying to pounce. 'Your mind will be poisoned forever! Come,' she seized Big Aunt by the arm, 'if you have anything to say, come with me.'

They left me alone sitting on the dust-sheet, clutching a picture of a horse. I stared for a long time and then, with tears rolling down my face and my heart thumping, I picked up a rag and went on rubbing at the urn.

They were away for so long that I went upstairs and wrote a letter.

'Dear Fowler,

I can't come to the circus with you and Priscilla on Tuesday. Can you take Rose? Big Aunt will be outside in a saucepan with disgusting pictures. DON'T LOOK; her temper's worse than Mrs. Hopkins.

Much love from Brother Ass and me. (Miss Diana).'

I added a drawing of us both.

I was tired of the Tate: we had walked for miles, Grand talking all the time and darting from one picture to another. It was as though we were chasing butterflies; there was always one further on.

'Oh, we must do the Turners!' she insisted, grabbing my hand and pulling me with her.

'Here we are.' She stopped and looked round. 'Turner was a shabby old man, with a very large head; slovenly in dress, as some great men are. Dear Holman was so fastidious, he scented his beautiful beard with sandalwood oil. He first saw Turner at the Academy Schools, when Turner gave Jack Millais a medal for drawing. He was two years younger than Holman, only a child.'

'It was the first time that Grandpa met Johnnie Millais,' I refused to call him Uncle Jack, 'and the Prince of Wales said he could have a wish.'

'A charming gesture typical of royalty, and the greedy boy asked for cream buns! He was too fond of the *worldly* pleasures, and later paid for them dearly; painting such nonsense as *Bubbles* and little girls in mob caps. I'm proud to say my Holman's motives were always of the highest order.'

'Oh no, you've got it all wrong! Aunt Mary told me his wish was to fish in the Serpentine; and when the policemen came, they said: "Now then, m'lad, you know it's not allowed," and he showed them his Royal Warrant. It had a huge seal and he kept it rolled up in a black tin box.'

'I think that was a different occasion, when he was even younger. He won many medals you know.' Half closing her eyes, she passed in front of one picture to another. 'To think some of these Turners were sold for a song!'

'I could do them,' I said, 'at least if the paper was wet. Mr. Russell Flint showed me how when we went there to tea. An alarm clock rang to remind him when the paper was ready.'

'You comical child.' She took my hand and squeezed it in her muff which hung from her neck on a chain. The butterfly fluttered on and on. 'I am so particularly anxious that you should understand the difference, learn to distinguish between, pre-Raphaelism and pre-Raphaelitism. Note the T.'

What did it matter? I swayed to and fro, watching my reflection bob about over a sunset. My head felt curiously far from my feet, and I had a pain.

'Pre-Raphaelism means copying the style of artists who lived before Raphael, slavish imitation, whereas pre-Raphael*it*ism . . .'

What did I care? My pain was getting worse. I could see my feet and hear them trudging on the floor but they were numb. Grand scurried through a room where some pictures seemed to shimmer.

'Don't let's waste time on this rubbish. Precious time: one golden hour of sixty diamond seconds! "Impressionism!" Material soulless chaos, as Holman said: "childishly drawn and ignorantly coloured!" Here we are on more familiar ground. You know who this is?'

'Oh yes, it's Guggums as Ophelia. She looks much prettier there than she does as Sylvia or even Isabella. Johnnie Millais painted a nice big rat on the bank—just here you said—but great-uncle Hunt made him paint it over with grass. I think it was a shame.'

'It looked suggestive, as if it might bite Ophelia's throat. The picture was painted at Ewell while Holman was painting *The Hireling Shepherd*. Did I tell you they were the first pictures painted on a wet white ground? Of course it was Holman's invention and much copied later by those unable to master the technique. After only one attempt, Mr. Frith gave it up. He botched a head in *Derby Day* and had to scrape down to the canvas and begin all over again.'

'The idea was meant to be a secret between Grandpa and Johnnie Millais but you said Johnnie didn't keep it and told Bruno when Grandpa was away. Bruno was what they called Madox Brown and you said he was "touchy".'

'You've got it all pat,' she said, nodding with approval. 'I reap my reward for perseverance. Here's Johnnie Millais' father in *The Carpenter's Shop*. He too mistrusted Rossetti. This is a new acquisition: I always called it Dickens's hullaballoo. He was an enemy at first but now I shouldn't say so. Holman's *Shadow of Death* was a far better picture. You've seen the Queen's letter about it? Dear child, you *do* look fatigued. Perhaps we should go and have tea. I'm afraid it's too late to pay a call.'

The pictures were spinning on the walls. 'I've got a pain and my boots are hurting.'

'I expect you laced them too tightly. Try not to think of Brother Ass. Ah, here are the eggs!'

'The eggs?' I was startled to attention with memories of breakfast.

'Such a splendid fellow was dear Augustus Egg! He saved poor Holman with a commission when he had sunk almost to despair, thanks to Gabriel Rossetti's treacherous behaviour. Try to remember the name: Augustus Egg. I shall test you later at our quizzing. Ivy Cottage was a centre for artists of every description, and actors. He had a very good cook. I told you the sideboard once belonged to him?'

'Yes, a good cook and a good egg,' I murmured faintly. I was unlikely to forget.

I always felt embarrassed when Grand asked the waitress for two cups and saucers and a jug of boiling water. Sometimes a haughty one, sneering over her notebook, would say in a loud voice: 'You don't want to bust yourself do you?' Our neighbours would titter when they caught her cheeky wink and stare at us rudely.

Today the waitress was polite and only asked: 'Nothing to eat?'

'I should like a bun,' I ventured, glancing anxiously at Grand.

'A toasted bun for the little girl?' encouraged the waitress with a smile.

'Yes, perhaps,' conceded Grand. She knew Helen would provide potato soup as soon as we got home.

Grand's bag was called a 'reticule'. It had a silver clasp and was made of smooth black velvet, shaped like a narrow sack. From its depth she produced a box of saccharin, a muslin bag of tea-leaves, and a creased manilla envelope of powdered milk. I spied through my fingers to see if anyone was looking.

In case the milk wasn't boiled, we made our own by stirring the powder with our spoons in a little water at the bottom of the cups. Grand dropped the tea-bag into the jug and wound its string round the handle. The saccharins fizzed in white splodges on top of the grey hot water. Although it was 'wholesome' life trickled into my legs and my feet began to tingle.

Grand's purse was so shabby that it always made me sad. It held pennies and folded sheets of stamps. When she paid the bill I always looked away. In the street I was at pains to distract her attention from any pavement artist, who might be squatting, greasy cap beside him, amongst his coloured chalks. If she spotted one, she would never pass him by, but would retire discreetly to a doorway, or press against the railings with her back turned to the passers-by. Then, to my confusion, she would lift her skirts to find the chammy-leather pouch of money which she wore concealed, suspended from her waist. Flushed with effort, she would at last approach the artist and hand him a piece of silver, saying: '*If* you are ever desperate and need to earn a shilling, you can come and sweep the leaves out of my area and scrub my front door steps. My cook will give you a cup of soup. You need never starve, I am your friend.'

Most of the beggars knew her but she would hand a card to strange ones, adding with a smile: 'Prudent thrift permits the luxury of giving.'

As we walked to the bus, she would explain: 'Only a few have any talent, but I am haunted by the thought of my beloved Holman starving, and also, that one of these pathetic creatures might be poor Simeon Solomon, such a gifted man, about whose end all my friends are so reticent. I fear, alas, he fell on evil days.'

I imagined him to be an eastern king who had lost his golden throne, his sacks of jewels and slaves, and fled to England heavily disguised. I scanned each new unshaven face, curious to know if it were his. We never found King Solomon and no one except boy scouts ever came to scrub the steps. I detested the whole affair and was reluctant to allow her this luxury of giving.

When we got home there was a soup tureen standing on the trivet. I sat warming my hands on my cup with my unlaced boots flapping open to the fire; because my slippers were still in my hamper.

'Now let's play the quizzing game,' said Grand. She was never tired.

'All right.' I took a piece of paper from the coolie hat, on which to score our marks.

'Should we include our whole expedition, the Albert Memorial for instance?'

'Yes,' I said, because I knew it very well, 'your turn first.'

'Ah, let me see,' said Grand, pretending to be puzzled. 'Who stand each side of Raphael's Throne in the frieze round the base of the Memorial—the bas reliefs, or bas-relievi, as they are called in Italian?'

'That's easy,' I boasted, giving the answer. 'What are the animals in the groups of sculpture at the corners of the steps?'

She paused and looked thoughtful: 'A bull, an elephant, a camel . . .'

'You forgot the bison!' I said.

'Bravo, you win! What is the exact inscription on the equestrian statue at Albert Gate? Quite right, Napier of Magdala, such a friend of Holman's!'

'How many different wild flowers can you remember in Ophelia?'

'Oh, that's very difficult,' she protested. 'The grass in Ophelia is so brilliant, so wonderfully green.'

She cheated and changed the subject. 'Holman's art master, I think it was Varley, said: "My dear fellow, you mustn't paint grass *green* like a cabbage, that won't do at all! Constable? He had no sense of colour. True artists, like myself, paint grass as it is: brown and yellow."'

After twenty questions, we added up our marks. Grand had to write her journal and I was too sleepy to wait for Helen and the bells. I lit a candle and went upstairs alone. I wasn't frightened because there was no question of a bath, and I knew Edward Bear would be waiting.

On Sunday morning Grand rushed into the road amongst the traffic, waving her umbrella. I could hear the brakes screeching; I shut my eyes for a moment and stayed glued to the kerb.

'Come along child!' She beckoned from the platform of the bus. 'It's beginning to rain but I know you like to go on top.' Holding up our skirts we clambered up the stairs. I was dressed in velvet, as Sylvia was in Grandpa's picture in the Tate.

'Off to act at the the-ayter on the *Sabbath?*' chaffed the conductor, slapping my behind.

'Fowler says we should wait on the pavement at the bus stop; she says one day we'll get run over. "The manner of her death was thus, she was run over by a bus."'

'What nonsense! The drivers—everyone in Kensington knows *me*. *Omnibus* please. I dislike abbreviations, and if you sit so high no one will believe you're half fare. We'll have to change for St. Paul's, which reminds me, I must get out some collection. Bother this shower; put on this shawl and hold the umbrella.' I spread the black oilcloth apron which hung from the seat in front over our knees.

'After the service today, we'll visit the crypt. You're old enough now to enjoy it. One day my ashes will be there. I shall hold my passport to heaven in my hand. I've left strict instructions for Holman's words to be copied on a piece of paper. I shall show it to St. Peter at the gate.'

'What gate?' Would Helen riddle the ashes?

'The Gate of Heaven of course! I shall arrive with a reference and I like to think that dear Holman will be waiting. He wrote: "This is an insufficient tribute to Edith my wife, whose constant virtues ever exalt my understanding of the nature and influence of womanhood." Let us hope one day *your* husband will say the same of you.'

'Will great-aunt Fanny be waiting too?'

'You will see Johnnie's grave, your great-uncle Jack Millais whom he loved; forever loyal during the darkest hours and ungrudging with material assistance—of course we paid back every penny—no man ever had a better friend. Poor Millais, he was tempted at last to forget the noble dedicated cause to which they had aspired as young men; but I for one will never hear a word against him and I refuse to admit there *was* a scandal. Many's the time Holman has sprung to his defence—at what a cost! The Carlyles, amongst others, condemned him and of course Mr. Ruskin turned away from Holman, who was Millais's friend, and bestowed his praises on that sly Italian. It was years before Mr. Ruskin admitted how he'd been hoodwinked by undesirable people. Are you listening? I may not live much longer and although you're too young to understand, I know Holman would wish you always to defend his friend.'

She had talked like this many times before. 'But did Johnnie do something *bad*?' I was anxious because he was my hero.

'He did nothing *bad*, as you call it—pray spare me these Fowlerisms—nothing dishonourable. Try to remember what I say: Euphemia's first marriage was annulled and she was married to Millais from her father's house. *No* one can point a finger at a woman if she's married from her father's house. Give me your word you will remember.'

'I shall always remember,' I said. A pond of rain had formed in the oilcloth cover and a spoke of the umbrella was dripping on my head. I hoped Papa would have a nice house when I got married.

'And what's more,' Grand continued, 'when Jack Millais was dying—poor man, he had no voice, it was tobacco smoking that killed him—he had to *write* his dying wish. He wrote "I would like the Queen to see Effy." Good Princess Louise, whom you know so well, went at once that night to see her mother, and the very next day Euphemia received a Royal Command.'

'Of a regiment you mean, like Papa?'

'Fares please, fares please!' shouted the conductor, rattling the pennies in his bag.

'An invitation from the Queen—a privilege which hitherto, owing to evil gossip, had been denied Euphemia. Good gracious!' She turned to the conductor: 'We should have got off.'

It was pouring with rain. When we reached St. Paul's at last, the service was nearly over and we had to sit behind a pillar. Grand crossed herself a lot and bobbed up and down. I wasn't sure what to do, so I sat still.

She had herself made my vast, silver, gem-studded prayer book: 'Don't leave it behind; I hammered it with my own hands,' she whispered. It didn't look hammered to me. There was a design of peacocks drinking from a fountain on the cover like the fresco she had painted in the kitchen.

When the congregation shuffled out she whispered: 'Come, my pet, I see my friend the verger over there, but on our way to the crypt we will spend a few minutes as usual in front of *The Light of the World.* As you know, it is the only picture in the Cathedral. A suffragette attacked it with an axe but, I am thankful to say, the canvas was skilfully restored and now even I can't detect any damage. Look!' she cried, in a louder voice, to attract the attention of people prowling on tiptoe down the aisle. 'Look at the two lights of one conscience!'

'She means the lantern,' I explained to a family of gaping children who gathered round with their parents. 'It cost a lot of money.'

I was resigned to people staring but I drew the frowsty shawl closer round me, to hide my Sylvia dress.

'And do you see the golden crown is interlaced with thorns, and green shoots are budding from the wood?' Grand pointed with her umbrella. A small crowd had collected. She explained: 'I have the honour to be the artist's widow.' There could be no stopping her now. Resigned, I leant my back against the wall and she continued: 'The picture is full of symbols: the white robe represents the Power of the Spirit . . .'

'It was great-grandma's best damask tablecloth,' I confided to the boy on my left, 'she was very cross when Grandpa cut it up.'

'My grandchild is right in a way but it was the tailor who cut it up, and in spite of my husband's careful sketches and entreaties, he produced—what do you think? A fashionable frock-coat! It was really rather droll.' She smiled but no one else did, perhaps because they were in church. 'It all had to be unpicked and draped once more on the lay figure. You see the folds?'

Had Grandpa painted them himself? When they were young, he and Johnnie got bored with the tiresome parts of their pictures and used to swop round: 'Come and do this hand, dear fellow,' or 'Please, old boy, finish this tricky bit of wall. I'm bored to tears with it, let me do some drapery for you.'

'*Oi* doan loike it. Oi doan loike 'is fice,' murmured a little man, who looked friendly and reminded me of Arthur.

'Hit's hignorant, that's what you are,' retorted a fierce woman.

'Mr. Carlyle hated it too,' I consoled him quietly, 'he called it a Papistical Fancy, whatever that is.' It was obviously an insult. 'Mr. Carlyle said: "Don't paint *subjects*, paint what you see man, not all this — "' I faltered and glanced fearfully at Grand, who was lecturing more and more people, '"all this tommyrot." That's what he said, really, and whenever Grandpa tried to argue, Mrs. Carlyle stood behind saying "Shush".'

Grand turned to the children: 'When you're my age you'll be able to tell your grandchildren—perhaps your great-grandchildren—that you met the painter's wife.' With a gracious nod she dismissed the audience and led me to the crypt.

The door was unlocked by an old man in a black dress with a bunch of keys. We went down a dark and musty staircase.

'Ah! There's the Duke's tomb. No, no, child, not the Duke of Argyll—you've got him on the brain—the *Iron* Duke. I saw him as a child and waved my cup and ball. He was riding in Rotten Row and raised his hat.' She hurried on. 'Now here we are at last among friends in Painters' Corner. Turner, the shabby man, remember? Leighton, who begged Holman to join the Artists' Rifles—so many P.R.A.'s. I wonder if Frank Dicksee will come to tea today, such a fine-looking man—a handsome beard is so manly.' She looked round the walls. 'Van Dyck from old St. Paul's—what illustrious company I'll keep, with so few other women. Not all the men who should be are so honoured: poor George Meredith, in death as in life, how disgracefully he was treated, in spite of our petition that he should be buried in the Abbey.'

Meredith had been the model for the corpse on the bed in *The Death of Chatterton*. She had told me long ago that the painter Henry Wallis stole his wife, as if one could steal a person.

'Yes indeed, how tragic! He wrote to us: "The gods have robbed me of all but the strength to endure", or something very touching; and here is Millais. Holman rests,' her voice broke, 'Holman lies by his friend: close in death as in life, and I shall be here, at the feet of my beloved.' She tapped the spot with her umbrella and sank slowly to her knees.

'You'll have to curl up like a hedgehog to get under that stone.' I said, peering at the space.

'Hush! Kneel beside me and pray. I mean of course, my ashes.' Her lips were moving and to my dismay, her tears splashed in the dust and made stains on Grandpa's grave. I knelt beside her. The cold from the floor seemed to paralyse my knees and seep up to my stomach. Still she went on praying. Frivolous thoughts would come into my head although I was kneeling on a *grave*. To my horror I heard myself humming the song uncle Hubert used to sing, 'A foot in the *grave* young man, a greenery yallery, Grosvenor Gallery, foot in the *grave* young man. A Francesco Di Rimini, niminy-piminy, *je ne sais quoi* young man.'

'Hush dear. Say your prayers,' she whispered.

The man with the keys would have forgotten us by now. It was dark and damp and we were alone. Grand seemed to be asleep. I shook her arm: 'Do come, let's go!' Let's go! echoed through the vaults. 'We'll get shut in.' I got up, my legs trembled. She rose at last, leaning heavily on my shoulder.

'It's horrible here,' I said, 'if we're not quick we'll be trapped and have to stay all night.' I shuddered. How much better it was to be buried under grass in a churchyard. 'If we have to stay here, just think of the ghosts.'

'I should *enjoy* meeting them,' she said. 'We could commune with Holman and with other shades. There's nothing to be afraid of.' Shades? Her face was radiant but I knew Fowler wouldn't like it.

'We must go home.' I ran away, reached the stairs and, picking up my velvet skirt, scrambled up the steps. 'Let me out!' I battered my fists on the door.

'Now, now,' said the man in the black dress, who was still waiting. 'Now, now, you're very young and the old lady—I always wait for her—she comes nearly every Sunday.'

Grand was At Home every Sunday afternoon.

'Fowler said if you make me wear my classical dress, I must wear my shoes and socks. I've got some slippers in Mr. Gladstone's bag.'

'I fail to see why our lives should be ruled by a dragon with the views of an ignorant peasant.' Grand frowned with annoyance as she laid my classical dress on the bed. We were both in our petticoats.

'I want to wear my brown velveteen. It's nice and warm.' I had felt cold and had been stared at all the morning.

'My pet, I implore you to listen. This dress is so becoming.' I brushed away her hand in irritation.

'Let's compromise,' she wheedled. It sounded suspicious. 'I will lend you the white silk stockings which I wore at Court many years ago and *I'll* give in about the slippers!'

'Oh all right,' I sulked. I would have to wear the dratted thing.

'I knew you would! Give me a hug. But my pet, when you make a generous gesture, try to do it graciously. We must hurry. Let me tie your ribbons. As a treat, I thought we'd use the special tea-service.'

'The labelled one?' I groaned.

'Of course. You can get it out and put it carefully in the lift. Now, down we go to the pantry.'

Each cup had a tag tied to its handle: so-and-so drank from this cup: Lear, Dickens, Burne-Jones, Carlyle, Thackeray, Madox-Brown, Meredith, Gladstone, Millais, Patmore . . . There were twenty-four altogether.

'Our tea-set at home is quite different,' I said, blowing off the dust. 'The cups and saucers I like best are white and gold, with little views painted on in grey.'

'Apart from a few Spanish and Italian things, our china is all oriental. Holman held the strongest views on the design of domestic utensils, maintaining that the whole surface should be covered with symmetrical pattern. Mr. Gladstone owned a lot of rubbishy Dresden and Sèvres, and yet was most interested to hear Holman's opinions, and in principle William Morris agreed; he and William de Morgan were, in fact, inspired by the idea.'

The labelled tea service was a swindle because all these people hadn't come together. She didn't know that any particular cup was really Millais'. 'We never tie labels on our cups at home: Arthur wouldn't like it.'

'It's rather wearisome, my pet, to be so frequently regaled with Fowler's and Arthur's taboos.' She sighed, and then, summoning her patience, went on brightly: 'Not everyone has been privileged, as I have, to receive such a galaxy of stars, at one time or another. I won't dispute that your grandfather Freeman was a very brilliant K.C. Indeed, I've heard that at the Parliamentary Bar . . .'

'It's five to four, mum,' called Helen, 'and the new lads is here and they say they feel a bit silly and they'd like you to tell them what to do.'

'Good afternoon, boys. Please follow me,' Grand shouted to the scouts, who were waiting in the area. We climbed the back stairs. In the hall she turned to me with a roguish expression: 'Put something on your head—anything will do.' I tipped the paper bags from the coolie hat and put it on. 'Oh, that looks very odd with your classical dress but never mind; we'll pretend. We'll be the visitors and go outside and ring, and the boys can admit us.'

We stood on the front-door step and rang. 'Oh no, don't peer through a crack as if you expected a cut-throat! Open it wide, wide like this, in welcome. Now listen carefully, you take our coats and hats.' I removed the coolie hat and handed it to them. 'We might have canes or umbrellas; the hats must be left in the hall. Lead us to the drawing-room door, yes, you go on ahead and then ask politely: "What name, sir, or madam" and announce what they tell you in a loud, clear voice.' In ringing tones she cried: 'Lord Godolphin, Lady Thingummy, Professor So-and-So. Now we'll try again. You, my pet, must keep your eye on the kettle. When six people have arrived, infuse the tea and I will pour out and you can hand the cups round.'

I paid little attention because I'd done it all before.

'If there's a crowd,' she went on, 'I'll take half and leave you with the other. Do you remember your *facts*? Have you got them clear?'

'I think so,' I said, but I began to feel uneasy.

'You mustn't neglect the Gollancz children. They are *your* guests. I was thinking in church that to produce a diversion you can act a charade. I asked young John Rothenstein as well . . .'

'You know we quarrelled last time,' I protested.

'Good gracious, it's quarter past four. You'd better go and fill the kettle.'

I was filling the kettle in the cloakroom, when the first visitors arrived. I saw through the ventilator that it was Lady Ilchester from Holland House, and someone else I didn't know.

'You've got ter leave yer 'ats,' said the tallest boy-scout.

'Oh no, surely?' Lady Ilchester protested mildly and turned to the stranger: 'I think we'd rather keep them?'

'Oh sure, anything you say,' she answered in a funny accent.

'Oi can't let yer in with them 'ats,' the scout said again, firmly barring the door. 'Oi've got me orders.'

With a plaintive murmur, Lady Ilchester unpinned her bonnet and laid it on a chair. With a tinkling laugh, the other lady did the same. Her hat was a little brown bird and it perched beside the bonnet. I came out of hiding when both ladies were announced.

'I don't think you should take the *ladies'* hats. I mean not if hey want to keep them. Arthur never does.'

The scouts ignored me. They both carried staffs.

'Oh well, I suppose it doesn't really matter.' I shrugged and opened the drawing-room door.

'Ah, here's my little Goddess with the kettle. Say how-d'you-do. This is Miss Claire van der Zuite—an American lady who has come with an introduction.'

My first meeting with a Yankee. I would tell Arthur all about it.

'Mr. Woolley, Mr. Telfer Waugh, Miss Millais and Miss Morse and Dean Inge,' shouted the tall boy-scout.

'How are you my dear? How de do, how de do. You know Miss Van-den-boot?' All the ladies were hatless and some looked annoyed.

'Mrs. Casson, Lady Noble and Mr. and Mrs. Peacock . . . *and* Sir Frank Dicksee,' boomed the cockney voice. The room was filling up but the kettle wasn't boiling: I wetted the tea, feeling guilty. The sandwiches were stuck with pennants, on which 'curried fish' or 'cheese' had been scrawled as if by a spider. 'Would you like one, a sandwich, I mean?' I asked the Yankee lady, who seemed to be alone. 'Do have some Dundee cake.' Unless it was eaten it would have to do for next week as well. 'Do try!' I begged, shoving the plate against her ribs.

'What a thrill!' She crooked her little finger. 'My cup is labelled Browning!'

'I'm afraid Browning's rather chipped.'

'What an At Home it must have been—what a party!'

'They came at different times. It's Grand's idea. It helps people think of conversation . . .' I didn't add that the mistress must have her little fancies.

'You wicked child! Don't spoil it,' she pleaded. 'I like to think of them all, drinking tea in this wonderful room; the wallpaper and everything is perfect. I can't wait to tell my folks at home. Would it be all right if I wrote *my* name on the other side of this label? Claire van der Groot?'

'Please do, if you've got a pencil.' No one was looking and I could always rub it out. I left her and handed round the milk.

'I've brought you some souvenirs from Ur, for your museum,' said Mr. Woolley. 'Another scarab, an ear-ring which belonged to a princess, and a phial of sand from the Flood. Mrs. Holman-Hunt is so generous and subscribes to all our expeditions . . .'

'Sand from the Flood? Thank you *very* much.' At Sunday school Mr. Duncan had told us all about it. I ignored the dirty old ear-ring and the scarab. The sand was in a little bottle. I would put it later with my Pendix and the Jordan water.

Sir Israel and Lady Gollancz were announced. 'Ah!' cried Grand, pressing through the crowd with two dark, sullen-looking children, 'here are your little friends: Oliver and Ruth.' Oh, save us from little friends to tea! 'They don't want anything to eat and I've told them you're going to play charades.'

'Would you like to dress up?' They gave me a hostile stare because I was dressed up already. I led them to the Hobman chest. Hats clung like limpets and anemones to the rock-like tables in the hall.

'Whatever's this? Did it belong to a bishop?'

'No, it's a choir-boy's surplice; Papa wore it for *May Morning on Magdalen Tower*. This is an Arab's burnous and that's a wedding dress from Syria.' The room was soon littered with clothes.

'I shall wear this,' said Ruth, rattling the vest of chain mail which had once belonged to Mr. Frith. 'No I shan't, I like this better.' She picked up Claudio's cloak.

Oliver swaggered round in the Amaryllis hat. 'It's a girl's hat,' Ruth protested, snatching it from him.

'Whatever's this, a nightgown?'

'It's Isabella's dress for *The Pot of Basil*.'

'Hurry up, children!' Grand looked round the door. 'Only two more minutes. You're keeping us waiting.'

'What a fag! I wish we hadn't got to do it. I hope it's Dumb Crambo?' Ruth turned to me.

'Dumb Crambo?' What was that?

'Oh, come on,' said Oliver, 'we'll do three men in a boat!'

There was a hush as we entered. 'Our wits are about to be taxed,' said the professor.

'Go on, sit down, start to row,' hissed Ruth, squatting on the floor.

'What an incongruous trio! I'm truly bewildered,' said Mr. Woolley, 'a Greek goddess, an Arab and an acolyte? Their costumes have some deep significance I'm sure.'

'A religious synthesis maybe,' the dean suggested. 'I see a Greek goddess, a Mahomedan, a Christian . . .'

'Are they crossing the Styx?' demanded someone else.

'Feeble apes!' Oliver muttered in my ear. 'Go on, *row*!' I had never felt more foolish.

'Well, my pet,' said Grand at last, rising from her chair, 'I am afraid we must all give up.' They were looking at *me* for the answer.

'I'm not quite sure what it was,' I confessed.

Several gentlemen guffawed.

'It was three men in a boat,' said Oliver crossly, and turning on his heel he dragged us from the room. 'You ruined it! You made us all look idiots. You must have known it was *Three Men in a Boat*? A book *everyone* knows, by Jerome K. Jerome.'

'I'm terribly sorry.' It must be a Jewish book, to do with their religion. To hide my dismay, I began folding the clothes and stuffing them back in the chest.

'Alas,' cried Grand, 'your little friends must go. Lady Gollancz is waiting. Say good-bye and then come and help me—there are so many people. Here's my little guide,' she announced, 'as we're such a number I will leave half of you with her. She explains the pictures very well, and anyone who cares can come round the other rooms with me.'

Gradually my confidence returned. Dumb Crambo was just a silly game. Grand left with her party and I led my audience to a picture: 'This is Grandpa's *Lady of Shalott.*' We were all reflected in the glass. 'It was painted long after he did the illustrations for the poem. Lord Tennyson didn't like it and said he should have paid attention to the text; *that* didn't say her hair was untidy and the silks were in a muddle. He said it wasn't his idea at all, but Grandpa didn't care . . . '

'Out flew the web and floated wide!' recited Kenneth Swan.

'The wooden sandals are in the Hobman chest. I wear them when I sweep up leaves in the garden. That peacock feather blouse is upstairs in a drawer. It's really a cape and Grand's wearing it here in her portrait, called *The Birthday*. Big Aunt doesn't like it.' I wouldn't tell them why. They followed me across the room.

Our hostess: how handsome! What a lovely face!'

'A Fancy Head, I fancy,' said Mr. Edward Marsh, with an odd look at me. How did he know?

'*Christ and the two Marys*,' said the dean, 'begun in 1845 and not finished until fifty years later; but don't let me interrupt the guide.'

'When he started the picture, Grandpa'd never seen a palm tree, so he had to go to Kew. The gardener gave him a branch and he carried it all the way back to London. He felt something horrid wriggling down his collar. It was a bat!' I shuddered.

'Dear me, how very disagreeable,' muttered someone.

'That's a sketch of Leigh Hunt and *this* is Dante Gabriel Rossetti.' He was the villain of the piece.

'My! What wonderful eyes!' cried the Yankee lady. 'He's always been my idol. Wasn't it he and Burne-Jones who started it all. Pre-Raphaelism I mean?'

'Oh no, you've got it all wrong!' I was shocked, and thankful Grand couldn't hear. I had always hated Rossetti. It was his fault Helen gave us macaroni—slimy white worms. Grandpa had never eaten it before he met those sly Italians. Arthur called them Wops.

'He looks so *ro*mantic!' gushed the Yankee lady, craning forward to see.

'He didn't really look a bit like that. He was dirty and horrid, his hair was always greasy and he spilt soup and spaghetti all down his clothes. They weren't even his! He borrowed everyone else's, even Bruno's. He never gave them back, and what's more he was a cheat!'

'Come now, I think that's a little hard,' protested someone.

'Yes he was. He was Grandpa's pupil and never paid the rent and sent his picture—Grandpa'd painted most of it—to an exhibition, without telling him and Johnnie Millais, although he'd said he wouldn't until theirs were ready too. He ate Grandpa out of house and home and gave noisy parties, and shouted at the models. It was Grandpa and Johnnie who started it all and it was pre-Raphaeli*tism* with a T.'

There was a sympathetic murmur.

'Poor Grandpa got thrown out because he hadn't any money and Mr. Ruskin turned against him because he was Johnnie's friend. Everything went wrong and it was all Rossetti's fault because he told lies and took all the credit.'

'Well, that's a most interesting theory,' said Mr. Edward Marsh. 'Our small guide feels very strongly.'

'I feel mighty confused but I just can't wait to tell the folks at home. My, it's like living in the past!'

'Now,' said the professor, polishing his glasses, 'perhaps we should turn from this—ahem—controversial canvas, to this truly magnificent work, which cost poor Hunt his sight. A miraculous picture: in fact, *The Miracle of the Holy Fire*.'

'To give the young goddess a rest,' said Dean Inge, 'perhaps I might say a few words: this scene is the Greek ceremony as it took place on Easter Eve. You observe thousands of pilgrims who have come from far and wide, Egypt, Russia, Abyssinia. The shrine is the Holy Sepulchre, the traditional Tomb of Christ . . .'

'That little boy,' I interrupted, 'on this man's shoulder, is Papa and this is poor Step-uncle Cyril who was banished, and this is Big Aunt Gladys—wasn't she pretty then? This English nurse in the crowd is really Grand and if you could have waited and seen what happened next, in a few seconds the whole place would be steaming with heat and smells. This lady died where she sat. The dead lay in bloody heaps five feet high and everyone was screaming and fighting and all these people were trampled to death or murdered. It became a squelching pulp of people, like ripe squashed tomatoes.'

With a sweep of my arm I wiped out the foreground.

'Dear me, how gruesome it sounds,' said Lady Ilchester, holding some smelling salts to her nose.

'Alas, our guide is right,' said the professor, 'a truly remarkable picture.'

'I do hope my little Goddess has not given you all a tedious lecture?' asked Grand, sweeping into the room like a ship in full sail, followed by a lot of dreary little tugs.

'No indeed,' said Lady Ilchester, 'I have rarely felt less bored.'

She patted her hair and drew Grand to one side.

'Oh, how comical!' Grand clapped her hands together. 'I thought it singular when you arrived and then one hatless guest followed another.'

The ladies made a great commotion in the hall, trying to find their toques and bonnets, crowding round the Venetian mirror to stick them on with pins. The boy-scouts held open the door until everyone had left.

'Thank goodness that's over,' I said, stacking up the plates. The Dundee cake wasn't finished.

'What a pleasant gathering. Delightful people,' crowed Grand. 'The charade was rather a fiasco but it didn't signify at all. You'd better put the things in the lift and run down to help Helen.'

The boy-scouts were sitting round the range, eating the cake which Mrs. Hopkins had baked especially for me. 'But that's *my* cake!' I protested.

'Yes, the lads find it very tasty,' said Helen, plunging a knife into the remains, and carving them up. 'You were so long sending down that bit of Dundee, I thought you wouldn't grudge the lads a bite.'

I was speechless with indignation. I took the cups from the lift and carried them through to the pantry, where I swabbed them out with the little nigger-brown sponge, which was tied to the tap with a string. The labels got wet but I didn't care. I had had no tea and felt angry about my cake.

When I went upstairs I found Grand sitting gazing at the fire. 'I've just remembered that delicious fig syrup. I wonder if the scouts would like it? Considering it was their first attempt they did very well.'

'Of course they wouldn't,' I said.

'I'm sure they would, you greedy little minx. I believe you've hidden it upstairs!'

'It is upstairs,' I admitted.

'What an opportunity for an exercise in self-denial! Wouldn't you *like* them to have it?'

I nodded slowly.

'Yes, yes, put it into glasses and add enough water to make it go round; they'll be very touched and Helen might like a little too. Take the drinks in on the silver tray. So good for *you*, my pet, to wait on *them*.'

I mixed it carefully. 'Grand says you're all to drink this. It's orders.'

The boy-scouts looked suspicious. 'You'd better drink it up like good lads,' advised Helen, tossing hers down, 'the mistress will have her little fancies.

'These last ten days have simply flown! What a life of battledore and shuttlecock you lead,' said Grand, sadly surveying my luggage, which had never been properly unpacked.

'Yes, I'm just like a parcel; I'll be sent back soon, but now I'm going home.' I failed to hide my delight.

'It was so mild this morning, I told Helen not to light the fire, at least until the doctor has called, to see her—such an expense. Your grandmother is sure to wear her furs. I only hope your grandfather won't knock things over.' She moved a small table out of the way. 'Blindness is such an affliction. Surely I should offer some refreshments, but who can I send out for some coffee?'

'They don't like coffee. Grandfather drinks whisky and soda and she has her egg-nog at eleven.'

'Whiskey and soda? He won't expect *me* to offer spirits! What are you doing with that Ming bowl? Put it back at once!'

I had balanced it on the arm of the chair. 'It'll do for cigar ash,' I said.

'Cigars in the *house*? I've never heard of such a thing. Don't talk such nonsense! Now, there are several small problems I wish to discuss while they are here, so when they arrive you'd better run downstairs to poor, seedy Helen. Now where is my list?'

'It's here.' I had read it and made up my mind not to leave the grown-ups talking it over for a second. She had written: Timothy X? Undesirable friendships? Religious instruction? Regular exercise of self-denial? Swedish Drill and Indian clubs?

We sat patiently waiting. In my thoughts I could hear grandmother's voice, 'But my dear child, I'm only asking you to tell us, in your own words, what you've been doing! Can't you see we want to be amused? Don't be such a goose! *Nothing*, for ten whole days? Really, children are too extraordinary!'

I would make a list too, like Pheobe, Young Uncle's favourite *iolie laide*. I took a piece of paper from the hat.

'Dear me, how unpunctual they always are. I really think I ought to light the fire. It's grown quite chilly. Ah, do I hear the motor?'

'You wait here. Let me go—I'll go!' I shouted, and before she could stop me, raced down the steps.

They were tucked up in fur rugs in the back of the car, their heads almost touching the net, which bulged with parcels, and was suspended from the ceiling. Grandmother was scrubbing her nose with a sheet of Papier Poudre. Seeing me, she rapped on the glass with her rings.

'Open the door, my precious, and give me a kiss. How pale you are, and breathless.'

'You can't come in,' I panted, 'there's no whiskey and she doesn't like cigars. There's no fire and it's too cold!'

''Pon my soul,' grandfather exploded, 'I've rarely received a more hospitable welcome! I suggest we stay where we are.'

'I quite agree. In any case my feet are frozen. That fool Fowler can't have put *boiling* water in the bottles. Please George, you're burning my knitting! Run in, my love, and make our excuses: just ask her to forgive us. Say, alas, we're in a hurry.'

Fowler pretended not to hear. She was sitting in front and staring straight ahead. Whaler was already collecting my luggage—all theirs had gone on by train with Arthur.

I tore back to the house. 'They're terribly sorry,' I stammered, 'but they don't want to, I mean, they *can't* come in, not now—it's too late . . . we must go and he's smoking.' I was incoherent with relief. If I were lucky, Timothy, my private friendship, would be safe from interference.

'Oh, how sad,' said Grand, withdrawing from the door to the hall, 'but perhaps it's just as well. I am so emotional and these partings have such a terrible effect . . .' She was crying quietly.

'Don't cry. Please don't cry,' I begged.

'My beloved child, give me a hug and say that you love your Grand just a little . . .'

'Yes, of course I do. I love you.' I burst into tears and held her thin body in my arms. For one moment I wanted to be with her forever, but it passed; I wrenched away and ran down the steps.

I sat in the car on the folding seat. Grandmother leant forward and kissed the back of my neck. 'You coat needs brushing. Such a long journey ahead. You will help pass the time. George, you really must throw out that cigar. I'm suffocating.'

I wiped my eyes, took my crumpled list from my pocket and laid it on my lap. I could think only of Grand, all alone, crying.

The first item was 'Naked Lady': 'When we went to tea with Mrs. Swynnerton, there was a naked lady, all lumps, lying on the sofa with two fat bulges on her chest.'

'Good God, La vie de Bohême! I presume she had lumpago.'

'Don't be so stupid, George, it was a nude—simply a model. Even I know Mrs. Swynnerton's an artist.'

Mrs. Swynnerton had said: 'Thank you, Doris, you can go now,' and the naked lady had disappeared behind a screen.

'She drew me, but Grand says it's not as good as Mr. Peacock's and she's given it to you, it's in my hamper.'

'I hope your hair was dressed. I would love to see the Peacock. No wonder that American fell in love with Mrs. Peacock's sister, when he saw her portrait, long before he met her. I always thought it so romantic. He married her you know. Do go on.'

'Out of the window we saw a black dog. Mrs. Swynnerton said it belonged to her neighbour—she called him Mr. Creepy Crawley—she said the dog was possessed by an evil spirit and that this Mr. Crawley was a black magician.'

'I've never heard such rot! Black magician indeed!'

'Look, a Norman church. Not there—eyes and no eyes—over there!'

'We went to see Sir Henry Dickens. He read aloud for hours. I thought he'd never stop and some white Jews came to tea and we played Dumb Crambo and Cousin Telfer says that Cousin Evelyn is turning into a Roman Catholic, and I've got some sand from the Flood.'

'D'you hear that, George?' She prodded him. 'Jews and Roman Catholics, it sounds *most* unsuitable to me. It's so horribly stuffy, I think we'll have to open the window.'

I tugged and tugged at the strap, straining and pulling until I was scarlet in the face. Without the least warning the window collapsed, knocking me down.

'Look out! What the devil's going on?'

'Take care, you trod on my toe! Oh what a draught!' Her veil flew off and she clutched her hat. 'Shut it! Shut it quickly. We're going too fast. Whaler!' She yelled down the speaking tube, 'Whaler! you'll drive us all to our graves!' He must have been doing at least fifteen!

'Whaler said that Young Uncle and Phoebe went *forty* miles an hour the other day.'

'What folly! The damn fool will kill himself.'

'Well now, tell us something of interest.'

'My Big Aunt called when we were busy; I'd never seen her before but Grand said that she'd seen me when I was a baby.'

'Now that *is* interesting, George. They must be reconciled at last and I'm very glad to hear it. It was such a bitter quarrel.'

She poked me in the back. 'Tell us something else.'

There was only one thing left on the list and I was afraid it wasn't amusing. 'When we were walking down the High Street, a gentleman dressed like the station master raised his hat to Grand and started talking. She said, "I don't think I know you", and he looked very hurt; but she did know him really and told me he was the West Kensington Member.'

'That will be Davison,' grandfather said, 'I believe he's suing for divorce and it has offended some of his constituents. He's an extremely able lawyer but no doubt Mrs. H-H suffered many slights as a deceased wife's sister and therefore is now censorious of others and resents the unconventional. . . .'

'But it was quite respectable, my dear! I know the Hunts had to get married in Geneva but later it was all made legal. After all, her sister Fanny was dead.'

'Oh yes, poor old Hunt worked like a black to get that Bill through.'

'For once I agree with Mrs. H-H. I think she was perfectly right to cut the Davison man. It's most inconsiderate of people to get involved in scandals and divorces and then walk about in broad daylight, in Kensington too. He should go and live abroad; he could buy a villa in Florence.'

'I must speculate in Florentine villas, which clearly will soon be at a premium, unless people resort to false beards and only emerge after dark.'

'Don't be so frivolous, George—in Kensington I mean, where one has so many friends. Dear me, how dark it's getting.'

It took Whaler nearly an hour to light the car lamps. When one started to burn, the other went out and the smell of carbide was horrid. Grandmother sniffed a handkerchief drenched in cologne and grandfather sipped at his flask of whiskey.

'Good God, what a journey; I'll never attempt it again!'

CHAPTER FIVE

FOR days before my cousin Priscilla arrived the house was turned upside down.

'Isn't it wonderful, Polly!' I cried, rolling about on the bed in one of the visitors' rooms.

'My, aren't you excited! Careful, you'll crumple the pillows.' She swished a long feather broom round the cornice and then glanced slyly at me: 'I do believe you're sweet on Mr. Tom.'

'Tom!' I burst out laughing. He was Priscilla's brother and followed Young Uncle about and joked with the *jolies laides*. He like to talk cockney: 'It won't arf make you larf, Oi've swoiped a fag, Oi 'ave.'

Fowler would look very shocked: 'I don't know, I'm sure, what to make of Master Tom. If you ask me he wastes too much time with Arthur in the pantry.'

'Yes, it's Priscilla I love,' I confided, hugging my knees.

'Love! My! What do you know about love?'

'More than you, much more than you!' I retorted.

'A little bird told me,' she teased, 'was it Mr. Pim? He told me a certain party and your Miss Priscilla fought like cat and dog!'

'We don't! We never do—we won't!' I shouted. 'You're silly . . .'

'All right, all right, don't mind me. True love never ran smooth.'

I lay back on the bed and watched her polishing the chairs. The room would soon look very different. As a treat I might be allowed to help Rose, my aunt's maid, to unpack. While she darted about shaking dress after dress from clouds of tissue paper, Fowler would stand by ready to press the things my aunt would wear for dinner; even her nightgowns were ironed every day. Strange-looking underclothes would froth into the drawers.

'Brown lace on pink satin!' Fowler would sniff. 'You can't beat white lawn; more lady-like too.'

I would snap the dressing-case open and draw the blond tortoise-shell brushes from their snug silk pockets—there was a curly D in diamonds on them all. Swansdown puffs, one on an ivory stick, would spring out of their boxes. I would hand Rose the lace caps, with their ribbon rosettes, which my aunt wore in bed while she sipped her early morning tea and nibbled wafers of brown bread and butter. The crocodile bag would be left until last. Many times I had watched Rose polish the jewellery with rouge, and before slipping the rings onto their tortoise-shell stand, I would try them on my fingers, flicking my wrists to and fro under the lamp to catch the glitter.

Rose would whisk red velvet hearts from the toes of the slippers and unroll the pale silk stockings. Fowler would return with the dress warm from the iron and reverently arrange it on the sofa. It would lie, limp and lovely, like my aunt when she had a pain.

Uncle Hubert suffered from gout. He usually sat in the library with a fat white foot propped on a stool. My grandfather would leave his usual chair to sit alone in the study mumbling: 'God, Hubert's a bore.'

Uncle Hubert's pockets were stuffed with tattered bundles of paper, scraps of which were always falling on the ground.

'Be a good girl and draw up that chair, only a second, this is most entertaining. You know Robert Bruce? My dear, pull down your skirt—what was I saying? Ah, Robert Bruce. Look, not there . . . here. This is of *particular* interest—the result of much laborious research.' He would point with a pencil. 'See? Then the first cousin married—pay attention—and formed the collateral branch. . . .' Pages fluttered from his lap. 'Where's that letter from the College of Arms? Try not to fidget.'

The grown-ups would pretend to be busy and rush through the room with harassed expressions. His outstretched hand would fall unheeded to his side and he would gaze sadly at the closing door.

Like everyone else, upstairs uncle Hubert was different. He would shout to my aunt from his dressing-room, and sing loudly in the bath: 'Cobble all day and cobble all night!' The words would boom along the passage, until my aunt would cry: 'Hurry, Hubert, it's nearly time for the gong!'

When they all arrived the bell rang and the pugs ran yapping to the hall. A great noise filled the house, as if a choir had burst through the door. My aunt's shrill voice rang above the music, and strange exotic scents drugged the air. Her powdered face swooped into mine and I was smothered with caresses.

For months, it seemed years, I had looked forward to meeting Priscilla again, yet now she seemed strange. She stood quite still, like a butterfly on a rose. I hung back staring. Her coat wasn't creased after the journey, and the wreath of daisies round her hat was as fresh as the day when it was new.

'Hello, Di,' she said softly, a faint flush tinting her cheeks. When the pugs pranced on their little hind legs she drew back in alarm and implored them: 'Down, please, down!'

I tore up the stairs, two steps at a time, and shouted over the banisters: 'I've got lots to show you—such a lot to tell.'

'Hush, my treasure, don't make such a rumpus, look at cousin Priscilla. She's like an exquisite fairy!' Grandmother nodded with approval and took my aunt's arm. Uncle Hubert limped at grandfather's side. 'Good to be back, sir . . . most interesting letters from distant Scottish cadets. . . .'

Tom disappeared through the green baize door.

'I can't come now,' whispered Priscilla. She turned and walked quietly away to join the others in the drawing-room.

'How are you, Miss Diana?' called Rose. She was up on the landing wearing a new hat and coat. 'You *have* grown—not too big to give your Rosie a kiss?'

The luggage came up in the lift with Johnstone, and Arthur and Tom put it on trestles in the rooms. 'Blimey, old cock, it ain't 'alf 'eavy.'

I could smell my aunt's scent. My fingers trembled as I unclipped the dressing-case cover. Slowly the room grew alive.

'You are a dear. Look out for the sequins, they melt if you touch them with the iron,' called Rose, when Fowler scurried off with the dress over her arm.

When the family went down to dinner, Priscilla's nurse opened the door and walked to the end of my bed. 'I'm telling you, young lady, if you leave your room and wake up Priscilla, the Old Monk will come for you tonight.' She wagged her finger in warning. 'You'll hear him creep along the passage.'

I was well aware that the Old Monk existed, whatever grandfather said. Visitors made anxious inquiries about footsteps familiar to us. They described how doors opened in the night. They saw green lights flash on the marsh, and heard bells ring across the sea. If servants were present my grandmother whispered: '*Pas devant les domestiques*', and more, which I didn't understand. Otherwise she pretended they must be mistaken, but she never met my eye.

After the gong had gone Nurse Watson, Fowler and Rose went down to the Servants' Hall for their supper. We were safe until 10 o'clock when Fowler and Rose would come up to gossip by the sewing-room fire until their ladies needed undressing. Nurse Watson would stay longer in the Hall, grumbling with Mrs. Hopkins.

I stole along the passage to Priscilla. It was to this sacred hour when, warm and friendly, we whispered and giggled in the dark, that I looked forward during the long months I was alone.

Her hands were trapped in stiff canvas bags. She flopped two white paws up and down. The sun was sinking and birds were calling to each other in the garden. Nurse Watson's starched cuffs and belt lay neatly on a chair.

'I was afraid you wouldn't come,' she said, 'I really hoped you wouldn't in a way.'

I crouched under the quilt and untied the tapes which were cutting her wrists. She could gnaw them through but if she did she got a 'drenching'.

'You must promise to put them on again and tie them up before you go.' Her sore red fingers plucked fluff off the blanket. Her nails were bitten to the quick, although Nurse Watson dipped them in alum.

She looked like a small skinned rabbit. With a moan she laid her head on my knees. Her hair was screwed in hard knots of rag pulling her scalp from the bone. One by one I untwisted the curlers and did them up again.

'Roll them tighter, tighter, I can bear it.' I had done this many times before; they were always looser, but Nurse suspected nothing.

'I told my friend Timothy . . .' I began.

'Your friend? That dirty old man with the hook? You swore you'd never tell a soul.' Her eyes were dark with reproach.

'He's much cleaner now. I told him about the drenching, because he's got a ferret. I read about a ferret who killed a boy's aunt . . .'

'You broke your promise.'

'I told him how she holds your head under the tap.' I closed my eyes, I could hear Nurse shouting: 'Huh! I'll teach you young lady, just you come and have a drenching!' I could see Priscilla forced to lean over the bath with her head gripped under the tap.

'The more you kick the longer you'll be.'

'Let her go, let her go!' I screamed, battering Nurse with my fists. Priscilla fell back, gasping, sobbing, breathless, blue with cold and shaking with shock. Dripping rat-tails hung to her shoulders. Nurse pushed me out of the room. 'Oh, oh, the tangles!' groaned Priscilla. Nurse was dragging a comb through her hair making it ready for the rags.

'I've decided,' I said now, looking up. 'We've got to *kill* her. If we could get her into Timothy's boat, the three of us could do it—if only you didn't hate the sea.'

'No, no! Promise while I'm here you'll say you don't want to go *near* the beach,' she pleaded, clutching my arm.

'Deadly nightshade? I'll put it in the jam.'

'Oh no, that would be wicked.'

We had discussed the problem many times before. No one wanted any trouble. Priscilla thought if we told my aunt, Nurse would get a month's notice.

'But Lizzie was sent away the very *day* she burnt the mouse,' I said as usual.

'I've told you over and over again,' said Priscilla with impatience, '*she* was sent home to her mother. Nurse would have nowhere to go and she would bully me for four whole weeks. I should die, and anyway Tom told Mummy all about the drenching. She asked Nurse why she did it and Nurse said my hair was as straight as a poker and if she wanted it curly it had to be wet. Mummy said, "It's certainly very effective; *il faut souffrir pour être belle*."'

'I tell you we must kill her. I'll stab her with my knife and then I'll say why, if I'm brought before the Bench. If they send me to prison I don't care a fig . . .'

'No, no . . . you always suggest such dreadful things.'

'There's no other way. We can't go on like this forever.'

'There is, there is a way,' she said, looking very solemn.

'Well, what is it?' Had she thought of Young Uncle's gun? 'What is it, tell me.' I shook her.

'We must pray.'

'Pray? That's no good – like talking on the telephone to no one. You must be potty,' I said.

'Do listen – it says in the Bible, God says when two or three are gathered together he'll grant their request. It's no good praying alone. We must go to church and do it and we must *both* pray at the same time every single night. Put your hands over mine and say: 'Please God take Nurse to Heaven.'

'He won't want her! Please God send Nurse to hell, and look sharp about it would be better.'

'That wouldn't do at all,' she said crossly, letting go my hands.

'We must know what we want,' I said firmly. 'What about, "Please make her very ill?"'

'We can't ask for that, he likes making people better.' We puzzled in silence.

'I think we could say: "Please make her disappear",' Priscilla said at last, biting her nails.

'Do you mean vanish – into thin air? I don't think God could do it. Witches can. A witch could cast a spell and say, "Curse Nurse, curse Nurse and . . ."'

'Oh do be quiet, there's no such thing as witches. I told you we must pray.'

'Oh all right.' I was feeling rather grumpy. 'Hush!' Footsteps creaked along the passage.

'The OLD MONK!' we whispered as one.

'It's because you say such wicked things,' she hissed, clinging round my waist, her heart thumping on my back.

Someone opened the sewing-room door. 'I've just looked in to say good night. I can see I'm not wanted . . .' chatter, chatter.

'Quick, it's Nurse.' I jumped off the bed and ran for my life, my bare feet aware of each change of surface, until I reached the familiar carpet in my room. I lay awake in the cold linen sheets praying that Nurse would vanish before she discovered the bags were untied from Priscilla's wrists.

A few mornings later we were all sitting on the terrace. 'Such a bore, Nurse wants to visit her sister who lives somewhere near,' said my aunt. 'Apparently before we left London I did say she might. She says the carrier's going there today and could bring her back before Priscilla's bath.'

'I fancy that no one would be exactly disappointed if Nurse remained indefinitely with her sister,' said grandfather, blowing smoke rings from his cigar. 'From what I overhear, she should be drowned in a bucket.'

'Yes, your father and I can't think why you keep that detestable woman,' grandmother said. 'I always think sensitive people like myself must have amiable, pleasant-looking servants. Johnstone, in spite of his attacks of vertigo, is an invaluable butler, and has such a distinguished appearance; and I'm thankful to say, as soon as I enter the kitchen my treasure, Mrs. Hopkins, is *wreathed* in smiles. Dear Hannah is like a family friend and the under-housemaids are such pretty girls, so willing.'

'They certainly are, but Fowler,' my aunt interrupted unkindly, 'scarcely radiates charm, and Arthur . . .'

'Perhaps Arthur is a little uncouth,' grandmother admitted. She brushed my aunt's objections aside and insisted: 'You should get rid of Nurse. Think what you would save! Indeed, I'm sure you owe it to yourself. Don't you agree, Hubert?'

Uncle Hubert didn't hear. He was reading his family tree.

'She looks after Priscilla's clothes so wonderfully well and the poor child has such troublesome hair; no one else can do anything with it!'

'My dear, don't be absurd! I'm sure Rose could. Rose can look after little Priscilla, can't she, my love? Have you lost your tongue?'

She stroked Priscilla's frizz.

'It might look odd in the park,' said my aunt, frowning, 'not to have a proper nurse, and who would take her to school?'

'Nonsense, a brisk walk in the park every day is what Rose needs. When I saw her in the passage she looked quite seedy. It would be most tiresome if her health broke down when you've taken the trouble to train her.'

'We mustn't let Rose get a cold in her nose!' grandfather sang.

'Cosy Rosie's nosey posey. . . .' I giggled, to cover my excitement.

'Hush, you two! My dear, if you give Rose a little more I'm sure she could manage.'

'Give Rose a shilling and she will be willing!'

'I might have a word with Rose; my last bill from Callot Sœurs is really appalling.' My aunt examined her nails.

'Thank heavens that's settled. I think you've decided most wisely. I know she upsets the servants. Now, don't forget I've invited some people to tea: Mabel Pritchard's coming alone but Lettice Syragg is bringing her Major. I thought it would be tactful to ask Mr. Duncan, who hasn't met them since the wedding. It will help to break the ice. You and Hubert should have sent a present.'

'I can't think what Lettice needs,' said my aunt, 'her house is already fully furnished and being a widower, Major . . .'

'I should send her a *Book of Directions*,' said grandfather, 'in case the Major's copy is mislaid.'

'No, really, George!' grandmother protested, glancing oddly at me.

Duncan promised to bring some old Kirk Sessions Records which by good fortune he has in his possession,' said uncle Hubert, who had taken no interest before.

'Mabel said she was sending a party of young people to the beach, so I've ordered Whaler and the trap. Fowler and Rose can take a picnic for the little girls; it's so nice for children to meet. I hope dear Walter will be there.'

Priscilla gave me a nudge and after a pause I said, blushing: 'Oh, I don't think we want to go to the sea, I mean not today.'

'What nonsense! Don't be selfish, Diana. The sea air will do Priscilla good. She looks very pale. You'd like to go to the sea, wouldn't you my love?' She held out her hand.

'I'd rather go to church,' said Priscilla, gazing thoughtfully out of the window.

''Pon my soul, I must tell old Duncan! I have a grandchild who prefers church to the beach!'

'Don't be so stupid, Priscilla, you'll be going to church on Sunday,' my aunt said, glaring.

'Run along and get ready for luncheon. Really children are *too* extraordinary—nothing but treats from morning till night and . . .'

'Isn't it wonderful?' I cried, bolting up the stairs. 'The prayers are *working*!' I cocked a leg over the banisters and slid down the mahogany rail.

'Take care, you'll tear your drawers.'

Priscilla's face was white and, when I grabbed it, her hand was very cold.

'Good riddance to bad rubbish.' I meant nurse.

'You are silly, don't you see it means A Month's Notice?'

Patsy, the pony, tossed her head and the trap creaked as we loaded it with baskets and the carriage box of pennies. We balanced ourselves on the sloping seats. Once we left the village, with its shifting curtains and people nodding from the doorways, the marsh stretched out to sea. Brass squeaked on leather and the smells of saddle-soap and oil mixed with the muddy smell of the dykes.

Fowler and Rose withdrew the black pins from their hats. My panama, loose on its elastic, bumped against my neck in time with the trotting and Whaler, waving his whip, began to sing: 'K-K-K-Katy! Beautiful Katy! You're the only g-g-g-girl that I adore!' We all joined in, the warm wind blowing our hair. 'When the m-moon shines, over the c-cow shed, I'll be waiting at the k-k-k-kitchen door.' Patsy broke into a canter, and we rushed through the gates. The gate boys jumped from the rushes to open them in time. Laughing and shouting, we scattered pennies and Patsy kicked up the dust.

As soon as we reached the sea Priscilla felt sick. Rose spread some rugs for her to lie on in the hut. Whaler undressed in the open, and when Rose and I were ready, she pinned up my hair in a bun. We ran down over the shingle, crying out when the stones hurt our feet: our long black bathing dresses, embroidered with anchors, flapped round our knees.

Fowler sat under the breakwater in charge of the picnic. She took off her shoes, as her corns were cruel. Some ladies squealed and splashed each other on the edge of the sea, their bathing dresses stained wet to their waists and clinging to their thighs. Further out were the men who wore almost nothing and always bathed alone.

Whaler ran past, plunged in and swam through the breakers. Rose sat in the surf, kicking up spray with her heels. The tide was going out. Soon the waves would leave the sand wrinkled in an endless frown. I would look for sea urchins and shells and bits of coloured glass and lucky stones, and explore the slippery rocks for seaweed like red lace. I would tease the baby crabs and poke my finger into the yielding centres of the sea-anemones which would suck and draw, and change from floating flowers to little rubber lumps. I would search the high-water mark for cuttle-fish for Mr. Pim and find glass floats and squares of cork, adrift from Timothy's nets; these made rafts to sail in the pools.

'Time to come in,' called Fowler, waiting with a towel. My teeth chattered and she dried me quickly. 'You'll catch your death,' she said, and hurried back to put the kettle on the primus.

Rose had dressed long ago. Her wet bathing dress sprawled like a dead cat on the shingle.

Priscilla had been sick in my new tin pail. She looked very ill so I tried not to be cross. 'But *why* are you sick when you haven't been in?'

'I can hear it, even with my fingers in my ears; I can see it — moving and shaking like a rotten grey jelly. I told you I didn't want to come.' The hut smelt and a gull screamed in the sky. I turned away from the pail, and, deserting Priscilla, stepped into the sun. Shading my eyes I saw some strange children playing on the sands.

'Old Timothy's shrimping, we'll join him later,' said Whaler, rolling up the legs of his trousers, 'but it's tea first, by the looks of things.'

'I think it would be best if we don't say about Miss Priscilla coming over queer,' said Rose, slopping milk into our enamel mugs.

'Nothing deceitful mind,' added Fowler, topping it up with black tea and spoonfuls of sugar, 'but we don't want any trouble —it wouldn't do to upset Miss Watson.'

'She's a silly old pig,' I said. 'I wish Tilly's friend the carrier would throw her in a dyke; anyway my aunt's sure to give her notice, and when she does Priscilla's going to have a Pendix. She's being sick now.' I was proud of this solution.

There was silence.

'Don't talk poppy-cock,' said Fowler.

'Well, I know Nurse is going and that's that,' I said. Meaning glances were exchanged.

'Now Miss Diana,' said Fowler, 'how often have I told you, you don't want to repeat what you hear in the dining-room?'

'It wasn't in the dining-room, but it's true all the same.'

'Well I never, I don't know I'm sure . . . Just look at the tar on your dress!'

'Least said soonest mended is what I always say,' said Rose, giving me a friendly smile.

'You're right there,' said Whaler, emptying his tea-leaves on to the stones. 'Well, miss, if it's shrimps you want, shrimps you shall have.' Timothy was waving.

When we got home grandfather was sitting by himself on the terrace. 'Is that Diana? I'd like a word with you.'

I sat beside him and flicked the ash off his cigar. 'It was great fun on the beach. What was the party like?'

He grunted and cleared his throat. 'Mr. Duncan told me a singular story; he alleges that about a week ago, he caught you and Priscilla making an appalling rumpus outside the church. On investigation he found you both rolling about between the graves giggling in an unseemly, indeed he said an hysterical, manner. I trust he reprimanded you severely. It is no place for childish pranks.'

Old Mr. Duncan was a sneak.

'Later on the same afternoon he heard noises in the church. He opened the door quietly and an extraordinary spectacle met his eyes: you two children, wearing peculiar confections on your heads, prostrating yourselves at the altar, in front of a dead rabbit. His first reaction was one of horror at what seemed like desecration of the church—you should know it is a consecrated building. On closer inspection he was gradually convinced that you were both praying devoutly. He confessed himself strangely moved at the sight of two kneeling children, their eyes closed and their hands clasped together in earnest supplication. He quietly withdrew. It appears you left the rabbit on the altar and he gave it to some deserving person in the parish. He declares that you and Priscilla have returned several times to repeat this extraordinary performance . . .'

'It was my fault about the rabbit; I got it from Dan but Priscilla said it didn't count, as a sacrifice I mean. Giving up sweets or talking to uncle Hubert would be better. I wouldn't leave the rabbit at home and we argued all the way. She said I should kill Mr. Pim; I knew she was teasing but I was angry. Then we found we'd left our hats behind. There wasn't time before tea to go back and get them and she said we *must* go in as we were. I said it wouldn't count without hats and Fowler wouldn't like it. She clung to the door and I hit her with the rabbit. Her dress got bloody and she started to cry because Nurse would drench her. Then Mr. Duncan came and he was livid. When he went away I said: "Let's go across to Mrs. Jenkins' sweet shop; we can make ourselves hats with paper bags." They were sugar bags, dark blue and pointed. Miss Dolby said we looked like dunces but she sponged Priscilla's dress. When we explained, she and Mrs. Jenkins lent us their bonnets. We promised to be careful. Miss Dolby's was her second best with the blackbirds but now Priscilla always wears her hat with the daisies and I wear my old Panama.'

He said nothing for a while and stared blindly across the lawns. 'You must both want something very badly.' He jerked away the butt of his cigar and it lay glowing on the flags.

'I want a miracle.' I closed my eyes. 'Please God, make Nurse vanish but don't let her get a Month's Notice. If you can do it, I'll practise my scales for hours tomorrow and learn about uncle Hubert's Tree.'

I said it aloud and meant every word.

Johnstone appeared in the doorway. 'Who's that? What is it?' grandfather asked.

'I have a message, sir, for Mrs. Hubert.'

'Get on then, what is it?'

Johnstone spoke as if he were reading a lesson: 'The carrier has returned, sir, but it seems Nurse Watson did not accompany him. Her sister has had a stroke.' He pronounced all the aitches carefully.

'I see,' said grandfather. 'I hope there's a fire in the library and I could do with a whiskey and soda.'

'Very good, sir. I will send Arthur at once.'

'Don't slaughter the pugs and keep your foot on the soft pedal when you practise those scales.' He thrashed out with his stick. 'Off with you now and move another mountain!'

I ran indoors as fast as I could. The drawing-room was empty except for uncle Hubert. The visitors had left the chairs and cushions all awry. 'Ah Diana!' He raised his hand in salute. 'What a chance, now we are alone. Draw up that chair. What do you think I've got here?' He patted some books on his knee: 'Parish Registers!'

'Oh, I can't stop now but I swear I'll be back in a minute.'

Before he could speak I escaped to the boudoir.

'Have you heard?' I cried.

'For heaven's sake don't burst in like that. . . . My nerves!' grandmother complained.

'But Nurse . . .' I cried. 'God *must* be there!'

I put my arm round Priscilla and led her from the room. Hand in hand we walked slowly upstairs. I forgot about my bargain with God and my promise to uncle Hubert.

It rained on the last precious day of Priscilla's visit. After tea we sat in the sewing-room, watching puddles spread on the drive. Fowler was helping Rose with the packing.

'It's so dull, there's nothing to do,' said Priscilla, looking round at the heaps of sewing on the old iron bed and grandmother's dummy in the corner. 'It seems so odd not to have a nursery.'

She got up, rattled the button box and stirred it with a bodkin.

'I don't really want one,' I said.

She picked up the glove stretc'-ers, opened them wide and then let them snap. She was a fidget.

'Everyone I know in London has a nursery.' She turned the wheel of the sewing machine.

'Don't touch,' I said, jumping up.

'Why not?'

'Fowler wouldn't like it.'

I had seen Priscilla's nursery in London. I could see it still as I watched the rain. Over the fireplace was a picture of a fair-haired boy in a nightgown talking to some rabbits. She said it was Jesus. I preferred the print of St. George in armour killing a dragon, with a fat lady bound to a tree, pretending not to notice. The wallpaper was silly, animals in clothes were running round the top. The furniture was painted cream.

She had lots of toys. There was a rocking horse with no proper rockers. Her books looked new, whereas mine were shabby and had belonged to my aunt and to Young Uncle. Some of the pages were missing and Alice was scribbled all over; Young Uncle must have done it.

The London dolls sat in a row on top of the bookcase. Some leant forward staring at their broad stiff feet, others lolled back, stupidly rolling their eyes. The dolls' house was small but it had a staircase. The windows weren't divided into panes, and the curtains were painted on the walls.

Priscilla yawned and drummed her fingers on the sill.

'Shall we play draughts?' I asked. 'Or would you like snakes and ladders?'

'You know I hate games.'

I was anxious to amuse her. 'There are the Burmese things Papa sent.' I rummaged in the cupboard and dragged out a jointed wooden snake. I held its head and made it wriggle.

'Ugh!' She drew back. 'They're horrid and they smell.'

'Yes, they smell of scent, I don't know why.' I held a carved elephant to my nose and sniffed. 'Like fir-cones at Christmas.'

'You don't seem to have any real toys.' She flung back the snake and slammed the cupboard doors. 'Oh look, there's the old leper's skin—the family joke.'

'I think my dolls' house is nicer than yours,' I said, feeling offended.

'Oh! you and your dolls' house!' She walked over to where it stood and knelt down. 'It hasn't even got a staircase.'

'Don't touch anything!' I cried with alarm, as she put in her hand and picked a silver chair from the drawing-room.

'Why are the walls red velvet?' She peered in and scratched with her finger. She hadn't any nails.

'There were some scraps left over from a dress. Be careful, it's only stuck. I haven't polished anything since you arrived, so it's tarnished.'

'Is it real silver?'

A piece of red velvet curled off the wall and curled over my silver table. She plucked out the scrap of stuff and put the chair back in another room, knocking things over.

'Stop! You're spoiling it all. Don't *touch*!'

'Didn't you know,' she said, sitting back on her heels, 'that when other children play with your toys, you must let them, even if they break things?'

'I would never let other children break *my* things,' I exclaimed, breathing hard.

'Oh yes, you would,' she said, smugly patting her knees. 'If you didn't, you'd be thoroughly spoilt. You *have* to let other children do exactly as they like, and after Ill I'm a visitor.' She upset a bedroom on purpose. 'If you show you mind it's bad manners—Nurse always said so.'

'Nurse! I saved you from Nurse!' I shouted, smacking her face and pinching her arm as hard as I could.

'You spiteful beast!' she yelled, jumping up and running to the fireplace. 'Look at these silly shells—' She swept them off the shelf: they flew with my little brass screws all over the place, pattering down like a shower of rain.

'My shells . . . ' I stopped to pick up a favourite. She was too quick and gathered up some more.

'Silly old shells!' she sang, darting round the table. She put one down by the machine. It was my best, a frilly pink one, given me by Timothy.

'Come and get it!'

She was like a gnat. I lunged forward, banging my hip on a corner of the table. She was still too quick. I tried to catch her and I grabbed her dress, but it tore and she got away. Mr. Pim began to chirp and hop up and down in his cage.

'Silly old shells!' she hissed, throwing them up in the air. The frail ones fluttered like moths' wings to the carpet. I caught her by the knees and dragged her down. The button box fell with a crash. I knelt over her and reached for the yardstick. As I leant forward she thrust me away. I was off my guard. She sprang to her feet and rushed to the door screaming.

I was mad with rage and thrashed out wildly with the yardstick as if I were swatting a fly. I missed. I tried once more and hit her, with all my strength, on the legs. She yelped with pain and sprang in the air like a jack-in-a-box. The yardstick splintered and I was just going to hit her again, because I had her cornered . . .

'What the devil's going on in here?' grandfather asked in a terrible voice. 'The most infernal noise!'

Priscilla was hiding behind the door which had swung back against her.

'She hit me on the legs, the beast, she hit me on the legs . . .' she whimpered again and again, like a prayer.

He stood staring at me, although he didn't know it. The hand in which I held the yardstick was wet and sore.

'Well?'

Priscilla crept out and ran down the passage. Prodding with his stick he explored the unfamiliar room. I had never seen him there before.

'Is this a bed?' he asked, hitting the metal with a clang.

'Yes.' I moved forward out of habit to help him.

'Well?' he asked again severely.

'My shells . . .' I said, bursting into tears. What did I feel? I thought it was despair—I pounded round the room smashing them to grit where some lay whole. I stamped on them and ground them to powder with my heel. The fragile ones whispered faintly like tissue paper, the others snapped like rabbit bones.

'Are you destroying your collection?' he asked, in a conversational way.

'Yes,' I mumbled, 'they're all broken now.' I felt hot and muzzy in the head.

'If you're sure there's not one remaining, I should come and sit down.'

I pushed over a pile of mending and sat on the creaking bed.

'You loved your shells.' I didn't answer. Tears were running down my face. 'You will miss Priscilla when she goes. I expect she was teasing you—quite normal on a wet day—I was bored myself. Women chattering like magpies in the boudoir, all about servants and nothing. No one has read to me for days. Hubert's in the library of course—it's damp with no fire in the study. I knew it wasn't time to dress, as the clock hadn't struck, but I thought I'd come up all the same. Instead of ringing for that lout Arthur to put me in the lift, I walked upstairs; halfway up I heard the rumpus.'

I said nothing. It was soothing to hear him talk, and I felt a little calmer.

'Although Priscilla's older than you, you are the larger. If you had maimed or disfigured her, *you* would have suffered, all your life, and no one could have helped you. Everyone would have sympathized with her, not you. Recollect that!' He sighed. 'Your shells! Little girls who destroy the things they love become . . . Give me your hand.' He dropped his stick. His fingers were stiff and dry.

Love was very tiring. I leant against him crying: 'She's going tomorrow and all my shells are *broken*.'

The door opened. It was Fowler. She looked round in amazement. 'S-Sir!' she stammered. 'Excuse me. I didn't know you were here.'

'Come in, it's high time I changed for dinner. I was on my way up when I heard the rumpus.'

'The rumpus, sir?' She looked very startled.

'Yes, the *noise*. While you've been gossiping with Rose, the children have tried to murder each other.'

'I'm sorry to hear that, sir.' She frowned at me and the broken shells and buttons on the floor. 'I was helping pack for Mrs. Hubert. I thought the young ladies . . .'

'Young ladies!' He snorted. 'Young hooligans!' He got up and I handed him his stick. Fowler stood aside. 'We'll say no more about it. The mistress would only be distressed. Tell Rose what I say.' He made his way slowly to his room.

Fowler shut the door. 'Whatever have you done? Just look at the floor! The master in my sewing-room, a rumpus! I never did! I don't know I'm sure.' She sank in her chair and stooped to pick up some screws. 'Who's been touching my machine?' She knew I wouldn't dare. 'You can't expect Tilly to clear up this mess. The very idea!' She swung the magnet; some pins jumped from among the scattered buttons. 'Fetch a dustpan and brush from the housemaid's cupboard.'

I did as I was told. There was a nice smell from the polish. I reached up and gave it a stir with its wooden spoon. The Prince of Wales was smiling.

'It's a stiff brush you want,' she said, when I handed her a soft one. 'I don't sweep up after you this time, young lady! I should think not. You do it yourself, and see you don't leave a speck on the carpet for Tilly!'

'Next time Priscilla comes, I shall be nicer,' I said, as I knelt down and brushed the tinkling splinters into the pan: 'nice and polite, like they are in London.'

'Poppycock!' She puffed and blew into a white kid glove. 'You'll always act daft. You'd better go and tell her you're sorry.'

Priscilla was sitting up in bed drinking her milk; her hair was bound in loose white rags. They formed a halo round her head.

'I've come to say I'm sorry.' Would she make room for me to sit beside her? I knelt on the floor and rested my arms on the quilt: 'Please say that you forgive me.'

She put down her empty glass, and rolled up the cuff of her nightgown. The twin bruises of my pinch stained her arm with a small blue moth. Nothing mattered except her forgiveness.

She was like a goddess—I knelt beside her begging. I could

see the poor people in the Bible taking their pet lambs and doves and killing them for God. The lambs thought they were going for a walk, when suddenly a knife swished down and slit their throats. Blood trickled over their curls, their legs crumpled, and they lay staring at nothing with glazed bewildered eyes, like the snared rabbits. The doves were coaxed from their cages by inviting fingers and then their necks were twisted and their bodies flung to quiver on the temple floor. I could hear the bleating and the flurry of wings. I buried my eyes in the quilt. The only comforting thought was that Nurse had disappeared.

'What a beast!' I cried. 'Nurse was a pig—a pig's bottom!'

'A what?' gasped Priscilla.

'A pig's bottom,' I repeated. 'Nurse was, and still is, a pig's bottom.'

We burst into frantic giggles. I had only to say 'Pig's—' and a fresh madness attacked us, until our convulsions were such that a mere spluttered 'P—' was enough to set us off; crazily we rolled about the bed.

Tom put his head round the door. 'What's the matter with the dear little girls? You are kickin' up a shindy! You won't 'arf cop it.' He was changed for dinner and puffed at a cigarette.

'Oh do let's try,' I begged, jumping out of bed, 'is it nicer than cigars?'

'You'll be sick!' warned Priscilla, 'and if you're caught there'll be trouble.'

'Mummy'll be livid and Fowler wouldn't like it,' he squeaked, and held out the cigarette for me to have a puff.

'He called her the Jewel of Asia, of Asia, of Asia,' boomed uncle Hubert in the bath. We all stopped talking and listened. 'For she was the Queen of the Geisha, the Geisha, the Geisha.'

My aunt's door opened and she called 'Ro-o-ose! I can't find my petit-point pochette!'

Rose ran along the passage. I could almost smell the dress, fresh from the iron. Was it the mauve one with fringes of pearls?

'Love, love, something love,' sang uncle Hubert, 'mischievous cupid with amorous dart!'

'For heaven's sake hurry, Hubert!' called my aunt. 'It's nearly time for the gong.'

Oddly enough the result of Nurse leaving was disastrous. Priscilla was sent to boarding-school and the gap between our ages seemed to widen.

At school Priscilla found a friend whom she called 'my chum, Wendy Malcolm'. Everything to do with Wendy Malcolm was objectionable to me; but all enchanted Priscilla. Wendy's mother was divorced and wore Russian boots, Wendy's hair was permanently waved and she read detective stories. Her favourite word was 'ghastly' and she could play 'Tea for two' on the piano. Priscilla had never enjoyed going to the beach or getting dirty in the garden, preferring to walk along the road or to the village, but now, on the hottest summer afternoons we sat indoors, caged like canaries. She, who had never liked reading, read for hours; or wrote what I presumed must be a diary. Sometimes she would gaze out of the window, biting her fingers and thinking of things she could say or do next term to impress and please Wendy Malcolm.

'Let's go and get some watercress for tea. Shall we ask Mrs. Hopkins to let us cook some fudge, or help old Dan make a bonfire in the acre?'

'Di, *do* leave me alone! You go. Can't you see I'm thinking? For goodness' sake shut up. Play with the dolls' house—polish your silver—clean out Mr. Pim's cage. Don't be such a *baby*.'

'I did it all this morning.' I was in despair when, after a long silence, she jumped up and said: 'We're going out. We shall need a telescope, some money, two pairs of gloves and some wax.'

'Whatever for?'

'Field glasses would do, and putty, but wax would be better.'

I knocked politely on the pantry door in case Johnstone was resting. 'Oh Johnstone, d'you think I can borrow these?' I held up the field glasses in their leather case. 'They were hanging in the gun-room.'

He was slumped in a chair. 'Eh? What's that, Miss Diana?' His eyes were bleary. 'Young master's binocu—' he belched and staggered to his feet, knocking an empty decanter to the floor.

'Oh dear, what a pity, it's broken!'

'Plen'y more o' them. Port's finished, f-finished!' He whistled through his teeth and steadied himself with both hands on the table.

'I'll be very careful, I promise.'

He lurched towards me, crunching bits of the decanter under foot.

'You're tipsy again,' I giggled. 'Just you try and stop me.'

He tried, and we fought for the glasses, he breathing in my face. I pulled away, revolted, and swung the heavy leather case on its strap, round and round like a sling. 'You can have it. Catch!' I let it go. He caught it but it hit him in the stomach. 'You little bit . . .' He tottered to the lead sink and started coughing.

I left him to be sick alone and rushed along the still-room passage, past the row of bells. The green baize door sighed when I flung it open; I had reached the boudoir before it hissed and thudded to. I knew there was a pair of opera glasses in the cupboard, elegant mother-of-pearl, on a slim gold stick. I took it and on my way out through the hall I grabbed some gloves and a few of the gate boys' pennies.

'What hours you've been. Did you bring the wax?'

'Oh dear, I forgot, and these were all I could find.' I put the opera glasses on the table.

She picked them up and pressed them to her eyes, twiddling at the little wheel. 'Better than nothing, but we'll have to melt a candle. Go and get me one from the housemaid's cupboard.'

She had become very bossy.

'Because I'm older you must do as I say! I s'pose you've heard of Edgar Wallace and I s'pose you know that your policeman, Percy, is just a silly ass?'

I sprang to his defence: he had found Polly after all. 'Who's Edgar Wallace?'

'Never heard of Edgar Wallace? The books you like are so ghastly and old-fashioned. Mummy says it's high time you went to school. She says it's bad for your sight, reading all that tosh aloud for hours in such a smoky room. Mr. Duncan told her you can't even do long division!'

'I don't care a fig for long division.'

'Give me your knife.' She sawed at the candle. 'To think you haven't heard of Edgar Wallace! What *do* you read? Even Daddy's read them all.'

'Talking of books,' I said, suddenly inspired and determined not to miss my cue, 'in London only a week or two ago I found the *Book of Directions*. It isn't called that but it says what people do if they *want* to have a baby.'

'Botany tosh about plants . . . I know, all about butterflies and roses!'

'About people,' I insisted.

She put the bits of candle on the trivet.

'It's ghastly—much worse than we thought last summer—a sort of operation.' I tried to explain. 'When *I* get married I shall have an anaesthetic.'

'Really it sounds too ghastly.' Her face was flushed. 'I've known for over a year—Wendy Malcolm told me.'

I sat in silence cursing Wendy Malcolm, while I kneaded the warm grubby lumps of wax in my palms. Priscilla bent down and rolled back the carpet, revealing a red notebook lying in a heap of fluffy dust. 'That pig Polly must have read it!' Her voice trembled.

'Poor you, is it your diary?' I was curious and of course sympathetic. I kept mine well hidden.

She put on some gloves and took the notebook to the window. 'Give me your magnifying glass.' She snatched it and peered at the red limp cover.

'No, she didn't after all. Look, the hair's still binding the pages.'

'Let's see.' I leant over her shoulder. 'Private Criminal Investigations,' I read aloud. She turned the page.

'I believe this house to be a Hotbed of Vice and Crime. Suspects as follows: Daniel Pettigrew, Robert Johnstone, Mary Hopkins.' She slammed the book shut.

'A Hotbed of Vice and Crime!' I was appalled. 'Vice . . . what do you mean?' Sodom and Gomorrah?

'It jolly well is! Now come on, I'll take the notebook and the opera glasses. Bring that clock and put the wax under your arm; it mustn't get cold. Put on your gloves and get out the box that's under the bed.'

I opened the box to put in the clock. A bottle lay inside wrapped in a face towel. It wasn't lemonade.

'Don't touch!' she warned. 'It's a clue; covered with fingerprints. I bagged it from the backyard.'

I decided to humour her as we walked through the village. The wax felt horrid in my armpit, and the clock and the bottle rattled in the box.

'Keep your eyes open for anything suspicious. Quick! It might be evidence.' She scribbled in the notebook: 'One brown Morris Cowley A 52. What's the time?'

'About half past three.'

The motor slowed down beside us. 'Having a nice game, kids?' asked the Major grinning. He was now *married* to Miss Letty. I looked at her with interest. Our Elsie was scowling in the dicky.

'It's not really a game.'

I gave them a foolish smile when the alarm clock exploded in a buzz.

'What's that?' Elsie glowered through her goggles.

'By jingo, it's a time-bomb! You'll be blowing us all to smithereens!'

'Oh, do come on,' said Priscilla. 'We must hurry. We've got to go to Miss Dolby's and it's half past three.'

'I shouldn't do that, dears,' said Miss Letty, 'not today.' She turned to the Major: 'Rather touching, Henry; the children were going to inquire.'

'Come *on*,' said Priscilla, pulling me away.

I followed and waved at the Major. He had got out to wind up the motor and it soon jerked off in the opposite direction.

The blinds were drawn.

'She must be resting,' said Priscilla, knocking on the door. 'Oh good afternoon, Mrs. Perkins, we've come for upstairs.'

Mrs. Perkins' eyes were very red. 'My poor Amy,' she gulped, 'didn't you know? She's passed behind the veil this morning, but seeing as you're passing you'd better step in, as I've got something here for Miss Diana. A bit of company is welcome, seeing folks leave one alone to do the baking, but you'll see, they'll all come to stuff themselves after the rites.'

'It means she's dead,' muttered Priscilla, pushing me into the darkened shop. The sweets were covered with paper. 'Ask to go upstairs. I want to see the rolls of silk. She told Mummy some of them were French.'

Mrs. Perkins stopped crying and was suddenly alert.

'You can't go up there, it wouldn't be right. Amy was moved into the front when she was ill so I should hear if she tapped with her umbrella. Mr. Duncan came. "Have you any requests, Miss Dolby? Any commissions or omissions which you would like me to attend?" Poor soul, she was sinking.' Mrs. Jenkins was convulsed, like the sea, with sorrow.

'Oh dear,' I said.

'"I'd like Miss Diana to have my lambs," said Amy, "see you do it, Freda." Just you wait here, miss, and I'll go up and get them.'

'Lambs? We can't take her ghastly lambs now, she must be loony.'

'They're china lambs. They were her mother's.'

Priscilla was bristling with impatience.

I took the lambs from Mrs. Perkins and put them in my pocket. Their curls pricked through the tissue paper.

'What a curse she's dead,' swore Priscilla, trotting down the street, past Mrs. Rook's shop. 'She would pop off just as the noose was closing round her neck. Thank goodness I've got an old dress on, because now we must go to the cliff.'

'The cliff?'

I was frightened; the full horror of our quest was dawning on me slowly.

'Miss Dolby's silk is smuggled, like the brandy. They get it from that old man you used to know on the marsh. I'm sure he sells brandy to Johnstone and hides it under the fish in his basket. Mrs. Hopkins is an accomplice and you've always said that he and Dan are thick as thieves. We'll watch through the glasses. If there's no one on the marsh we can search the premises for clues. There'll be fingerprints and we must wear our gloves. Timothy's the head of the gang. We'll write a report and get Percy to arrest him. We'll round up the others. Pity Miss Dolby's dead; they'll be marched, handcuffed, through the village. They'll be up before the Bench and *our* names will be in the papers, even *The Times* and the *Daily Mirror*, and Wendy and Mrs. Malcolm will read all about it.'

We were sitting on the cliff. She focused the opera glasses.

'But Johnstone doesn't like brandy,' I protested, 'he only drinks port,' I snatched the opera glasses from her, 'and Mrs. Hopkins only takes sherry for her headaches.'

'D'you mean to say you know that Johnstone *drinks*?'

'Yes, of course! I don't think anybody *minds*!'

'You really are the limit. See the smoke? Timothy must be at home. What a shame, we'll have to try again another day.'

A plume of smoke rose from the huts. I would warn Timothy tomorrow. If he were guilty, his hook might have left scratches on the bottles.

'It must be tea-time.' I fumbled in the box for the clock. 'It must be half past four.'

'Oh goodness, my dress is dirty. I'll have to change for tea. Mummy'll be back from Lady Pritchard's. I'll run on ahead.'

I let her go. For once I didn't care about tea. I sat alone, holding the opera glasses. The wax was still under my arm. I threw it away. I had a pain like an ice-cream, freezing my stomach.

The bell rang without any warning; it pealed and pealed. I froze all over. It couldn't be the church bell, it sounded too close. Below on the marsh, Timothy's dog began to bark, and a small black figure emerged from the huts. The bell was still ringing. It must be the Estate bell which hung in the kitchen backyard. In my mind's eye I could see its huge clapper swinging to and fro. Something ghastly had happened. Perhaps the house was on fire? I scrambled up the cliff. I felt the china lambs in my pocket bump with each step against my thigh. Timothy and his dog overtook me. There was no time to talk until we reached Snakes' Wall, when he wedged his hook in a crevice and I used it as a step.

I was panting: 'I must come and see you tomorrow. Priscilla thinks you sell rolls of silk to Miss Dolby—she's dead you know—and brandy to Johnstone . . .' I avoided his eyes. 'She's loony of course but—well, we don't want any trouble . . .'

'Quit worriting, I baint no fule.'

He patted my arm and we peered between the trees. The bell stopped ringing but its echo lingered.

Old Dan's spade stood abandoned, upright in the earth. I left Snakes' Wall and stumbled through the acre, ignoring the paths and trampling the spinach underfoot.

When I turned the corner of The Ruins, I saw Dan and Whaler lifting a body on a gate.

At once I knew what had happened. I could hear grandfather groaning. Arthur and Johnstone were there but Fowler was giving the orders. They moved like puppets and at last all marched slowly with their burden towards the back entrance of the house.

My first instinct was to run and join the procession but on second thoughts I stayed where I was. The thing we had dreaded for years had come about: grandfather had had a fall.

I felt dazed but not surprised. I wandered vaguely among the hazels and then sat in my swing; the seat was too small, but I rocked on one hip between the ropes, thinking about love and death.

Much later the sun went down and, feeling cold, I left the nuttery and walked up the steps past Cherub to the drive. I turned right at the fork to the tradesmen's entrance. In the backyard I noticed three empty bottles in a box. I stooped down and wiped them, one by one, on my dress. Then I stood for quite a long time staring at the bell. It looked harmless enough, but it was evil.

I entered the house quietly and sank on the wooden bench in the still-room passage, beside a trug full of scrubbed potatoes.

Through the door of the Servants' Hall, I heard the clink of cups and saucers. Someone was sobbing.

'Now, Polly, don't give way, there's a good girl. We must keep our heads.'

It was Hannah talking.

'The mistress. I knew she'd have one of her attacks—her lips was blue!'

'The 'ole blinkin' place is packin' up. What with Mr. Johnstone givin' 'is notice—when I shows Mr. Duncan out, the master, 'e says: "Send Johnstone *hat once*!" Winkin' merrybugs!'

'It was all in the Sunday tea-cups,' Polly moaned, 'a Death, a

Change, and wasn't it a Courting? I'm sure I remember the coffin and the heart.'

'Don't talk soft,' said Tilly, 'that coffin was Miss Dolby's.'

'As for the heart,' said Hannah, 'the Young Master's new lady seems very nice to me, and that maid of hers is quite refined.'

'A cut above that Mrs. Phoebe!'

'Seeing as the mistress contents herself with slops, *I've* no fancy to be taking orders from any young lady, what thinks she's the Queen of Sheba,' announced Mrs. Hopkins, who'd been silent until now. 'You're welcome to Annie's cooking, very welcome I'm sure, unless of course she betters herself and goes as a General to the Vicar or as number four at Knole. The carrier says as they're short-handed in the kitchen.'

'You wouldn't be thinking of leaving, Mrs. Hopkins?' asked Tilly, her voice betraying agreeable surprise. 'Why the place wouldn't be the same!'

Mrs. Hopkins exploded: 'There's gratitude! Some folks know when they're not wanted. If Annie's cooking's as good as mine—you're welcome, very welcome!' She banged the scullery door.

''Ark, 'ark the lark! and good riddance!' muttered Arthur.

I got up and opened the door.

'My little love,' said Hannah, 'where have you been?' She coaxed me towards the fire and looked me up and down.

'My word, she's in a pickle,' said Polly.

I burst into tears.

'P'raps Arthur should cut along,' said Tilly. 'There goes the phone.'

'Come along dear, it's bed time. We'd better go upstairs.' Hannah took my hand and together we tiptoed through the silent house to my room. I didn't want to see Priscilla.

Fowler's bun had collapsed. She and Hannah whispered together in the passage.

'I can't stay, you'll just have to manage,' said Fowler, frowning and peering at my face. 'The mistress keeps asking: "Where's Miss Diana?" I don't know I'm sure; perhaps she had better go and say goodnight. Mind now, she's not herself—she's rambling—she's had one of her attacks and quite three of them dratted pills. You don't want to stay too long or pay much attention.' She wrapped me up in my new kimono.

Grandmother's room was almost dark and smelt of doctors. 'My precious, draw up that chair.' Her mouth was mauve and had some white powder caked at the corners. Three fat leeches clung to her neck. 'Poor George, crippled now as well as blind. It's really tragic . . .'

'I thought he was dead.' Perhaps everything would come right after all. 'Miss Dolby died this morning and gave me her lambs.'

'Children are *too* extraordinary. This is no time to talk about Miss Dolby—of course I was very sorry . . .' She shaded her eyes. 'The latest news on the telephone is good. They think he will recover, but at what a price, crippled! That bell! The way it rang and rang.' She shuddered. 'I knew it was the end.'

'But if he isn't dead, it isn't the end.'

'Yes it is. Nothing will ever be the same. Thank heavens in a few years you will be married!'

'Married!' I clenched my toes.

'I dislike the idea but you will have to go to school. Thank God for my beloved. I must write to your father . . . tomorrow. He'll have to come back and take responsibility for once. You can spend more time with Mrs. H-H. If only you were older, if only you'd been born soon after they were married.'

If only they'd drowned me in a bucket.

'Mrs. H-H. is as strong as an ox, so at least she can present you. You'd better start walking backwards with a sheet round your waist and a bag of beans on your head. You must learn to kick it aside without bending—only a knack—I could do it very well. I hope you won't grow any taller and look like that unfortunate Gladys . . .'

'I shall never get married. *Never!*' My heart was pounding. 'D'you mean I'm not going to live here any more?'

'Of course, my love, you will come here now and then.' She held out her hand. 'You know you are the apple of my eye. "Like to the apples on the Dead Sea shore, all ashes to the taste." And don't be such a goose, of course you'll get married. I must have a word with Mabel Pritchard, her Walter's such a dear.'

'Walter!' I was aghast. 'Walter won't want to marry *me*!'

Under the door, cracks of light shone round Fowler's feet. When she eased her corns the pattern changed.

'What rubbish! He'd be very lucky. My dear child, you must realize you're an heiress. You know that Grand has skimped and denied herself everything for you—yes, Walter! Thank goodness that's settled. Such a pretty wedding in our exquisite church, which reminds me—Mr. Duncan called this afternoon—about Miss Dolby. So tiresome! Who will make the bridesmaids' dresses now? And then he told George that Johnstone was drinking . . .'

Fowler's feet changed position.

'Oh dear, will he have to go before the Bench?'

'Heavens, no, it's gone on for years; he's saved me such a lot of trouble.'

Fowler came in without knocking. 'It's high time Miss Diana went to bed and you turned in.' She, only she, would dare to talk like that.

'See how I'm bullied?' Grandmother smiled and didn't seem to care.

Hannah was waiting in my room. 'You snuggle down, my little love.'

'Oh dear, Papa's coming home, I've got to go to school and get married and she doesn't really love me . . . not like Young Uncle. And Priscilla's so *changed*.'

'Don't talk daft, you know the mistress said you was the apple of her eye,' insisted Fowler.

I saw the apple; it had cankers and was eaten by wasps. It had fallen in the mud. I hugged Edward while Hannah held a glass of milk to my lips. Fowler sank on the bed and undid her shoes.

'She only likes rosy apples!' I whispered, looking at the door.

'You don't want to talk like that. She's my lady,' said Fowler, 'my lady, and don't you forget it.' With dignity, she hobbled from the room.

Part Two

CHAPTER SIX

THE headmistress was drinking something which she always referred to as her medicine. I was relieved to see that her pink and discreetly powdered cheeks were not suffused with rage, as my conscience was never clear. With a false smile she invited me to sit beside her; at once I was suspicious. Grandmother Freeman having died the year before and Fowler having left, there remained only one probable disaster; perhaps grandfather had had another fall? No. My heart jumped when I saw a letter from Papa lying open on the table.

Her eyes followed mine and she smoothed out the creases, saying: 'It came some time ago.' Here and there the nib had pierced the paper with savage downstrokes and underlining. I dreaded Papa's letters with their stern instructions for extra drill, special coaching at lawn tennis or some other horror, like more frequent riding lessons on the downs. They always ended: '*My* daughter must look A.1 in the pigskin.' Only recently I had learnt that the pigskin was a saddle; for years I had supposed it to be a symbol for some idyllic state to which one day I might aspire.

'How long since you saw him? *Really?* Not since you were twelve and you're fifteen now; he'll find you very changed.'

I was doubtful. I was just the same to me, and poor Papa had always wished that I were an athletic, horsy boy. On his last leave I had been a failure.

She grimaced. 'Well, he's here, he's waiting in the lounge and he wanted it to be a nice surprise.'

A nice surprise indeed! I froze with shock: he should have been eight thousand miles away. She got up briskly and pushed me towards the door. 'Smooth your hair and pull down your tunic . . .'

The lounge was a hideous room reserved for parents' visits. A huge brown man, with shiny shoes, crouched like a cricket on the sofa. He sprang up to a colossal height and strode across towards me. I took a step back but he flung out his arms and crushed me to his buttons.

'Hello,' I said, 'did you have a good journey?'

He thrust me away and stared. 'Crikey, you've grown. You look tophole! How tall are you now? You'll soon be bigger than Big Aunt Gladys. You're not the namby-pamby little kid I left behind, and you've bobbed your hair—I never liked those cissy ringlets.'

'I'm only five foot ten: I hope I don't grow any more.'

'Will your old girl mind if I have a gasper?' He lit a cigarette and paced round the room, grabbing up the hockey cups and banging them down again on the table. Ash scattered on the floor and the clock ticked sadly.

At last he blurted out: 'I know I've been a rotter not writing; but letters are so, well—you know—and it's been rotten of me not sending any presents.'

'Oh that doesn't matter. The leper's skin was very nice—ages ago, I mean . . .'

'Oh that!' he shrugged. 'I owe you two or three, no several, counting birthdays and Christmas. Now's your chance.' He slapped me on the back. 'Anything you want!'

'*Anything?* Anything at all?'

'Up to a hundred quid. Honest Injun.'

I was amazed and my mouth went dry, while I perched on the edge of the sofa, thinking.

He collapsed beside me. 'By jingo!' Somehow the tension between us broke with the springs in the seat and we laughed together.

'What I want costs eighty-something, at least that's what the other girls say.' It wasn't fair; poor Papa thought I meant a pony. 'I want to leave today.' I stared straight ahead so as not to see his reaction.

'You mean this place? You want to leave today?'

'Yes, that's what I mean.' I hastened to explain it would cost next term's fees because we hadn't given notice.

'You're a rum kid. That's just it, you're not a kid any more, neither fish, fowl nor good red herring.' He shook out a handkerchief to dab his brow. 'I always thought this school was A.1, what with the games and well, you know, the riding. No one likes work, I was sacked from Wellington myself—'superannuated'—he pronounced the word carefully—'that was what they called it. The Guvnor came down and bailed me out of scrape after scrape—betting and so on—he was very cut up about my leaving. To celebrate I set fire to some barrels of pitch and rolled them down the hill. I told your head the work didn't matter. Can you do a swallow dive? How's the jumping getting on?'

'Oh, all right. Never mind, I knew you didn't mean it.'

A bell rang in the hall and the headmistress came in. Had she been listening at the door?

'Although it's a week-day, as it's such a special occasion, I'm sure you'd like to take Diana out to lunch? The Grand or the Cavendish are good.'

'Um er . . .' said Papa, going very red. I held my breath. He glanced at me and then pulled himself together. 'As a matter of fact, I know this place is tophole, but I'm taking the kid with me back to London.'

Her face too went crimson. She glared and was, I could see, quite confident of his defeat.

'Perhaps if you've time,' she said with forced politeness, 'the two of us should have a little chat.'

'Yes,' said Papa, jutting out his chin, 'she'd better get ready.'

They both sat down. 'Have a gasper?'

'What a racket! Why aren't you in class? Are you ill?' asked Matron, peering through a chink in the cubicle curtains. She was the nicest member of the staff.

'I feel wonderful,' I cried, throwing my thick stockings and serge bloomers on the floor.

'Pick up those things! Have you taken leave of your senses?'

'Yes, I've gone absolutely potty!' I sang, rummaging in a drawer for the silk vest, petticoat and knickers which we were allowed to wear for dancing. 'My Papa's arrived and I'm leaving now for ever. He's the most wonderful, the bravest, best looking, tallest man you've ever seen and he's taking me with him back to London.' I stripped off my scratchy combinations, 'Good riddance to those foul things!' I kept on the broad tight piece of elastic which I wore day and night to squash down my bosom. Fowler had stitched it and others, under protest. 'What you want is a proper bust bodice.' The poor old-fashioned dear!

'If it's really true you're leaving I must go and get your trunk,' said Matron, bewildered.

'I can get all I need into my suitcase,' I said, vigorously brushing my hair and rubbing talcum powder on my nose.

'You'll take your trunk whether you like it or not,' she retorted, 'and don't sit on the bed. In my humble opinion your Papa, as you call him, is a prize silly ass!'

'Prize silly ass, prize silly ass,' the train puff-puffed to London. It was Matron who was silly, not he. Nevertheless, it was strange to think that this jolly overgrown schoolboy, sprawled asleep across the carriage, was really my Papa, whose stern letters had filled me with dread. Once, before my grandmother had time to *pas-devant*, my grandfather, blind to my presence, had called Papa 'not only obstinate and weak, but an unmitigated bore'. I had crept out of the room blushing and everyone had pretended not to notice. Grandfather was of course mistaken. An obstinate man would have argued with me or at least insisted that I stayed until the end of term. And there was nothing weak in the way he had tackled the headmistress, or the head waiter at the Grand, who had said luncheon was over.

'What, no tiffin?' he had roared. 'Tell the cook to ruddy well fry some bangers and eggs and bacon!'

We had devoured mountains of food amongst the potted palms under the disapproving gaze of grey-haired ladies, while a dark man played the violin.

'Tell that dago to stop that squawking on the fiddle!' Papa stormed to a quaking little page.

'Oh no, please,' I implored, crossing my fingers. 'I love it, really.'

He now awoke with a yawn. 'Crikey, I shall get awful stick from the Mater when she sees you; but you'll have to take the blame. Don't you worry, when it's all over we'll make whoopee, you know, have a jolly . . .'

'Oh I'd love to see *The Matriarch* with Mrs. Pat Campbell or would you like the Russian Ballet?' I dared not suggest *Young Woodley*.

'Sounds ruddy high-brow to me,' he objected, 'now Cochran's *Wake up and Dream* is a tophole show, I've seen it twice already. On our way to the club we'll get a brace of whiskey seats at Ashton and Mitchell—gangway seats—you know, quicker to get to the bar. The club's a cock-and-hen place and I'd like you to come and meet the pals.'

'Do you mean the Athenaeum?' Grand had always boasted of Papa being a member.

'Crikey, no! Never set foot in it. Getting me in was the Guvnor's idea.'

On our way from the station, as well as the whiskey tickets we bought a gramophone which only needed winding once for two records. The taxi-fare was enormous. 'Here's ten bob,' said Papa, throwing me a note, 'get him to help you with the luggage. We're late, so I'd better go ahead.'

The cabby carried in my case. 'Oh don't bother with the trunk,' I said, 'I don't want it any more.'

'Don't want yer trunk, miss? Yer must be barmy! This 'ere trunk's worth a packet!'

'No, really. It's only navy blue clothes. I shall never wear them now. I *hate* navy blue.'

'An' supposin' I don't fancy it?' he grinned, stuffing the ten shillings in his coat. 'Navy blue! Blimey! I ain't a somethin' sailor!'

'Couldn't you give it to the poor and needy?'

I turned and ran, knowing Fowler would have disapproved.

The cock-and-hen place was full of brown men like Papa and beige women with blue eyes and faded hair.

'Meet the kid,' said Papa. 'Make your salaams. Pongo, Puss, Dot and Carry, Jumbo, Rag and Bones.'

'How d'you do.' I refused to bob. I was grown up after all.

'More chotah-pegs all round? Boy!' Papa thumped on the table and snapped his fingers.

An elderly waiter rushed up: 'And the young lady?' he asked, giving me a little bow.

'Missy Sahib would like a ginger pop,' Papa announced to the room, just as if I were a child.

Furious at my blushes, I turned to Mrs. Bags or was it Mrs. Bones? 'Have you been in England long?'

'A damned sight too long—if you'll pardon my French,' she answered.

'Pongo's a sahib,' said Papa in the taxi, 'but the others are box-wallahs we picked up on the boat; you know, one loses touch with people over here.'

He had a key to Grand's front door. Once inside the hall he strode to the top of the basement stairs and, instead of blowing on the whistle, shouted: 'Soup, soup, beautiful soup.' What a way to speak to Helen!

'Hadn't we better shake hands and explain?' I began to feel anxious; and all the portraits were frowning.

'No, leave it to the Mater.' He threw his hat at the Burmese gongs and opened the sitting-room door: 'Guess who's here?'

Grand's voice answered at once: 'Diana!'

'I hope you won't be cross,' I said, when she gave me a hug, 'it's all my fault, but Papa let me leave school today.'

'Bravo for him! Cross? My pet, why should I be cross? I applaud your father's decision! Indeed, I have prayed for this moment: I have always deplored and regretted the influence of your school.'

'It's wearing off already!' In fact it seemed a million miles away.

'Well, Mater, we're off to a show after dinner so I'd better go and change my togs.'

'To the play? How delightful! *Mary Rose*? I see they are giving *Hiawatha*. Now there's no time to dawdle: I must have a Little Talk with Helen.' She patted my arm. 'Dear child, you can sleep in my bed as usual.'

Left alone, I realized sadly that I had nothing suitable to wear. My jumper and skirt wouldn't do and the white confirmation dress, which I wore for dancing and had packed in my case, was really too young, and very tight across the bosom. I decided to try the Hobman chest, and its store of models' clothes. My classical tunic was dirty round the hem and some of the beads were missing. The sari would be pretty but wouldn't go with my blazer. The gold embroidery on Julia's dress, which Grandpa Holman was supposed to have done, was horribly tarnished and there was a nest of mice in the shepherd's cloak. I closed the lid and plumped for my confirmation white crêpe de chine with black silk stockings. Perhaps if I wore my school patent leather belt set fashionably low, I would look less frumpy.

As I changed in the gentlemen's cloakroom, I heard the food lift rumble up from the kitchen and then Helen's footsteps on the stairs. I was soon ready and ran to seize her by the hand.

'How d'you do, Helen?'

'Only so-so, miss,' she said, pressing her side. 'It's not that I grudge Master Hilary a bite, but a three-course dinner comes very heavy after all these years.

'Oh, do tell, what's for tonight?' I sniffed at the dishes in the lift.

'Well, it *was* Bovril, scrag and sardines, but there was only just enough for one—I weren't expecting you and he's an eater. From now on, all crusts is to be saved for Miss Diana, said the mistress; and baked slowly in the oven. Rusks she said. Rusks and a dish of boiled bones at every meal as extras.'

'It's not true. You're joking.'

'Cross my heart! It's no concern of mine but the mistress says you face is going wrong and chewing is what's going to make it better. I expect you think it looks all right but then we never know, do we?' She carefully set a teaspoon on the table. 'No more big spoons for Miss Diana and you're to drink your soup from a teapot. Orders is orders; the mistress will have her little fancies.' She looked me up and down. 'I've heard it said high foreheads aren't the thing for ladies. Perhaps you ought to grow a fringe like the Duchess of York.'

'My—my face!' I stammered, peering at my reflection in the glass of Titian's portrait of his daughter.

'Diana!' called Grand. 'Is this your caboodle in the hall?'

'What's all this about my face and boiled bones and teaspoons?' I shouted.

'Oh hush!' she whispered.

Papa was coming down the stairs. He wore a tail coat and carried an opera hat.

'Look how handsome he is,' she said, proudly. 'See the fine mouth, the splendid line of the jaw.' She turned to me. 'My pet, your chin is too small and the remedy is mastication.'

'The Mater's right. If you want a decent jaw, mastication's the thing. Crikey, I should know, she made me and Gladys chew every mouthful over fifty times.'

'But you can't chew porridge,' I objected.

'If you chew rusks and gnaw bones for two or three years,' said Grand, stroking my hair, 'your mouth will improve; alas, it is far too wide and a large spoon will only stretch it; a teaspoon and a narrow spout will be better when we are alone.' Her voice was coaxing. 'After meals I shall dip my finger in salt and massage the gums of your lower jaw exactly as I did my children's, pulling the jaw forward so . . .'

'No you won't!' I cried. 'I don't want to look like a gorilla! I shall grow a fringe down to here and no one will see my face at all.'

'If you want to be a stunner, you must listen to the Mater,' said Papa. 'She was a famous beauty. All the Miss Waughs were stunners but the old Guvnor knew a thing or two and brought off a double.' He chucked Grand under the chin.

'Some people did think my sister Fanny quite good-looking,' she admitted, sinking gracefully into a chair, 'but the poor creature's eyes got very sore and she was always bathing them with boracic. I hate to boast, but, just between ourselves, Cyril's looks are—well, I don't like to say, because her brow was rather low and her nose a little crooked.'

'Oh *poor* great-aunt Fanny. I think it was awful that she died giving birth to uncle Cyril and I think it was ghastly to give him that horrid second name, just because . . .' My voice broke with pent-up indignation: 'I've always wondered how they could!'

'Who's "they"? What rot! Old Cyril didn't give a damn.'

'It was my idea,' Grand said proudly, 'a beautiful Arabic word and such a *fitting* name: Benone, child of sorrow.'

'Cheer up, kid,' said Papa. 'If aunt Fanny hadn't popped off, we three wouldn't be here. She got in first after all—it's my bet the Mater always had her eye on the Guvnor . . .'

'You wicked boy!' She pretended to slap his face.

'You know you did,' he teased, and waltzed her round the room.

'Not until Fanny was dead and I offered to look after Cyril,' she protested, breathless. 'Of course I worshipped my father but I must confess I longed to get away from home. The music was incessant. I should say the *thumping* on the piano. Seven of us had to practice for an hour and the youngest started after breakfast. I shall never forget when Holman came back from Florence with his baby. I used to sit in the conservatory painting silk fans, or pressing flowers out of Bentham and Hooker. The scales were so distracting and he knew how sensitive I was. The first I knew of his attention was when he painted on my fan a tiny little fly.' She smiled, 'I tried to brush it off . . .'

'But the Guvnor was caught . . .'

'Caught!' I cried. 'Like Byron said: "caught within the subtle snare, I burn, and feebly flutter there".'

'Caught!'

With his hands round her bony waist Papa lifted her up as if she were a doll.

'Wicked boy, put me down!' she begged.

'May I smoke my gaspers in the house? Promise us steak tomorrow?'

He went on laughing and whirled her round and round.

'Oh Pax! You'll make her giddy!'

'Reprieve!' cried Grand. 'Steak it shall be.'

'Grilled, not stewed?'

He was a giant. It was grotesque to see him shake her like a puppet in the air.

'Grilled,' she whispered.

He set her down and she clung panting with her hands clasped behind his head gazing up at him with rapture. I was astonished. Was it love? or were we both besotted with Papa? Uncertain I left them and sat down in the dining-room without another word, to sip my Bovril from a little china teapot.

It was pitch dark in the hall when we got back from Ma Merrick's. She owned the night club we had gone to after the theatre. Papa was feeling rather giddy and had collapsed on a Waugh chair under Grandpa Holman's portrait.

I wished that after all I had not chosen to wear my confirmation dress. I had heard of night clubs of course; it was clear that they were places where gentlemen went when their wives had run away or were dead or simply busy. The ladies looked like actresses to me but Papa had said in the taxi: 'They're joy-girls really.' I felt sleepy and sank on the other Waugh chair.

'Wake up and Dream,' I sang quietly, giving him a prod. He went on snoring.

When he had introduced me to Ma Merrick, she had screeched: 'We've heard all about *you*,' and handed me a ghastly fat doll with a pink fuzzy wig. I had left it in the taxi. What *could* she have heard about me?

Papa and I had had one dance together, while everybody clapped; but he was really too big to do the Charleston and had kicked my shins and laddered my black silk stockings. Then I had seen my white lock-knit bloomers reflected in the floor, which was made of mirrors—and had said: 'I feel rather hot,' and left him talking to a person who said her name was Betty.

'You'd better give me your matches,' I now whispered, nudging Papa.

'Can't find the ruddy things,' he growled, dropping the latch key on the floor.

At last he handed me a box and I groped my way about, trying to avoid the Burmese gongs. 'Oh, hush; stay where you are until I light the gas.' Pop! We blinked as the flare lit up our faces.

'I want a snifter before I doss down,' he said, lunging towards the drawing-room door.

'Look out! The bells are hooked in place. Do come to bed. You know there's nothing to drink in there.'

'Yes there is, I hid some Johnnie Walker in the piano.'

Before I could stop him the bells had crashed jangling to the floor. 'For goodness' sake take care,' I pleaded, 'look out for the tins. Grand promised to give up the trip-wires, but, oh dear, what about the police?' I rushed blindly up the stairs to stop Grand blowing her whistle.

She had lit the candle and was already out of bed, clutching the rattle and wearing the police whistle round her neck on a string.

There was a frightful crash below followed by a lot of noisy swearing. I shut our bedroom door.

'Good gracious, my pet, it's you. What an uproar! It's three o'clock. Where have you been?'

I sat on the sofa. 'We've been to a party at Ma Merrick's.'

'But Hilary never said you were going to a party?'

'Well we did, but I spent most of the time in the cloakroom, talking to someone called Doris. She said she was a hostess . . .' I sighed. 'She was lovely, and she wore a *backless* black velvet dress, very tight, and a pink and black feather boa.'

'Backless? How immodest! A hostess? Who could that be?' Grand asked, scratching herself.

'As I said, her name was Doris. She was sitting at the dressing-table, rubbing her face with a harefoot.'

She had licked her hair into kiss-curls and stuck them to her cheeks.

I had said, 'I do wish my face wasn't all wrong,' and she had said: 'It's not bad, but you're sallow—better try some of this—and you've got a rush of teeth to the head. You ought to go and see my uncle.'

She had written his address, and shown me 'how to make the best of what I'd got'.

There was another bang from below and Grand, who hadn't been paying much attention to me, pricked up her ears.

'She sounds a very stupid woman and rudely outspoken: what they call a flapper, I suppose, but what was Hilary doing?'

'When I left him he was going on and on to Betty about the last night at the Empire . . .'

'Oh yes, the last time he was home—such a fleeting visit! You had some infectious disease and were almost unconscious when he saw you in the sanatorium. The last night at the Old Empire! He was staying here. What a night that was!' she mused, gazing at the ostrich eggs which hung from the ceiling. 'It was all reported in the press. I bought the papers and pasted the cuttings in my scrapbook—only sentimental souvenirs, but how I love to read and re-read accounts of his boisterous exploits. The Prince of Wales was there in a box with Adeline Genée. On that last night the old so-called chuckers-out came back, Bunkle and Bungay. Dear me, he was more than a match for them.' She smiled indulgently. 'They threw him out *six* times, and chalked his coat with a sign, but he came back to hurrahs. He even confounded the police with his high jinks and climbed up on the stage. It said in one paper that the orchestra pit was very low and a smaller man couldn't have done it, but perhaps I shouldn't give his pranks away. . . . Ah! I remember all his favourites of the old days—Vesta Tilley, Dan Leno, Marie Lloyd . . .!'

'Oh do. Go on!' I begged.

'It was just high spirits. And once up there behind the footlights,' she continued proudly, 'with people cheering and hanging out of their boxes, he picked up the huge pots of palms, which formed a decoration on the stage, and hurled them at the audience.'

'Yes, I know, and Papa was telling Betty that he nearly killed some ruddy fool. The pots parted from the roots and earth flew all over people's heads and somebody's eye got . . .'

'But the *Daily Telegraph* reported that pots and trees were all fielded with remarkable dexterity. Come now, my pet, Holman rightly disapproved of tittle-tattle.'

We went out onto the landing. She wrapped her black kimono round her skinny legs and picked her way barefoot down the stairs.

Helen appeared from above dressed in red flannel. She was holding a poker and a candle. 'Oh mum, is it Master Hilary again? Is he playing the giddy goat?' Toothless she gazed at me. 'Look at Miss Diana: cross my heart, her face is all painted!'

'Painted? Come, come,' said Grand, creeping on and flapping her sleeves like an old black bat, 'she's a little flushed.'

'Hell's bells!' roared Papa. Tins shot across the hall as he kicked them through the drawing-room doorway. There was a terrific bang, followed by a noise of breaking glass. The piano wires were humming.

'Merciful heavens, what a shindy! My good Helen, this is no

concern of yours, you had better go to bed.' Grand glanced anxiously at me.

'Papa isn't feeling very well and I think he must have eaten something *bad*.'

'Calamity!' She clutched my arm. 'Where *did* I put that stomach-pump, the one my mother gave me when we went to Palestine? It sounds so *un*like a crush at Lady Perrick's, her buffet suppers are delicious.' She raised her voice, 'D'you hear, Helen? Poor Master Hilary is *seedy*.'

Helen sniffed and made her way upstairs.

Papa strode into the hall. 'Sorry, Mater—spilt something in the piano.'

'Poor boy! See how he staggers with fatigue!' Helen wasn't looking. 'It has clearly been far too long a day. Take my arm. Perhaps you'd like a little brandy?'

'Or vaseline or senna pods?' I ventured.

At the blue bedroom door I gave Papa the matches. Stooping to kiss Grand on the forehead: 'I'm O.K., Mater,' he said.

She clung to him with her candle dripping on the mat. 'God bless you, my precious boy.'

Once he had safely lit his gas and shut the door, she instructed me: 'Say your prayers and hop into bed in your chemise.' She tucked up her feet in the scratchy blanket on the sofa.

My pyjamas were still in my suitcase. I took off my confirmation dress and rolled it into a ball. I would give it to someone of the right age tomorrow. I yawned and was just about to snuff out the candle when the door was flung open by Papa. I drew the sheet over my shoulders to hide my bust-elastic.

'Some ruddy poodle-faking, interfering fool has mucked up my blueprints!' he stormed, smashing his fist into the ostrich eggs. They jiggled up and down. 'Crikey, I'd have thrashed my native boy and kicked him all the way back to the compound.'

'Oh, poor thing, I mean, poor you!' I said.

'Some unclean something, son of a pig-sucking, something fool,' he raved, and banged on the table, 'has wrecked a solid week's work, *tidied* up,' he made a face, 'and thrown every ruddy thing away.'

'Try not to fash yourself, dear boy—I know it's catastrophic. Tomorrow I will have a word with Helen. Holman allowed no servant to meddle in the studio and only *I* might use my little feather brush. Now remember, you're bilious and fatigued: I implore you, go to bed.'

'Calamitous,' she whispered, when at last he went away, 'she interfered unwittingly, of course, but the road to hell is paved with good intentions.'

'Is it a plan of a bridge or a canal, with lots of awful sums?'

'Not exactly,' she conceded, 'but so *intricate*: it's a design for an elaborate piece of baggage.'

'D'you mean a suitcase?' I choked.

'I see nothing comical about it, Diana. All the travelling caboodle he requires is weighed and placed carefully on the floor. Then the detailed outlines are meticulously drawn on sheets of paper—like Holman, your father is so *thorough*. Epsom salts, macassar oil, shoe-horns, brushes and quinine and flasks and shaving tackle; the plan for their disposal is marked to scale on blueprints. Dear me, I hope she hasn't thrown out the leather samples—they might do for polishing the door; and now I come to think of it, I believe I did see her with some graph papers in the kitchen. . . .'

I smothered my giggles in the pillow.

'It's ten o'clock, miss,' said Helen crossly, 'but seeing as you was up half the night I've let you lay in. The mistress went shopping, after her and I had a Little Talk. She said, if Miss Diana sleeps late, she won't want to spoil her luncheon, so there's no need for any breakfast; and Master Hilary, well! it's no concern of mine, but he's got a headache; so I didn't go in, I just put his cup of tea on the landing. I wouldn't set foot in his room, not after what the mistress said, because I'm not one to meddle. The mistress and others must have their little fancies—there was broken glass in the piano that I'll have to bury in the garden. If I put it out what would the dustman say?'

'I shouldn't worry,' I said.

As if it mattered!

'The mistress says you're to wash in the cloakroom; you can

fetch a kettle from the kitchen.' She broke off, staring: 'That's a queer bodice! And just look at the sheet.'

It was covered with rouge. 'Oh that!' I shrugged, it was no good explaining. 'I must unpack and wash my hair, because it's greasy. I don't want to use the cloakroom: I'd rather have a bath.'

'A bath! Master Hilary's in there every morning for two solid hours! What with breathing and swinging Indian clubs that break the windows, and all the fiddle-de-dee with tooth-picks and eye-baths and rubber syringes—what the mistress calls grooming Brother Ass—you'll never get in there. I was sweeping up tea-leaves this morning, "Cheer up, Helen," he said, when I told him *sharp* that I had such a lot to do, "Miss Diana will help you with the ironing." He didn't speak about his room. Too seedy.'

'Oh dear, I've burnt it *again*.' In a second the iron made a large black ace of spades on the shirt.

'Gracious, you'll have to patch it, and this one doesn't look much better. It's all spots,' said Helen, sniffing. 'So *that*'s how Miss Fowler taught you to iron?'

I felt hot and tired and my wet hair kept getting in my eyes. 'She only let me watch. The iron is so heavy and it gets dirty on the range. I don't see how anyone can iron a shirt on a table. Perhaps I should have wiped it first.' I stooped for a bit of paper from a pile in the fender.

'Now, out of my way, miss, please. I've got to fry this bit of shin, so I'd better start it early. Pity really, it would have made a nice jug of beef-tea.... You leave those filthy papers alone. I shall burn the lot. They were thrown out with the rubbish but I wouldn't soil my hands; cross my heart, I couldn't put them in the bin ...' She pulled the damper out.

'Oh do let's see.' I grabbed a handful and read the title: *La Vie Parisienne*.

'You put that down, miss. You give it to me.'

I was interested to see in the pictures the girls wore no elastic. 'Oh dear, what an awful smell ..'

'There goes the kitchen whistle and you've burnt another shirt!'

'Is that Diana?' Grand's voice quacked down the tube. 'Come, my pet: your father suggests we have a pow-wow.'

'When I returned from Hammersmith Market I wrote out an agenda,' said Grand. 'There are one or two items I feel we should discuss all together, as Diana's growing up. First: domestic economy, the organization and division of labour.' She adjusted her pince-nez and turned to Papa. 'Pay attention, dear.' He was reading, and puffing at a gasper.

'I'm afraid I'm no good at ironing,' I said. 'I'm terribly sorry, I'm afraid I've burnt some shirts and a . . .'

'Burnt a shirt! How vexatious!' She put on a prig's face.

'What the hell,' drawled Papa looking up from *Tit-bits*, 'why don't we get a dobey. I don't want the kid to be a slave.'

I liked him more than ever.

'A slave, how wrong you are! It is a feminine delight to tend the helpless male. The joy I had from darning and mending Holman's clothes. How he depended on me! But all good wives respond to such masculine appeals. Even Mrs. Carlyle was most touched by her husband's comic telegraphic message: "Send buttons by return of post."'

'I don't mind sewing and cleaning,' I said, 'I know Helen has an awful lot to do. But why don't we get a char?'

'My dear child, the cost—*sixpence* an hour! No, no, it's out of the question. The working classes work no longer. The more they're paid, the more they squander on such evils as betting. As Mr. Watts said, just before he died—alas! Holman and I called at number six that afternoon—the loyal old-fashioned servant has almost disappeared. We were all three diametrically opposed to the corrupt, demoralizing practice of paying by the hour. I consider it our duty . . .'

'Sixpence an hour isn't very much. Think what it costs to buy a dress.' I refrained from adding 'backless black velvet'.

'Kid's right,' said Papa, peeling a five-pound note off a wad from his wallet and handing it to Grand. To my surprise he tossed a few at me. 'Buy yourself some togs. Toodle-oo, I must go and see a man about a dog.'

I got up, as it seemed the pow-wow was over.

'After lunch I must go and telephone a friend,' I said.

Grand sat in a trance stroking the money. 'Yes, perhaps between us we have found the solution: a strong malleable girl, at *less* than sixpence an hour, and under constant supervision. I will have a Little Talk with Helen.'

It was very stuffy in the telephone booth and complicated putting in the penny.

'Hello, is that Mr. Corthorpe? Oh, this is Miss Hunt—Miss Holman-Hunt—I've got too many teeth. I should like to have some out this afternoon. No, they don't *ache*. I should have said it was your niece, yes, Doris, she said I should come to see you. What? Oh no! I may sound young but I'm not—I left school ages ago. Four o'clock? Oh good! I've got to do some shopping. Thank you *very* much. Yes of course I can take a taxi.'

'I've rather lost touch with Doris,' said Mr. Corthorpe, 'my sister says it's too bad how the hospital keeps her on night duty when others never take their turn. She's too good natured.'

'Oh yes, she's very kind,' I said.

'Open wide! Well young lady, *you* should have worn a plate, but even that might never have succeeded. I see what you mean, but if I remove, say, these four teeth—all perfectly sound,' he tapped them with his little mirror, 'for several months, perhaps for years, the gaps may be unsightly. In fact there is a risk that the remaining teeth may never pull together. Tut! It would be drastic and of course your parents would have to be informed.' He stood back and looked expectant.

'Oh no,' I gulped, 'not them, I'm an orphan. There's only me to say.'

'An orphan, young lady? Tut, *tut*, how very sad.' He pursed his lips and stared. 'But I suppose you have a guardian?'

'Sort of,' I admitted, taking time to think of something convincing, 'but he's blind and not quite right in the head. He never goes out because his keeper is lame.'

Please God and Fowler forgive me.

'Well, in that case—' Mr. Corthorpe dithered, 'in that case perhaps . . .' He rang a bell.

I took a taxi home and Grand opened the door. 'My dear child,' she gasped, falling back in horror, 'you've had an accident? Good gracious! What a lot of blood!'

'I've been to Doris's uncle,' I mumbled, spitting into a sopping scarlet rag.

'The scoundrel! What has he done to you? We must stanch the bleeding—Hilary!' she called Papa. 'Come at once. Calamity!'

'He's a very good dentist, so I had some teeth out,' I said.

'I can't understand it. Were your teeth *decayed*?'

'They were absolutely rotten,' I lied, hoping the means would justify the end.

'Crikey, what a stink!' said Papa. 'I suppose you had gas, like a cissy. I had some fangs out the other day—buckshee. The little poodle-faking ass wanted to give me an injection. There he was tugging away. "Give me the ruddy pliers," I said. The fool was sweating. I pulled out two and threw them on the floor. He hadn't got the nerve to charge.'

'You're wonderful, dearest,' said Grand, gazing up at him in wonder, 'how proud you make me feel.'

'I think I'll go and lie down,' I said, retching, 'I feel a bit sick.'

Because Papa thought I looked under the weather, I had been told to rest on Sunday afternoon. I could not do so and was impatiently waiting for Grand to come upstairs and get dressed for the party. At last she appeared, looking innocent enough.

'I'm livid, it's the ruddy limit!' I shouted, hugging Byron to my flattened chest. 'It's mine—it's leather bound and grandfather gave it me for Christmas.'

The gaps in my teeth made it difficult to speak. 'Dishgraceful! Pages and pages cut out and all this beastly Indian ink blotting the paper.' My tears splashed on the mutilated book. 'Look what you've done to *The Forsyte Saga* and . . .'

'I've never heard of Hugh Walpole or this Galsworthy man,' Grand said calmly, putting a bundle of stuff on the table.

Rudely, I retorted: 'Well you've heard of Byron and I'll never forgive you, never!'

'Come, come, that's no tone to use to Grand. Try to remember who you are.'

'How *can* I forget! And how I wish I wasn't.' I threw the Hugh Walpole on the floor.

She frowned. 'I can only think it is the shock of losing your teeth,' she shuddered, 'and the dreadful haemorrhage that followed, which has caused a mental aberration. You should wipe your mouth, I see it's frothing.' A pink stain joined a smudge of rouge on the sheet. 'Indeed I have heard of Lord Byron and it distresses me to think that such an *evil* man should be your hero. I know that Holman would agree.'

'I don't care a fig if he was bad and I don't believe it. Look what you've done to this sonnet. It said "Love . . ."'

'Love, you call it love! Mawkish sentiment you mean—impure and unlawful. As Holman used to quote, "Lilies that fester smell far worse than weeds".'

'Unlawful? What about you and *your* love and *your* marriage? Even Fowler said it was illegal.'

When I looked up I could see I'd gone too far. Her eyes were gimlets but she clenched her fists and recovered her control.

'How hateful.'

I flushed with shame and started sobbing. 'I'm terribly sorry.' I threw my arms round her waist. What could I do to make amends?

'Poor child,' she sighed, 'corrupted innocence. The modern novel is to blame. Come and be forgiven, let bygones be bygones.' She patted my head. 'Keep what's left of Lord Byron if you will. Mr. Trelawny told Holman that even his swimming was a fraud. He described the feeble effort, the fiasco . . .'

'Oh well, anyone can swim.'

'So you would imagine. Cyril, of course, showed no aptitude at all, but my Hilary is a very fine swimmer.' She did up the clasp of her cloak, having during this scene somehow got ready for the party. 'Your father won a life-saving medal; I expect he was too modest to tell you. The dear brave boy dived fully clad into the river to save a Burmese woman from drowning. He tried to grab her by the hair but it was oily.'

'How revolting. Then what happened?'

'She kept slipping away but he dragged her to the bank exhausted and then, of course, left her to his servant. Alas, the native boy saw his master's topi floating down the river and rightly fearing a beating, he dived in to retrieve it, leaving the wretched girl face down in the mud.'

'Oh no! D'you mean she died after all?' Tears started in my eyes.

'Now my pet, this is no time for further tantrums; unless we exert ourselves the scouts will steal a march on us and that would never do.' She started untying the bundle. 'In the omnibus on our way to St. Paul's I saw you smile at the conductor. Poor child, perhaps you did not hear his observation? If only those raw infected cavities would heal—but I have had an inspiration for the meantime. You can wear a yashmak! It would be so discourteous to distress or agitate our friends.'

'But I want to wear my new green dress from Selfridge's,' I objected.

'No, no, my pet; think how exciting! You can be a Turkish slave and wear a yashmak. Here are the trousers, bangles and anklets, and the gold ear-rings that the model wore in *After Glow* and *The Bride of Bethlehem* head-dress.'

'But what is a yashmak?' I asked, feeling suspicious.

'A veil worn below the eyes. We will darken your brows and lashes with the kohl from your museum. We must spare our guests embarrassment, you see.'

'I should rather like to paint my eyes again,' I said, glancing in the mirror. I reached for the trousers. For once Grand had had a sensible idea.

Neither Papa nor his pals had turned up at the party and the last visitor had gone. Grand and I were sitting by the fire.

'I suppose Turkish slaves never see what they eat,' I said, blindly nibbling some stale Dundee, with my veil tossed over my eyes.

'Should I tell the boy-scouts to clear? No, perhaps not, in case . . .' Grand dipped her crumpled handkerchief into the kettle and squeezed it over a plate. 'To freshen them we will sprinkle the sandwiches with water.' Their corners wouldn't lie down: the bread had curled and parted from the cheese.

A boy-scout's harassed face looked round the door. 'There's

some rowdy blokes comin' up the front luggin' some 'eavy boxes.'

'What a commotion,' Grand protested at the squeals and roars. Seeing her frantic signs, I pulled down my yashmak to hide my mouth full of cake.

'Here we are, Mater,' said Papa. 'The others couldn't come, only Pongo, Dot and Carry.'

'Ever so sorry but better late than never,' said Dot. 'Salaam and pleased to meet you.'

'How-de-do. Any friends from our Empire are very welcome here. My grand-daughter will add some hot water to the tea.' With a roguish smile Grand led them to the table. 'Perhaps coffee would have been appropriate from a Turkish slave. May I press you to a sandwich?'

'Crikey, we don't want *tea*. I brought a case of bubbly from the club.' Papa heaved a large scratchy crate onto the polished piano. There was a sound of splitting wood as he wrenched the lid off the case and tossed some straw bottle jackets in the air.

'Moët Chandon champagne, what a treat!' Grand cried clapping her hands. 'Our Turkish slave must fetch the glasses.'

'Gosh, in that rig-out you should be doing a stomach dance,' said Dot, wriggling her behind. 'You know, wiggle, waggle, *pom*.'

'My pet, not the Venetian goblets!'

'They'll do. Fetch the gramophone, kid, and we'll show them how to Charleston.'

'Before we trip the light fantastic, might we be privileged to see the pictures?' asked Pongo politely.

'Oh yes, Mrs. Hunt,' said Carry, 'while we're here you must see my Patty's work. This was the calendar she did last year . . .' Two faceless black cats with their tails entwined were sitting on a horseshoe under a crescent moon. 'And this is the one she sent to Auntie Iris—Pip, Squeak and Wilfred.'

Pongo broke the silence: 'Jolly good! I think they're jolly good!'

Carry was delighted: 'I think they're dinky. When Patty leaves school, she wants to study art in gay Paree. Mrs. Hunt, do you think that's a good idea?'

'Alas, in spite of her brilliant heritage, my own grandchild shows no special gift,' said Grand, turning from the calendars and smiling consolingly at me, 'but were she, or even your daughter, to develop one, I would wish it to be unsullied by the evil, indeed *licentious* influence of a foreign school. When my beloved husband went to Paris he was aghast at the depravity he found, and deeply shocked by the immorality of the masters, not to mention the students. Great men like my husband and Mr. Watts kept their pure, English talents untainted; but in these misguided days the Tate Gallery demeans itself so far as to hang all that foreign rubbish from the Courtauld Bequest; even here, our children's innocence may be exposed to the insidious French corruption of ideals. I forbid Diana to waste her time on the daubs of a madman, although I trust the dear child is not so warped as to admire a crude study of a dirty kitchen chair . . .'

'I suppose you mean the Van Gogh,' I broke in; 'but you and Papa agreed I could go to school abroad and I'm going to Italy next month—Papa said so this morning.'

'The Eyeties' art is A.1,' announced Papa, getting up again to fill our goblets, 'but it's a waste of time to learn the lingo. The kid wants to go to Florence.'

'Is Florence on the Po? Ah no,' giggled Dot.

'That's a jolly good portrait,' said Pongo, staring at *The Birthday*.

'It is most gratifying that you recognize the sitter,' Grand said coyly. 'Alas, no one would wish to paint me now; perhaps I should wear a yashmak to disguise the ravages of time.'

'Don't say that! Think of Whistler's portrait of his mother,' said Pongo, with a gallant bow.

'Don't mention Mr. Whistler or his work to me!' Grand cried, wagging her finger. 'Small wonder that his pictures show no profundity of thought; he was such a superficial man. Pictures indeed! As if such a word describes his loose, trashy smears of paint! I recall the disgraceful levity he showed when dear Holman, ever solicitous, commiserated with him over his well-merited financial crises. "Save your sympathy for my creditors, dear fellow. Pity the poor devils who won't get their money." Holman was profoundly shocked.'

I yawned. Grandpa Holman's eyebrows were always up in his hair.

'Well now, I fear I must leave you, as I have just remembered my boy-scouts will be waiting for their shillings. Diana can show you the rest of the pictures. My friends tell me she does it very well and can entertain you with capital anecdotes about my husband.' She shook hands and said good-bye.

'Whew!' whistled Dot, before the door closed. 'Talk about high-brow . . .'

'Yes, come on kid, do your stuff and be the Mater,' urged Papa.

I had already torn off my yashmak and swigged my second goblet: I got up and imitated Grand. 'One day I went down to the studio with my little feather brush—only *I* was allowed to meddle—and what do you think I found?'

I was sure I looked provocative. I paused and felt a bit giddy. My gums were throbbing.

'What?' they cried.

'Alas, Holman, disgustingly intoxicated, rolling on the floor with a model. How catastrophic! Are you seedy? Have you forgotten who you are? Where are the senna pods, the vaseline . . .' I collapsed, hysterical with giggles.

'Kid's tight,' said Papa. 'Don't you dare poke fun at the Guvnor.'

'I'm terribly sorry,' I gasped, 'but I've always hoped one day Grand would tell us something *bad*.'

'It's you who are bad,' teased Papa, 'at least that's what that old bee Fowler used to say: "I don't know, sir, I'm sure, but sometimes she acts real bad!"'

'What a shame! I should drink some water,' said Pongo kindly, handing me another dusty goblet, filled with gritty dregs from the kettle.

'I won't hear a word against the Guvnor,' said Papa, 'he was a real sport. He paid up my debts and got me out of dozens of jams without splitting to the Mater.' He flicked ash on the Persian rug and looked towards the door. 'There was a bit of a dust-up, you know, long ago, but well, I don't think there was anything in it.'

'Oh, do tell,' I pleaded.

'I suppose there's no harm,' he said, lowering his voice and drinking some more champagne. 'An old bee, my Aunt Emily, wrote the Guvnor a proper stinker after she read something in a rag called *Household Words*—I think it belonged to Dickens. It was some story about the Guvnor being a bit of a dog and seducing his favourite model, Emma Watkins. Crikey, she was a stunner, if ever there was one. He painted her as the Temptress in *The Hireling Shepherd.* She's giving the lamb a green apple.'

'That's one thing to call it!' Dot interrupted, winking at me. 'Pore thing, I expect it got a pain in its tummy.'

'Anyway,' went on Papa, 'he and Johnnie Millais got off with her at Ewell and somehow got her to come to London. They were all potty about her, the Guvnor and Millais and Stevens and Rossetti; but it was the poor old Guvnor who got the blame—her mother kicked up a shindy and it all got in this ruddy paper. Old Wilkie Collins—his brother married one of Dickens's daughters—said it was a rotten libel and told the Guvnor to write them a stinker. Dickens wrote back and said it would be best to let sleeping dogs lie, and that's just what he did, and of course the Mater burnt all the letters. Perhaps there wasn't much in it.'

'Oh, I do hope there was,' I said, 'I think it's thrilling and I do hope he . . .'

'Diana!' called Grand, from the other side of the door. 'If our guests will excuse you, I think perhaps it's time we went to bed.'

'But it's only eight o'clock and we haven't played the gramophone!'

'You'd better hop it, kid,' said Papa. 'You still look under the weather. An early night for once won't do you any harm.'

'Isn't it splendid that I'm going to Italy?' I said to Grand. Avoiding the paint-work, we slowly climbed the stairs.

'Your father is wonderful,' she said, taking my arm. 'He has made a very wise decision. In Florence at least you cannot fail to learn the appreciation of art and I have suggested that after that, you spend a year in a *gemütlich* family in Prussia. My sisters and I had a fräulein, who came from somewhere on the Elbe.'

This didn't sound a good idea to me but for the present I decided to ignore it.

'Don't you think if I'm going abroad for so long, I should go home and say good-bye to grandfather and all my friends?'

'My pet, I have told you before that *this* is your home and your father and I have decided a visit to that sombre household is not so necessary now that your other grandmother is dead.'

CHAPTER SEVEN

BECAUSE of fog, my boat from Hamburg arrived several hours late at Southampton. It was snowing, and it was one o'clock in the morning when I arrived on my aunt's doorstep in Hyde Park Square. I rang again.

'It's so cold, you'd better go,' I said to the cabby, to whom I had given my last half-crown.

'Who's there?' asked uncle Hubert's voice through the letter-box.

'It's Diana.'

'Diana? My dear child, but you're in Germany. Wait and I'll unlock the door.'

Stamping snow off his boots the cabby lugged in my belongings. Uncle Hubert looked like a pixie in bulging bedsocks and a tasselled nightcap pulled over his ears.

'I sailed in the *Europa*, it's the biggest ship in the world.'

I threw my beret on the table.

'Whatever is it, Hubert?' called my aunt, from the landing.

'It's Diana, back from Germany,' he said.

'Good heavens!' she cried, billowing down the stairs in a cloud of pink swansdown and lace. 'My sweetest, a kiss!'

I grinned with pleasure and ran my fingers through my hair.

'You *have* improved! Still a little too tall, perhaps, but dear Mother would have been delighted. Smile again and let me see your teeth. A miracle! See, Hubert, how they've grown together? Don't stand there doing nothing! Is that her dressing-case? Heavens, how shabby, and poor lamb, your cheek is frozen. Come and get warm by the fire.'

Grandmother had come to life again.

'I'd better take her bag up to Tom's room as he's still up at Cambridge,' grunted uncle Hubert, limping up the stairs.

'Oh do let me!' I grabbed it from him.

Aunt's own room was a warm, rosy taffeta bower. Golden cherubs, clutching electric lamps in their fists, fluttered from the ceiling and hovered round the bed. It all smelt delicious. When I looked more closely, I saw that her face was painted white with some lotion, and her wavy hair was stuck with tortoiseshell-combs and bound with plaited ribbon. She wore cotton gloves and a pink rubber strap under her chin.

'D'you always sleep in gloves?' I asked, seating myself on a sheepskin rug.

'Yes, of course, and so will you at my age, unless you want wrinkles and horrid brown spots like Mabel Pritchard—quite disastrous, my dear. Her hands look hideous playing bridge.'

'I think I'll toddle along,' said uncle Hubert, with a longing look towards the door.

'Don't be so stupid, Hubert. Of course you must stay and hear her amusing adventures. Sit down over there and if your foot hurts, put it up on the sofa.' She kissed me lightly on the forehead. 'Now, my love, begin.'

'Well, for weeks and weeks no letters came from Papa and he owed the Baronin a frightful lot of money. My own bank account was so overdrawn that even the manager complained, so I wrote and said he'd better close it—it was just a dress allowance. I wrote and wrote to Papa, and every morning it was ghastly, because they were all looking for an answer and it never came. Of course he *was* eight thousand miles away.'

'You should have gone on writing to your father,' said my aunt, greasing her eyelids.

'Well, I didn't want to make any trouble, but we waited so long, I thought he must be dead—he's quite all right really,' I added quickly, seeing her horrified expression, 'but I think he must be *bankrupt*.'

'What rubbish! Are you listening, Hubert? Disgraceful! I told you he'd gone quite mad—I shall certainly write to . . .'

'It would be most unbecoming for us to discuss or criticize her father,' broke in uncle Hubert, frowning.

'Well at last, only a week or two ago, this came,' I rummaged in my bag, 'but no cheque and no letter.'

'Let me see. How too extraordinary!' She reached out for the tattered cable and read aloud: '"Return to Grand and get a job."'

'Does he mean earn your own living? I've never heard of such a thing! And as for living with that dotty old woman in a damp mausoleum with no servants, it all sounds *most* unsuitable to me.'

Grandmother was talking.

'And where else do you suggest she should live?' asked uncle Hubert, carefully adjusting one woollen bed-sock over a lumpy bandage. 'For a young girl your own father's house is scarcely more suitable now.'

She bit her lip and stared at the fire.

'Oh dear, it's *most* unfortunate. What would Mother say? You know, we should love to have you here, but this year it's out of the question. Of course it will do for a few days, but you see Priscilla's coming out, and as this year, you, my poor lamb, aren't being presented, it would be so terribly awkward.'

'Do tell, how is Priscilla? Better out than in?'

'Exquisite—quite exquisitely lovely. The way she puts her clothes on . . .' My aunt threw up her white cotton hands. 'The season's only begun, but the invitations, the dances, the parties . . . the house is besieged by young men! And do you know Simon . . .'

'Is she engaged?'

'Let us hope not to Simon,' said uncle Hubert. 'There's bad blood there—his mother's a Blodweb.'

'Of course she has winged *several* birds,' my aunt said darkly, flicking a hair off her lap.

I could see Priscilla pretending not to notice the wounded pheasants, with their drooping wings and their heads down, crouching in the grass, knowing the one she picked would be a runner.

'Talking of birds,' said uncle Hubert, 'your aunt doesn't want a decoy on the pond just now.'

'Don't be so stupid, Hubert. What a thing to say! Heavens, it's two o'clock and Priscilla has a lot of debutantes lunching here tomorrow. Hubert and I are going to the Berkeley and you, my love, can have something on a tray. Now, don't wake her up! Dear child, your turn will come.'

Very quietly, I opened the door between Tom's room and the nursery. I found it completely changed. Animals no longer romped round the walls, which instead were painted custard. The shiny story books and the row of silly dolls had all been swept away. Some glass tulips sprouted from a pot, and a Lalique vase filled with shell flowers stood on a lacquer table. A Medici print of 'Primavera' had replaced the one of Jesus in a nightgown talking to the rabbits. A shimmering dress of green and silver sequins hung like a beautiful herring from a hook. I peered closer: it even had a tail.

Shaking with excitement, I opened Priscilla's bedroom door. The light shone in to show her sitting up in bed.

'Hello, Di,' she said. 'I knew you'd come. I heard everything. I was sitting on the stairs. Sit here.' She patted the eiderdown. Her hair was pinned in little curls and her face was lovely.

'So you're having a wonderful time,' I said.

'It's ghastly,' she shuddered, 'but I have to pretend I like it because it's so expensive.'

'Aren't they odd to pay so much to get rid of us?' I said.

'Daddy looks everyone up in Burke—not that I care; but Tom wants to marry Wendy Malcolm. You know Young Uncle's married and living in the old Manor up on the hill. I loathe young men and I'm madly in love with Henry.'

'Henry who?'

'You must *promise* not to tell—Henry Wildash. You know, he married Lettice Spragg.'

'You *can't* mean the Major?'

'Why not? He's only forty, but she had pots of money. If only she'd married Mr. Duncan.'

As her fingernails were buffed and pointed, she chewed the pad of her thumb.

'But does the Major know?' I was astounded.

'He doesn't know a thing.' She sighed and lay back against the pillows. 'I met him again at grandmother's funeral.'

'But he's so old!'

'Old! At that rate, so is your Papa, but—oh dear, I swore I wouldn't tell you!'

'But he can't marry. Can he?'

'You wait and see. You know what stepmothers are? I expect it's her who sent that telegram to say you'd got to get a job and I bet Lettice is foul to Elsie.'

'I hope she is. I don't care a fig for Elsie.' I was furious and kicked my shoes across the room.

'S-shush! If Mummy hears us—'

'She'll be livid! Oh, why didn't they drown us in a bucket.' I stared wildly at the lacquer wardrobe.

'Sh, don't! You always say such dreadful things.' She flinched and turned her head away.

My aunt was lying on the drawing-room sofa, wearing a tea-gown. 'While I was having my treatment, my masseuse suggested that in case your letter went astray, you should go and call on Mrs. H-H. before arriving with your luggage—I'm sure the bed won't be aired.'

'I would also suggest,' said uncle Hubert, 'that we consider some career. I had a word with my friend Rouge Dragon at the college, hoping there might be an opening; it seems, however, that even for research females are not welcomed. Some quite well-bred women become governesses you know, and hospital nursing has become a more respectable profession.'

'Oh no, that sounds terribly dull,' cried Priscilla. 'With her figure I think Di should be a mannequin. In the *Evening Standard* they're offering thirty shillings a week at Reville's, and someone else wants pretty girls to be photographed in hats and shoes at five shillings an hour.'

'Really Priscilla, you had better go and lie down if you can only contribute such frivolous suggestions. You are doubtless unaware that *mannequins* is just a euphemism—' grunted uncle Hubert.

'Oh yes, Tom lent me a wonderful book called *Poule de Luxe*; if I were Di . . .'

'My manicurist is *almost* a lady,' broke in my aunt, viewing her white hands with satisfaction.

'I refuse to spend my life doing people's nails. I'd rather be a char!'

'My sweet, *do* try and show a little more co-operation . . .' The telephone rang. My aunt unhooked the receiver and clamped it to her ear. We could discern Young Uncle's voice, very faintly.

'Hello!' she shouted. 'Oh, it's you, darling! What? Yes, of course. . . . Good—Father will pay? Rabbit and thing? For heaven's sake, Hubert, don't sit there doing nothing, find a pencil. Gabittas and Thring? Yes, I'll go tomorrow. How clever you are . . .'

I relaxed while my future was decided.

'Well, thank heavens that's settled and we can go and dress for dinner. I wrote to Father, and he says she's to take a course of secretarial training as she speaks German and Italian. Why didn't it occur to us before?'

Always I seemed to be ringing door-bells. This time there was no answer, so I walked back into Melbury Road. I peered through the railings and seeing a dim glow in the kitchen, groped my way down to the area. The steps were covered with slush and leaves —no King Solomons had swept them lately for potato soup and half-a-crown. Skirting the coal-house door and the dustbins, I rapped with cold knuckles on a pane.

A glimmer from the range showed Helen asleep in her Windsor chair. The cat lay like a black pool in her apron. I tapped a second time. She spilt the cat and got up to open the door—cautiously at first, until her eyes were accustomed to the light from the street lamp.

'Who's that? Gracious, what a start you gave me!'

'It's me—Diana,' I said.

'But I thought she was in foreign parts. Aren't you tall, miss, and haven't you changed? Wait, I'll come up to the front.'

'Don't let's bother. It's warmer down here.' I sniffed the usual stale cabbage.

She poked the sluggish fire. 'Burn now, will you! I don't like to use another match.' She knelt and blew through the bars. 'Burn now, do.'

It did at last and she lit the gas with a pop.

'Brutes!' she cried, stamping her feet. 'Brutes! Look at them everywhere.' The floor was heaving with beetles.

'Oh well, they're only the black ones.' I trod here and there to crack them underfoot. 'The frescoes are very faded. You can scarcely read "Hitch your wagon to a star." I hope Grand is all right.' I ran my finger round the ace of spades on the table. 'What a burn that was.'

'She is and she isn't,' said Helen. 'Most days she's in bed, but she gets dressed for a funeral, and last week she paid a call on the Princess, but she never takes a cab. "It's not safe," I said to Miss Gladys, "her memory's gone." She reads *The Times* every day over and over but doesn't open half the letters, and, well, she messes on with a lot of fiddle-de-dee. Cross my heart, how I wish Mr. Hilary was back: all she wants is a letter from him. Of course she won't see him again. "I want to die, Helen," she said. "I want to join the Master." There's days when she's talking to herself. I'm not one to meddle, but her room is, well . . .' She gave the range another savage poke.

'Oh dear, it sounds even worse than usual! What about the Sunday parties?'

'The lads won't come. One or two people call and, unless she's dressed, I go up and say: "Not at home, madam."'

'I see.' I couldn't see at all. For a while I was silent. 'I'm coming to live here but I shan't be any trouble as I shall be out all day at an office.'

'Coming to live here, miss? That wouldn't do at all! It's no concern of mine but I'd say you'd far better stay with that aunt of yours—your mother's sister.'

'It's impossible, I've got to live here, it's orders. Papa sent a cable.'

'You stay with your aunt, miss,' she repeated.

'I can't.' Nothing would induce me to confess to her that I wasn't wanted. 'She's got a catching disease. They're all going away so you must help me.'

'Well, it's no concern of mine,' said Helen, tipping up the

wretched cat, 'you'd better go and see the mistress. It's been one of her bad days so I shouldn't stay long.' She lit a candle with a spill.

Grand was sitting in bed hooded in a blanket. In two years her face had shrunk to a skull.

'Hello Grand, how are you?' I shivered as I bent to kiss her – just an old tortoise, a slice of life poking from a shell.

She drew back in distaste. 'How stupid of Helen not to say it was you! She's getting very absent-minded. As you can see I'm not at home.' She waved a claw at the chaos of unopened letters, scrapbooks and diaries round the bed. 'Don't sit in that chair. It's Holman's and he'll be up from the studio as soon as he's finished the donkey.'

'Your nails look very Chinese,' I said, nervously backing away. They were discoloured and twisted and, except for a few that had broken, at least two inches long. I moved over to the sofa and pushed some rubbish aside.

She ignored me and, putting on her pince-nez, picked up a book on Egypt. The clock had stopped. I began folding some disordered copies of *The Times*. Amongst the unopened letters was mine but none with an Indian stamp.

'Have you heard from Papa? He says I'm to come and live with you.'

'A likely story!' she snapped, giving me a hostile stare. 'I have no accommodation and my staff is overworked.'

'But he sent a cable,' I protested, searching in my bag. 'You don't seem very pleased to see me.'

'Under the circumstances I really cannot say I am. You'd better go now, Norah. It's very sad but, you must realize, there is nothing more to say.'

Norah was my mother's name. I began to shout: 'I'm not Norah, I'm Diana! I'm not – I'm not!'

'Diana indeed! You can't deceive us, we know the child's abroad.'

'No she isn't! I'm here, I'm Diana.'

How could I prove it?

Helen came in. 'I expect the mistress is tired. Out of my way now, miss, you'd better get along.' She added in a whisper: 'See? Sometimes we have our little fancies.'

'How often must I remind you, Helen, to tell all visitors when I'm indisposed,' Grand complained.

I left them and went to sit on the landing. It was more peaceful thinking in the dark.

'This is my *home*,' I said aloud.

By the time Helen came out with the candle my plans were made. I hope that my voice was firm, like Fowler's.

'I'll return with my luggage this evening. I shall come today as I start work in an office tomorrow. The blue Morris room will do—the one Papa had—and you could light a fire. There's one other thing,' I added, blushing. 'You must show her this cable from Papa and tell her to give me some money. I shall need the bus-fare to Baker Street and back and must pay for my lunch every day.'

'Money?' Even by candle light I could see she was aghast. The air was so cold that our breath was cloudy. 'I'll do my best, miss: but Rome wasn't built in a day.' We shook hands and then I walked back to collect my belongings.

'Here I am like a bad penny, Helen.' I shook hands again. 'There's not much luggage; that's my gramophone and this box is only records and books.'

'A gramophone, miss? You can't play that noisy machine!'

I paid the cabby out of my tip from uncle Hubert, who had said smiling: 'I'm sure Mrs. H-H. was delighted to see her only grandchild again.'

'I think, miss,' said Helen, sniffing, 'that you and I had better have a Little Talk. The mistress is settled and I've waited for my cup of tea.'

'Yes, let's go and sit by the range.' I followed her candle, through the freezing hall and down the stairs, to the kitchen.

'Cross my heart, it wasn't easy,' she said, scooping the cat off her Windsor chair. 'I couldn't light a fire; the chimney's never been swept and who could carry up the coals even if there was enough? There's been no fire since the master died in that bed. I expect it's damp, and you mustn't turn on the gas, because of the leak. I'll put a clean sheet outside Mondays, but I won't come in. I'm not one to meddle.'

'Oh that's all right. I like cleaning.' I plucked up courage: 'D'you think she really knows it's *me*?'

'Well,' said Helen, pouring some more hot water into the teapot, 'I do and I don't. It's no concern of mine, but you're changed, miss, in two years you've changed very much. There's a look of your mother—I needn't say more.'

'But everyone else says I'm much more like Papa,' I protested.

'There's a *look*,' she said again, 'it's your teeth what's done it, and, if I was you, I wouldn't sit under the light. Your voice is the same, a bit hoarse, but what the eye can't see . . .'

'Oh dear, it all sounds very difficult. . . . Is there any sugar?' The cat looked thin. 'Did you ask about the money?'

'I did and I didn't. A shilling a day. I'll put it out with your breakfast by the gong.'

'But that won't be nearly enough! The bus-fares alone are eightpence, and that leaves only fourpence for lunch. What about stamps and toothpaste?'

'Well, miss,' she poured herself another cup of tea, 'if you walk home you can save a fourpenny ride—it's the best I can do. There's potatoes and tea and candles and soap and bones and oatmeal and semolina and washing and gracious knows what fiddle-de-dee out of what's left from a pound. Thirteen shillings I make it and that won't go far.'

'Thank goodness I'll be out to lunch on Sundays.' I stopped short, remembering my aunt had a disease. 'If I had a latch key it would save a lot of trouble.'

'A latch key and you seventeen! It would save my legs but you'll have to talk to the mistress.' She got up and pushed in the dampers and then strained the tea-leaves and put them on a bit of paper. 'This lot'll do tomorrow if I dry them overnight on the range. Out of my way, miss, please. I lock up at eight and then I hang the bells. After that you won't get in, so it's no good playing the giddy goat.'

'If I can't get out I *must* play the gramophone.' I rinsed the kitchen cups under the tap.

'What you do, miss, is no concern of mine, but the big rooms is underneath the mistress and the Morris room, as you call it, is right next door and all the others is locked. I suppose there's the attics and they're no colder than the rest, but in all these years since the master died, no one's set foot in them.'

I arranged my gramophone, my records and my books up in the attic on a trunk. It bore Grandpa Holman's initials and was labelled 'NOT WANTED ON VOYAGE'. There were some drawings of great-aunt Fanny amongst a lot of other rubbish.

Having sold my plaited pearls for thirty shillings, I bought a packet of Woodbines, and plenty of candles which I stuck into old Bovril bottles from the dustbin.

A gigantic rocking-horse stood in the corner; he must have been specially made for Step-uncle Cyril, Big Aunt and Papa, when they were children. Horses had always alarmed me and this one proved no exception. When my torch first caught him in its beam, I was shocked by his evil expression. His ferocious upper lip snarled and twisted over huge, chipped, savage yellow teeth. His nostrils were red and flared. He was angry at being disturbed because the attic belonged to him.

I was dismayed to find an enemy installed and determined to get possession. For at least two days the problem occupied my mind, while I shivered over my macaroni pudding in the hall or struggled with my typing lessons at the office. When I decided to ignore him I found it impossible to do as, even under sheets of paper, his presence was overpowering.

At last I tied his face in a bag and knotted the tape below his eyes. It was a boot-bag made by Fowler long ago. 'Now you're a Turkish mare eating wholesome oats out of a yashmak and your name is Fatima,' I said. When I pulled her tail she nodded; then the attic belonged to me.

After supper I would lie across Fatima's back rocking and swaying to the music and singing softly out of tune: 'And he'll be big and strong, the Man I Love.' He would be cleaner than Timothy and look like Ramon Novarro. We would make love and read Byron together and eat delicious meals.

If I played something dramatic, Fatima reared and plunged amongst shadows fighting on the wall. My feet in the stirrups and clinging to her mane, I rode her with abandon, swinging the huge arcs of the rockers back and forth to their tips, so that we were propelled across the room leaving stripes in the dust which covered the floor.

On very cold nights I would dance: 'Dance, dance, dance little lady.' 'Charleston, Charleston, Charleston.' Sometimes smoking cigarettes, I read in silence, with *The Times* or my book propped against Fatima's ears. The candles went out one by one and now and then I fell asleep on the floor curled in some blankets. I dreamt of food: dressed crab and whipped cream on chocolate soufflé, treacle tart and . . .

In the morning, sneezing with dust and stiff from the boards, I would hobble down to wash at the sink and, snatching my shilling from under the Burmese gong, rush to work without eating any porridge.

'You look very anaemic, Miss Hunt,' Miss Smith, the office principal, would say, 'and you're so drowsy in the afternoons. I always tell my girls that it pays to have a good lunch.'

For fourpence at the A.B.C., I could buy suet roll and a pennyworth of cream, baked beans on toast or devilled sardines. I never left a tip. If I did without lunch to save up for some essential from the chemist, I went to sit in the church in George Street. The candles under the Madonna looked warm. I sat watching them glow, in a hungry dream. Fowler would have called it 'mooning'.

In April the spring came, and I enjoyed my Sunday walk across the park, through the lovers and shrivelled snowdrops, to lunch with my aunt in Hyde Park Square.

'My sweetest!' she cried, 'why wear that frowsty old frock on such a fine day? And heavens, your shoes are quite shabby!'

'I sold my summer clothes in Hamburg to buy my ticket home because I couldn't ask the Baronin for money.'

I brushed my skirt which did look rather dusty in the sun.

'You do look a frump! What would Mother say? You must buy a light coat and skirt at Harrods and a silk dress and some foulard blouses.'

'But Mummy, I told you poor Di has only a shilling a day – no allowance – and she's so tall that none of my clothes will do . . .' Priscilla was wearing her pleated crêpe-de-chine.

'A shilling a day! Hubert, d'you hear? Don't sit there doing nothing!'

'What's that?' uncle Hubert looked up crossly from a dirty bit of parchment.

'A shilling a day. Disgraceful! And no answer to any of my letters. I heard by pure accident the other day that he's in Hong Kong!' She went to her satinwood bureau. 'Here's a cheque for Easter, darling. Spend it on dresses and tell Mrs. H-H. that pin money is essential. Of course Mother never liked her but I suppose it's true she has a lot of fascinating friends?'

'Mummy, I told you, poor Di never meets anyone at all. There's no telephone and she doesn't know people's addresses. While Tom's at Cambridge she ought to come and live here . . .'

'I feel at the end of my tether!' cried my aunt, pouring herself another glass of Madeira. 'The middle of the Season and parties every night—too much!'

'Di's got lots of young men abroad. I think she ought to go back at once and get married . . .'

'My dear Priscilla,' said uncle Hubert severely, 'you make far too many frivolous suggestions.'

'Yes, my dear, what use as husbands are foreigners and Roman Catholics?' My aunt waved a Turkish cigarette and its smoke left a query in the air.

'Perhaps we should put an advertisement in the paper, "Protestant Bride of Seventeen Heiress or Bankrupt Failed for Bank of England",' I said. Priscilla and I burst into giggles.

'It's no laughing matter! Children are too extraordinary! What was that about the Bank? I must write to Father. I thought it was all *settled* . . .'

'Di says that shorthand is like Chinese and all the other girls are ghastly,' said Priscilla.

'I'm afraid I'm not very good at the office and Miss Smith is very cross.'

'This is grave news indeed, my dear,' said uncle Hubert, 'your grandfather paid a lot of money for your indenture. However you have at last been accepted as a *candidate* for the Foreign Department of the Bank of England? I venture to think he will be very gratified at that.'

'Oh no, it's all off!' I explained. 'Last Saturday I went to tea with the Montagu Normans—I hadn't seen them for ages but I met them on Campden Hill . . '

'Now that *is* interesting,' said my aunt, 'why didn't you tell me before?' She turned to uncle Hubert: 'You see I have to drag out every word!'

'Well, when it was time to go I said to Mr. Norman: "I'm coming to work in your bank," and he stared and said: "But that is out of the question." He had added, while solemnly stroking his beard: "I must think of my clerks, and the bank is no place for a Botticelli angel."'

'Out of the question?' she cried.

'And on Monday, Miss Smith got a message to say the bank wouldn't have me after all.'

'How disastrous! You must have made the worst possible impression, but don't worry, my dear,' my aunt added kindly. 'I shan't dream of telling Father.'

When I got home Helen said that Grand had been up for several hours, turning out the drawing-room as if she were expecting to have a party. She had tied or pasted labels on all the vases and cabinets and pictures saying: "Now Helen, this belongs to Master Hilary and this was *given* to him, don't you forget, and this is Miss Diana's.'

'It's no concern of mine,' grumbled Helen, 'but cross my heart, when the day comes, what *will* Miss Gladys say—you know she's adopted a little girl?'

'Yes, isn't it exciting!'

'That's not what the mistress calls it,' she said, sniffing.

'I think it's far nicer for Big Aunt to have a baby than all those cats. Grand says there were holes cut in the doors to let them in and out. Now the holes will have to be bigger. Well, if she's back in bed I must go up and see her, because I've decided it's high time we had a Little Talk.'

'Good evening, Grand,' I said boldly, squatting on the prie-dieu where she couldn't see my face. 'My aunt says I'm to tell you that a shilling a day isn't enough. You see the bus-fares and . . .'

'Is that you, my pet? I've had a capital idea! Now that the evenings are drawing out, you can indulge in a healthy recreation and cultivate the garden. A delightful pastime, don't you agree?'

'Yes, but there isn't a spade and you can't dig without a spade. Dan said . . .'

'Fiddlesticks, of course you can. Holman and I used to work most effectively with the shovel and Helen still has it for the coals. There is no need to squander a fortune on unnecessary tools. Talking of digging . . .'

'But we weren't! We were discussing the *shilling*, and more pin money,' I said, curbing my exasperation.

'Ah yes.' She reached out for a bit of paper and putting on her pince-nez, read aloud: '"The precious legacy of a constant example . . . the unwearying helper of her husband, the cheerful sharer of his anxieties, the wise and faithful counsellor of his children, whose infancy and childhood bore testimony to her *laborious* yet willing toils and whose matured experience of her tenderness, piety and thrift leads them to cherish this last sacred deposit." Very moving.' She sighed.

For a moment I was silent. 'I don't understand. Is the last sacred deposit the Ashes? Is that what you want Papa to write on the stone?' I faltered. 'When the day comes, I mean.' It would never fit in the space.

'My pet, you misunderstand me. This was a fitting memorial to my beloved mother. Alas, I am unworthy of such a tribute but I suppose some epitaph . . . ' She broke off and tears trickled slowly down her face. 'I hope I shall not be entirely forgotten.'

'Of course you won't; but what about the shilling?'

'Holman sculpted a magnificent sarcophagus for Fanny with his own hands when she died in Florence. He stayed there for weeks chiselling away, while we all waited at home. . . . The idea is so disturbing—that all these years he and Fanny have been united in heaven, perhaps as they never were before. I have tried to keep him with me, but if only I could join him now! I long to die but here I am burdened with my cursed Brother Ass!'

A fig for the shilling! I jumped up in concern.

'Oh Grand, please don't cry. I'm sure Grandpa Holman has been here in this house with you, far more than he's been in heaven with great-aunt Fanny. I *know* he's here, he always has been. Everything will be all right. Papa will see that your'e not forgotten. Now what would you like me to read to you tonight? More Mr. Woolley or Tennyson again?' I wiped her cheeks and held her bony hand. 'Since I cut your nails your hands look very nice.'

'Dear child, although I must confess that once or twice a certain person's visits have been distressing, as I said to good Helen today, your reading aloud, our little talks and especially our prayers together, have comforted and sustained me, so let us pray together now.'

'Praying always seems far worse, more difficult I mean, than ringing someone up.'

'Hush, my pet. Help me to my knees.' She struggled and tried to reach the floor.

'You stay where you are. I'll kneel.' I buried my face in the plaid.

'God, are you there? It's Diana speaking. Yes, do you remember me? *Please make Papa come home, and send us some money. Make something happen.* If you do, I promise . . . I promise . . .'

'There's a letter for you, miss,' panted Helen, the following morning as she knocked on my door with her broom. 'I've put it on your tray by the gong.'

'For me? God must have *heard*! Has it got an Indian stamp?' I rushed downstairs. 'No, it isn't from Papa and I'm *so* sick of porridge!'

'Cross my heart, miss, I'm sick of cooking it,' she said.

A card fell out of the letter. 'Lady Pritchard at home. Dancing.' With it was a note: 'Dear Diana, Forgive this late invitation but from what your grandfather says I can't make out if you are *out*? I am giving a small dance for Walter in Cadogan Square. I had hoped you might come with your aunt and Priscilla but as they are already engaged, perhaps you would bring a partner and dine first, quite informally, with us? Eight o'clock! Affectionately, Mabel Pritchard.'

I pushed my breakfast aside and announced to Helen: 'This is a most important letter. I'm not going to my office today.' As I had promised in my prayer, I made my bed before escaping to the attic.

'Fatima!' I cried, jumping into the saddle: 'Miss Holman-Hunt thanks Lady Pritchard and God for their wonderful, thrilling invitation. She regrets she cannot bring a partner but hopes to meet the Man I love.'

I stopped rocking and laid my head on her mane. It would need planning. I would cash my aunt's cheque and buy a backless, black velvet dress and a feather boa. I would leave the house before Helen locked up and spend the night at an hotel. No, that would be extravagant. Perhaps I could sit up for nothing in the waiting-room at Victoria? Or at the end of the dance I could pretend to faint . . . I saw myself swooning gracefully into the muscular arms of Ramon Novarro.

I had never looked forward to anything so much as Lady Pritchard's dance. The shop-girl had said: 'It fits a treat. It's only reduced because no one buys velvet in the spring.' I had replied, 'I do!' and produced a wad of notes from my bag with a flourish.

I had also bought some rouge and a yard of pink and black feather trimming to make a boa. How I longed to try it on! Clutching my treasured parcels I rang at the front door. Helen was slower than usual. She was, I supposed, in the middle of cooking something wholesome for supper—fish balls or tapioca cheese.

I was just about to brave her disapproval and descend the area steps, when the front door opened abruptly, as far as the chain would allow. Instead of Helen in a print dress, a huge woman in blue glared down. Had I come to the wrong house?

'What is it? Are you from the Press?' she boomed. Her voice was faintly familiar. 'I'm sorry, I can see nobody from the Press,' she went on, trying to shut the door.

'What do you mean? I'm Diana and you are my Big Aunt Gladys!'

'But it's not possible,' she said suspiciously, 'Diana's a child; in fact I believe she is abroad.'

I tried to be patient.

'No one thinks I'm me. Ask Helen. I'm seventeen.'

Would she never let me in? I was still outside the door. When I took a step forward she didn't move.

'I can tell you no more than you've read in the evening papers.'

'But I haven't seen an evening paper. I read *The Times* every night with Grand.'

'You'd better come in for a minute,' she said, frowning.

I followed her into the hall.

'This is my husband.'

A small dark man, with gentle eyes, shook my hand and murmured: 'My dear, prepare yourself for a shock.'

'Yes, your grandmother was run over in Kensington High Street today.'

I dropped my parcels.

'Was it a bus?'

To my horror a grin split my face from ear to ear. 'The manner of her death was thus, she was run over by a bus.'

'Fowler's always right. She knew.'

I sank down on the stairs. I had prayed for something to happen and now it had. I stared at Grandpa Holman's portrait and his eyes met mine. My heart thumped while a frightful query grew and twisted between us. Did she kill herself for you? Was it because of great-aunt Fanny?

'I'm not sure if it was an omnibus,' said Big Aunt. 'I think the wretched man told the police he was driving a heavy van or a truck. Mother ran into the road waving her umbrella . . .'

'Are you sure? Did she warn him?' I put my head in my hands. 'She always did, but Fowler said *one* day the traffic wouldn't stop.'

'I don't know who Fowler is,' said Big Aunt, 'but you must go at once if you want to see her—she's at the hospital in Marloes Road. Helen's with her now.'

'D'you mean she's alive?' I was amazed. 'Of course I must go, but how shall I get in? Shall I wait for Helen?'

'You'd better go at once,' she said again.

Her husband put his hand on my shoulder and led me to the door.

'Here are your parcels,' she said.

'I'll be back.' I brushed them away.

She handed them to me again. 'When you get home you'd better send a cable to your father.'

'I *am* home. I live here!'

'You *live* here? Since when?'

She pushed some wisps of grey hair off her forehead.

'For months. This is my home,' I repeated, grabbing my parcels and putting them down on the table.

'But how odd of Helen not to tell me. When I've come to see Mother, she's never said a word and I've never seen a sign!'

'I'm out all day. I don't use the sitting-room,' I said.

'But you can't stay here alone with Helen.' She turned to her husband, 'Really!'

'I suppose Cyril will come?' he whispered.

'I must stay, Papa says so and I've nowhere else to go.' I was in a panic, and hurriedly added, 'I must be off to Marloes Road.'

I shook hands and let myself out. Silently they watched me hasten down the steps.

Luckily, when I returned I found the back door open. I made my way up to Helen's room. She lay in her coat, heaving on the bed. Above was a print of *The Light of the World.*

'Poor Helen!' I took her in my arms.

'She went to buy a Dundee because she thought there was going to be a party. It's all my fault for letting her go!' she wailed.

'Are you sure she only went to do some shopping? Don't you really think she wanted . . .'

'I do and I don't,' said Helen.

We would never know; was it my fault?

'You stay here, I'll go and make a cup of tea.'

The range was out: I had no idea how to light it. I pushed the dampers in and screwed up a lot of paper. After half an hour I was black and not a glimmer showed amongst the coals. At last, stamping on the beetles and wild with frustration, I filled the kettle at the sink and took it and the two remaining matches out into the garden. I lit a bonfire, as Timothy had taught me, using dry twigs from the Thackeray tree and laying them the way of the wind.

I sat on some sooty bricks and waited as Grandpa Holman had done, when he tried to boil a horse.

The young doctor at the hospital had said, 'Grandchild? The only one?'

I had nodded.

'She's conscious, poor soul; I'm afraid we'll have to amputate tomorrow but she may pull through; these Victorians are very tough.' He patted me kindly.

'Amputate what? Oh *no*!' I was filled with indignation. 'You must *help* her to die!'

The sister led me up the ward, past rows of patients, to Grand.

'My pet, how frightened you look. Your eyes are as big as saucers: I can't hold your hand because mine are useless.' She smiled.

'Oh Grand, how wonderful of you to know me! I love you so . . .' I collapsed sobbing on the bed until a nurse led me away.

The kettle boiled and it dawned on me that I would miss Lady Pritchard's dance.

For the next few days the house was besieged by the Press and telegraph boys and friends calling to inquire. Dozens of letters for Miss Holman-Hunt flopped onto the mat, but few were for me. It was clear that many people didn't know that Big Aunt was married.

'One of you must always keep guard,' she instructed Helen and me in the hall. 'Whatever happens don't go out together. Your Step-uncle Cyril—Mr. Cyril—may arrive any time from Dorset—a room must be prepared. On *no* pretext is anyone else to be admitted, and never open the door, except on the chain. Beware of the Press! Nothing is insured and, as you know, once it gets about that the house is full of priceless things . . .'

'The thieves will come! We know!' I glanced smugly at Helen.

'Burglars,' corrected Big Aunt, pinning a straw and satin saucepan on her head, which made her seven feet high. 'I'll see you tomorrow.' She grabbed a pile of letters and left.

'We can spy callers through the keyhole,' said Helen, ramming home the bolts.

We slunk down to the range. I read to her aloud from copies of *The Times*: 'Listen to this—"Victim of a serious street accident" —ghastly to think she's still alive—"Mrs. H-H. aged eighty-four".'

'More like ninety!' said Helen.

'Hush! "In a very serious condition after the amputation of her arms on Thursday." Isn't it awful? Poor Grand. "The daughter of George Waugh, widow of the great painter" etcetera. "She brought to his genius *great* sympathy and notable social gifts . . . her only son abroad, Captain Hilary Lushington H-H. of the Indian Army." It's very odd we haven't had a cable.' I picked up another page. 'Yes, here it is: "Mrs. H-H., well-known figure in society; one of the last links with the past; her home Melbury Road; a meeting place of the most distinguished of the day" and rats and beetles and silver fish,' I added, stamping. '"Vital personality and dignity of manner." Look, here's a photograph of Mrs. Swynnerton's portrait of Lord St. Davids and all about the banquet and the private view at Burlington House—Grand and I would have gone. The Woolleys are still at Ur—I hope he brings me back a present—The Stavordales' wedding, old Lady Ilchester was there. How I would have loved to see Sybil Thorndike as St. Joan!—She sent us tickets you know. Priscilla's been to Ruth Chatterton in *The Right to Love* and Ronald Colman in *Raffles* . . .'

'It's nearly visiting time. I've no time for all this fiddle-de-dee,' said Helen. 'Out of my way, miss, now.' She pulled out the dampers and heaved a sooty iron pot onto the smoking range.

'Stew *again*. Couldn't we get something to roast?'

'We could and we couldn't. The oven's cracked. Don't forget to lock up.' She brushed past the frescoes and stumped up the area steps, after slamming the scullery door.

Alone at last! There was not a moment to lose. I tore upstairs to put on my feathers and black velvet dress. I sat before the glass but now there was no Grand by my side. I rubbed my cheeks with rouge and was pleased with Brother Ass while she, not far away, was shedding him for ever.

The bell! Blast the blinkin' bell! I threw my hairbrush on the bed and, picking up my skirts, danced down the stairs, past Grandpa Holman's portrait, to the door.

Through the keyhole I spied a *young* man, wearing a trilby and carrying a large box and a tripod. I unbolted the door.

He raised his hat and asked in gloomy but sympathetic tones: 'Am I addressing Miss Holman-Hunt? I wish to extend the condolences of my paper for the tragic ordeals of your family.' He looked up and his face lighted with a smile. 'I wonder if you could spare a few minutes? A nurse at the hospital told me that you live here alone and there's no phone and no electric light and the house is a fabulous museum, full of treasures. Aren't you nervous? Would you like a watch-dog? Do me a favour: let me come in and take a photograph of you in that dress against a Greek statue. Or is there an oil painting of the Grand Old Man of the World?' His eyes were pleading.

'Oh no, there's nothing but rubbish,' I said, by now thoroughly alarmed.

'You wear that long black dress already, but . . .'

I explained that I had always longed to wear modern clothes, instead of being dressed like the people in Grandpa's pictures.

'You know you *do* need a watch-dog,' he said.

'Oh no!' I let out a peal of laughter. 'I keep a fierce horse in the attic.'

'I see!' He looked me up and down and backed away with his boxes, mumbling: 'Poor kid, very sad!'

A telegraph boy ran up the steps. 'Holman-Hunt?'

I nodded. The young man had gone so I closed the door, and opened the telegram, which for once was for *me*!

'Shocked by tragic news your return here imperative after funeral telegraph arrival Grandfather.'

I had somewhere to go.

I began to feel excited when the wailing of gulls diving over the train jarred on the throb of the engine. I pulled down the window, and a salt breeze blew in from the sea. The setting sun painted the dykes in gaudy streaks and a heron stood poised near some lambs.

I longed to see my friend Timothy again. When I crept round

the huts to surprise him, he would shout 'Ahoy!' then wave his hook and, winking slyly, press it to the side of his nose.

Whaler would be at the station to meet me with the motor. The old carriage-box of gate boys' pennies would be clipped to the door under the window; the glass would still be scratched from the repeated rapping of heavy diamond rings. A little book of papier poudré would be tucked in the fitted leather pocket at the side, between the smelling salts and cologne.

I would sit in front, instead of yelling down the speaking-tube for gossip. When I arrived, the pugs would run yapping to the hall, their paws skidding on the parquet. Arthur would open the door: 'Winkin' merrybugs, 'aven't you changed?'

It was already nearly dark, so the library chandelier would sparkle; and because it was spring, the hall fireplace would be banked with arum lilies. There would be silver and cut glass bowls with haloes of carnations and roses, their colours reflected in the tables; and a warm jumble of smells: violets, wood smoke, cigars and beeswax.

When we reached the station I grabbed my luggage and jumped down to the platform.

'Miss Diana? My little dear, I couldn't believe my eyes. If only the mistress . . .'

'Oh Hannah, it's wonderful to see you.'

She was smaller than I remembered, thin and dignified in black. I kissed her as she bent to take a case.

'Here's Miss Diana,' she said to a stranger. 'You remember Tommy Rook, dear, don't you?'

'Yes, of course.' I put my gramophone down and shook his hand. 'I hope Mrs. Rook is well.'

'The master sold Tommy the motor—it's the village taxi now—he's ever so modern, our Tommy, and thoughtful too; just look, he's even put a flower in the vase. There's no stove plants or flowers in the house since the mistress died—the poor master doesn't miss them . . .'

There was no carriage-box of pennies, but when I explored the pocket the papier poudré was there.

'Since the mistress died, there's been a lot of changes,' Hannah went on. 'Since his fall the master's always in pain. It's cruel: if you ask me those doctors don't know their business. Mr. Johnstone left—least said soonest mended—and how I miss Miss Fowler! Mrs. Hopkins got unsettled, not that Tilly and me were sorry, and Annie bettered herself and went as cook to Miss Letty what married the Major; she's expecting now and seeing she's no chicken . . .'

'And what about *you*?'

'Cook-housekeeper! *Me* who's never been trained in the kitchen! The drawing-room's shut and the boudoir under dust-sheets. The master never goes in there and Tilly . . .'

'Oh dear, it all sounds quite different. Is Timothy well?' Was anything or anyone the same?

'*Old* Timothy down on the marsh? He's dead, dear, lost at sea. Oh, it must be all of two years ago. Now I come to think, Dan brought a box up for you—lucky stones and shells and some green glass balls.'

'Floats,' I murmured. We rolled down the hill to the porch.

'Oh no, dear, put your purse away. You don't want to hurt his feelings. Most like, Arthur will give him some beer in the pantry. What, *me* come in at the front? Never! In all my years of service . . .'

'It's high time then! You're the housekeeper now.' I pushed her forward.

No pugs barked but Arthur was there: 'Good hevening Miss Dihannah,' he said, with a pompous little bow.

'Good hevening Harthur,' I mocked. 'Did you know all the time that 'Ark, 'ark the lark and winkin' merrybugs were Shakespeare? It's *Cymbeline* and they're marybuds really.'

'Fancy Arthur talking Shakespeare all these years.' Hannah dived for the green baize door.

The house had shrunk and the smell was different—only smoke and cigars. The rugs had gone and the dull parquet floor was scarred with the marks of rubber wheels. I walked quickly to the library door and Arthur announced: 'Miss Diana, sir.'

I fumbled for the light while he piled more logs on the fire.

'You were sitting in the dark!' I exclaimed, swooping to kiss the pink head huddled in cushions.

'So you're back! Dark? All the same to me.'

'Where are the pugs?' I pushed aside *The Times*, which was no longer ironed, and sat on my stool.

'They tripped me up. The mugs and the pugs and the rugs all got in the way.'

'I see.'

'I have anticipated your arrival with the greatest pleasure: I have sadly missed our reading. Has that fool Arthur brought in the whiskey? If not, ring the bell.'

'I'll get it—I expect he's busy with the luggage. Would you like a cigar?'

'Can't feel the glass, you'll have to hold it,' he said gruffly.

I had lost my knife long ago so I bit off the end of the cigar and put it alight between his rigid fingers.

'You must puff,' I said.

'That's better.' He winced with pain and moved his leg over the crutch. 'I'm glad you're back. I was thinking today we can progress to Flaubert and Balzac. I trust you've not neglected your reading?'

'There was no library and very few books . . .'

'So Mrs. H-H. is dead. I recollect old Hunt's funeral very well: thousands attended and a great concourse was obliged to remain outside on the steps, representing his millions of admirers. It's remarkable to recall that in his lifetime he sold that hideous *Light of the World* for twelve thousand—colossal sum then. The pall-bearers were a distinguished lot: Tennyson, that old bore William Rossetti, Arthur Hughes, Lockyer, Forbes-Robertson, a fine-looking man, and Israel Gollancz. I take it you and Gladys were the chief mourners today?'

'Step-uncle Cyril walked with Big Aunt's husband behind. All the Sunday party people were there and I wore a camellia . . .' I told him all there was to tell.

'Go on, tell me more,' he said.

While I described my adventures he closed his eyes and chuckled now and then. The heavy ash from his cigar flopped to the floor; the butt glowed and the rising smoke melted in the haze.

'I recollect Byron's lines,' he said at last: '"And if I laugh at any mortal things, 'tis that I may not weep . . . " Until your father returns in a couple of years; I am your last remaining guardian and *this* is your home—a trifle dull I fear; but soon, let us hope, your aunt will come to the rescue. She's a gregarious creature so I daresay she'd give a ball. In the meantime you must console yourself with me and Walter Pritchard, your grandmother's favourite. She thought him very suitable I know, and there will be no harm in you renewing his acquaintance. I suggest we celebrate the end of what I might call this singular chapter with champagne.' He banged his crutch on the fender, 'A little drop of sherry and a little drop of cham! I hear the clock strike; my wheel-chair is rumbling on the parquet and it's time to go and dress.'

My room was almost as I had left it. Edward, and Miss Dolby's lambs were still in places of honour, and Timothy's box stood squarely on the table. I raised the lid. Inside, as well as shells and floats, was a beautiful piece of yellow silk. I held it to my cheek and walked over to the window to look out at Cherub. The curtain was patched where for years a hatpin had stabbed my list of tasks to the stuff. The patch was the same size as the familiar list which had faced me every day: 'Date eggs, label packets for bazaar, dead-head roses, learn *Maud*, Kings of England . . .'

On the bathroom shelf, the bear's grease in the china pot had shrunk to a rancid blob and the Pomade Divine was dried and cracked. When I picked up the ivory box I could almost hear Fowler rattle on the door and shout: 'Hurry up do! You don't want to moon, it's nearly time for the gong.'

I had drunk lots of champagne and Hannah was waiting upstairs to undress me. 'I told Tilly you'd see her tomorrow; you know Polly left and got married.'

'There aren't any violets.' I collapsed on the bed in tears.

'My little dear,' she said, 'if only the mistress was still in her room next door. We never knew how happy she made us, but as I said to Tilly, there's better times coming for you; next year the master says he hopes Mrs. Hubert . . .'

My list of tasks spun round and round on the curtain. I stared but couldn't stop it spinning.

'I can see you at your ball, dressed in white satin. The Prince of Wales—He'll be there. You're sure to catch His eyes . . .'

'Oh, no!' The music began, tick-tock-tock. . . . It was a waltz. The ballroom was full of *jolies laides*. My bed began to dance, and the end where Hannah was sitting rose and fell, rose and fell. Her face was close, then far away.

'You'll see, everything'll be all right.'

'Are you sure?'

Why was the bed heaving up and down?

'Why, Miss Diana, I do believe you're tipsy!'

'Tipsy?'

I shouted for Arthur. The bed whirled round again. I rolled onto the floor and fell through the house, down to the cellars and the furnace: Johnstone's room exploded in a blaze and shot me up in the air. I was on Fatima's back, flying after Cherub, over the lawns and trees. I clutched at Edward. Instead of the lambs I found the ivory box in my pocket. When we reached the sea we began to fall . . .

'Mercy—it's the wine,' cried Hannah.

I fell on my feet and danced slowly between the shells on the frowning pattern of the sands.

HAMISH HAMILTON PAPERBACKS

'Among the most collectable of paperback imprints . . .'
Christopher Hudson, *The Standard*

All books in the Hamish Hamilton Paperback Series are available at your local bookshop or can be ordered by post. A full list of titles and an order form can be found at the end of this book.

QUEEN VICTORIA
Her Life and Times 1819–1861

Cecil Woodham-Smith

A new conception of Queen Victoria emerged from this biography. Mrs Woodham-Smith had access to previously unused information and her book established once and for all the true character of the young Victoria. Its publication was a landmark in historical research. Intensely readable and sympathetic, this biography deals with the Queen's wretched childhood, her passionate nature, her devotion to the Prince Consort and her native shrewdness in politics. Sadly the author did not live to complete the second volume of this life, but her word on the young Queen is unrivalled.

'. . . unlikely ever to be surpassed.' Michael Ratcliffe, *The Times*

'. . . quite indispensable to any student of this peculiar sovereign.' Paul Johnson, *Guardian*

ALBERT, PRINCE CONSORT

Robert Rhodes James

A man of outstanding ability, Albert, Queen Victoria's Consort and husband, has had a lasting influence upon this history of his time and on the development of the British Constitutional Monarchy. His achievements were innumerable: the reformation of Cambridge University, the organization of the Great Exhibition of 1851, the building of Osborne and Balmoral, and his promotion of social reform and town planning, to name but a few. In this extremely readable biography, Robert Rhodes James does full justice to this talented, complex man.

'Prince Albert was a man of great character and of noble achievement. In Robert Rhodes James's book he receives a worthy tribute. Indeed this is one of the finest biographies I have ever read.' A. J. P. Taylor, *Observer*

HUGH WALPOLE

Rupert Hart-Davis

'Rupert Hart-Davis's book is a remarkable feat of understanding and restraint. . . . He shows us the man himself, and the spectacle is delightful.' Edwin Muir

'Fully to appreciate how remarkable an achievement is Mr Hart-Davis's biography of Hugh Walpole, it is necessary to read the book. No summarised comment can convey the complexity of the task accomplished or the narrative skill, restraint and self-effacement with which it has been carried through.' Michael Sadleir

'The most entertaining book about a writer of our time.' Terence de Vere White, *Irish Times*

THE LIFE OF ARTHUR RANSOME

Hugh Brogan

For a man who longed for a quiet existence, Arthur Ransome had an extraordinarily adventurous life comprising two stormy marriages, a melodramatic libel suit, and a ringside view of the Russian Revolution. In this absorbing book, Hugh Brogan writes with sympathy and affection of the author of some of the best loved books for children.

'The wonder is, from Mr Brogan's enthralling account, that Ransome ever got down to writing *Swallows and Amazons* at all.' A. N. Wilson, *Sunday Telegraph*

MARY BERENSON:
A Self Portrait from Her Letters and Diaries

eds. Barbara Strachey & Jayne Samuels

This superbly edited book of extracts from Mary Berenson's letters and diaries provides an absorbing picture of her extraordinary complex relationship with Bernard Berenson, and of their life and work together in Italy.

'Mary . . . writes with a startling, unsettling, often hilarious candour which makes it hard to put the book down.' – Hilary Spurling, *Observer*

A DURABLE FIRE:
The Letters of Duff and Diana Cooper, 1913–1950

ed. Artemis Cooper

For long periods before and after their marriage in 1919 Duff and Diana Cooper were apart, but they wrote to each other constantly, witty, gossipy letters that have been admirably edited by their granddaughter to form this delightful collection.

'It is rare to find a correspondence duo in which both sides are of equivalent verve and strength . . . a unique, inside account of a charmed circle whose members governed England between the wars.' – Anthony Curtis, *Financial Times*

NANCY MITFORD
A Memoir

Harold Acton

Nancy Mitford never completed an autobiography. Fortunately she was a voluminous letter writer and had a genius for friendship and laughter. In this delightful memoir, Sir Harold Acton has been able to show us, largely in her own words, almost every aspect of her personality, and her immense courage during the years of her final painful illness.

'Sir Harold Acton has memoralised a very gifted writer, and a unique personality, with affection, skill and truth.' Anthony Powell, *Daily Telegraph*

'The main lesson I derived from Sir Harold's stylish and loving evocation of Nancy Mitford's personality, is that she gave just as much pleasure to her circle of friends and relations as she gave to her readers.' Antonia Fraser, *Evening Standard*

ANOTHER PART OF THE WOOD
A Self Portrait

Kenneth Clark

Kenneth Clark's sharp witty account of his eccentric Edwardian upbringing and his swift success in the world of art after leaving Oxford is a classic of its kind and a pleasure to read.

'An immensely entertaining memoir . . . rich in deliciously dry tales . . . all told with perfect brevity and wit.' Michael Ratcliffe, *The Times*

'A stylish, dazzling work flecked with touches of learning and imagination, wit and malice.' Kenneth Rose, *Sunday Telegraph*

MRS PAT
The Life of Mrs Patrick Campbell

Margot Peters

Beautiful, witty, talented, Mrs Patrick Campbell became a legend in her own lifetime. Her theatrical career encompassed tremendous triumphs and unmitigated failures. Her private life was controversial and tragic. In this superb biography Margot Peters captures the magnetism of an outstanding actress and extraordinary woman, who remains today as intriguing as ever.

'The book has been researched with exemplary care and accuracy. The famous bons mots — nearly always witty, sometimes cruel and personal, but usually devastatingly apt — are quoted with appropriate relish. There is a wealth of material, never before made public, to enthrall the reader.' John Gielgud, *Observer*

TWO FLAMBOYANT FATHERS

Nicolette Devas

'A marvellous account of growing up in the artistic Bohemia of the 1920s with friends and mentors including the still-roaring Augustus John and the young Dylan Thomas, who was to marry her sister Caitlin. Candid, touching and engrossing: one of the finest autobiographies of our time.' Philip Oakes

MISSION WITH MOUNTBATTEN

Alan Campbell-Johnson

From 1947 until June 1948 Alan Campbell-Johnson was Lord Mountbatten's Press Attaché in India. The diary he kept of those dramatic and critical months was the first authoritative account to be published of one of the most important events of this century: the transfer of power in India by partition and consent. Both for those who remember that crucial time and for a new generation, this remarkable book provides a fascinating view of statesmanship at its most creative.

'A most revealing and graphic report of one of the most extraordinary and imaginative episodes in our history.' Arthur Bryant

ASQUITH

Stephen Koss

In this outstanding political biography, Stephen Koss traces with masterly insight the controversial career of H. H. Asquith, the man who has been regarded as both the victim and the agent of the liberal decline.

'This is the best biography of Asquith yet to be written and a book indispensable to every lover of political history.' A. J. P. Taylor, *New Statesman*

'Professor Koss's style is easy, and agreeably astringent. . . . His assembling of the materials conceals the enormous trouble he has taken both to evaluate the latest sources and to slip these almost effortlessly into context.' Andrew Boyle, *Listener*

A LATE BEGINNER

Priscilla Napier

In 1921, Priscilla Napier, aged twelve, left Egypt where her father worked in the colonial administration. In this funny and perceptive memoir she brilliantly recreates a child's view of the exotic surroundings of those early years. It was a world of comfort and security, of calm routine and Cadbury's Tropical Chocolates, with the excitements of scorpions in the nursery cupboard and black beetles in the garden, and long sea voyages to England, a country of endless green lawns inhabited by endless relations. But the impact of war was far-reaching and the world changed.

'She is a born writer. Mrs Napier displays the most professional skill in modulation between her childhood feelings and adult commentary.'
Raymond Mortimer, *Sunday Times*

GOD'S APOLOGY
A Chronicle of Three Friends

Richard Ingrams

In this very entertaining book, Richard Ingrams celebrates the friendship of three men: Hugh Kingsmill, writer and former literary editor of *Punch*, Hesketh Pearson, the biographer, and Malcolm Muggeridge. At the centre of the group was Kingsmill, whose lack of success as a writer was perhaps a result of his memorable success as a conversationalist and friend. The portrait that Richard Ingrams draws of the relationship between the three men is affectionate and compelling. In the words of Kingsmill: 'Friends are God's apology for relations.'

'Most readable and spirited. . . . A book that is so full of affection is most welcome nowadays.' Nigel Dennis, *Sunday Telegraph*

MRS PAT	Margot Peters	£5.95	☐
THE SECRET ORCHARD OF ROGER ACKERLEY	Diana Petre	£4.95	☐
ALBERT, PRINCE CONSORT	Robert Rhodes James	£4.95	☐
LORD RANDOLPH CHURCHILL	Robert Rhodes James	£6.95	☐
MARY BERENSON	eds. Barbara Strachey and Jayne Samuels	£4.95	☐
BISMARCK	A. J. P. Taylor	£5.95	☐
THE YEARS WITH ROSS*	James Thurber	£4.95	☐
THE DRAGON EMPRESS	Marina Warner	£4.95	☐
QUEEN VICTORIA	Cecil Woodham-Smith	£5.95	☐

All titles 198 × 126mm, and all contain 8 pages of black and white illustrations except for those marked*.

All books in the Hamish Hamilton Paperback Series are available at your local bookshop, or can be ordered direct from Media Services. Just tick the titles you want in the list above and fill in the form below.

Name________________________________

Address______________________________

____

Write to: Media Services, PO Box 151, Camberley, Surrey gu15 3be.

Please enclose cheque or postal order made out to Media Services for the cover price plus postage:

UK: 55p for the first book, 24p for each additional book to a maximum of £1.75.

OVERSEAS: £1.05 for the first book, 35p for each additional book to a maximum of £2.80.

Hamish Hamilton Ltd reserve the right to show new retail prices on covers which may differ from those previously advertised in the text or elsewhere, and to increase postal rates in accordance with the P.O.